The Mysteries Of Light

Illumination, Intention and Desire
In Photobooks

Robert Dunn

A Coral Press Arts original

Copyright © Robert Dunn 2023

All rights reserved. No part of this publication may be reproduced, stored in a retrieval system, or transmitted in any form or by any means, electronic, mechanical, recording or otherwise, without the prior written permission of the author.

Published by BookLocker.com, Inc., Trenton, Georgia.

Printed on acid-free paper.

ISBN: 978-1-935512-54-7
Library of Congress Control Number: 2020943169
Manufactured in U.S.A.
1 3 5 7 9 10 8 6 4 2
BookLocker.com, Inc. 2023
First Edition

Cover Design: Beth Bugler
Cover Photograph: Robert Dunn
Author Photograph: Daido Moriyama

www.ecstaticlightphoto.com

To Robert, William, Saul, Daido, Shomei ... all those photographers who inspired me, and keep inspiring me

Table of Contents

Introduction   15

Why I Love Photobooks   17

Why I Take Photographs   44

REVIEWS

Daisuke Yokota, *Taratine*   54

Time Ravages the Photobook:
Huger Foote, *Now Here Then*   56

The World in the Photobook:
Jacob Sobol, *By the River of Kings*   59

Fiction and Metaphor in the Photobook:
Marcelo Greco, *Sombras Secas*   62

Provoke: Between Protest and Performance   64

A "Storytelling" of Ravens:
An Appreciation of
Masahisa Fukase's Masterpiece   67

When Once Isn't Enough:
Chris Killip, *In Flagrante Two*   70

Beyond Black and White:
Katrin Koenning and Sarker Protick, *Astres Noirs*   74

Too Many Palm Trees
Intentionality and the Photobook:
Renato D'Agostin, *Archaeologies: Los Angeles*   77

True Intentionality:
Arthur Bondar, *Shadows of Wormwood*   80

Photobooks in Concert:
Daido Moriyama's *Never-Ending Tour*   83

Words and Photos:
Mikiko Hara and Stephen Dixon, *Change*   86

Autobiography and the Photobook:
Takahiro Kaneyama, *While Leaves Are Falling*   89

My True Story:
Jim Goldberg, *The Last Son*   93

We're Not in Japan Anymore
Politics and the Photobook:
Fyodor Telkov, *36 Views*   98

Disparate Harmonies, Tall Climbs:
Shane Lavalette, *One Sun, One Shadow*   102

Loving the Life:
Mao Ishikawa, *Red Flower: The Women of Okinawa*   106

The Photobook as Literature:
Igor Posner, *Past Perfect*   110

The Darkening Sky:
Masahisa Fukase, *Ravens*, Part 1   113

The Darkening Sky:
Mashahisa Fukase, *Ravens*, Part 2   117

Going Home Again:
Mike Mandel, *People in Cars*
Larry Sultan, *Pictures from Home*   123

Daido's Tour Keeps on Never-Ending:
Daido Moriyama, *Pretty Woman* — 129

Weird, Weird, Weird:
Feng Li, *White Night* — 134

Inventing the New Photographic Language:
Christer Strömholm, *Poste Restante* — 138

Joy, Mischief, Life:
Saul Leiter, *It Don't Mean a Thing* — 142

I Gotta Make a Photobook:
Stephen Gill, *Night Procession* — 146

Can You Make Too Many Photobooks?:
Nobuyoshi Araki, *Blue Period/Last Summer* — 150

Love Stories and the Photobook:
John Sypal, *Zuisha* — 154

Bring on the Literature:
Mary Frey, *Reading Raymond Carver* — 158

Back on the Road:
Vanessa Winship, *She Dances on Jackson* — 162

These Books Are Made for Walking:
Morton Andersen, *Fast Cities* — 167

Feed the Feed
Social Media and the Photobook:
Nick Sethi, *Kichari* — 172

Time and Street Photography:
Janet Delaney, *Public Matters* — 177

"The Presence and the Living Energy"
Three Weeks in a Foreign Town:
Anders Petersen, *Okinawa* — 181

The Defamiliarisation of Ephemeral Reality:
Issei Suda, *The Mechanical Retina on My Fingertips* 185

Yep, The Dream Does Spring Eternal:
Mark Power, *Good Morning, America* 189

Will and the World in Photography:
Alec Soth, *I Know How Furiously Your Heart Is Beating*, Part 1 194

Artistic Faith and the Photobook:
Alec Soth, *I Know How Furiously Your Heart Is Beating*, Part 2 198

Trusting Nature:
Stephen Gill, *The Pillar* 203

Literary Ambition and the Photobook:
Jason Eskenazi, *Black Garden Trilogy* 206

Going Through the Drawers:
Philip Perkis, *Mexico* 211

Photos to Books to Art Objects:
Laura El-Tantawy, *A Star in the Sea*, Part 1 215

Photos to Books to Art Objects:
Laura El-Tantawy, *A Star in the Sea*, Part 2 219

The Photobook as Pulp Fiction:
Tania Franco Klein, *Positive Disintegration* 223

Color Film Changes Everything
Fun Times in the Soviet Union:
Boris Mikhailov, *Suzi et Cetera (Part 2)* 228

We Are Family:
Masahisa Fukase, *Family*;
Guillaume Simoneau, *Murder* 232

Opening Up:
Matthew Spiegelman, *Transmitter*   238

In Your Face:
Street Photography and
Jeff Mermelstein's *Hardened*   242

Far More Than "Pretty Vacant"
Joji Hashiguchi, *We Have No Place to Be*   247

Daido's Progeny:
Subway Diary by Masakazu Murakami;
The Dreaming by Yasuhiro Ogawa   251

A Plenitude of Novels:
Stephen Shore's *Transparencies:
Small Camera Works 1971–1979*, Part 1   257

Getting Your Kicks on Route 66:
Stephen Shore's *Transparencies:
Small Camera Works 1971–1979*, Part 2   262

News That Stays News:
Gordon Parks, *The Atmosphere of
Crime, 1957*   267

Shelter from the Storm:
Jesse Lenz, *the locusts*   271

So Long Photography, Hello East Orange:
A Reissue of Daido Moriyama's
Bye Bye Photography   275

The Endless Afternoon:
Mimi Plumb, *The White Sky*   282

Vermeer Around the Corner:
Forever Saul Leiter;
Dorothea Lange, *Day Sleeper*   286

Night Prowl:
Joshua K. Jackson, *Sleepless in Soho*   292

The Raised by Wolves Bootleg Series No. 2:
Jim Goldberg, *Fingerprint*   295

Pick a Card, Any Card:
Daido Moriyama, *Random Walk*   298

FEATURES

Out on the Street: Rules of Street Photography   319

My Tokyo Photobook Trip   330

Introduction

MYSTERIES OF LIGHT IS a wide-ranging book on photobooks, what they are, how they work best, their place in the art world. The book is comprised of both essays of mine and reviews of photobooks I wrote for *Photobookstore Magazine* and *The Od Review*, though each piece is not simply a review. Thanks to both *Photobookstore Magazine* publisher Martin Amis, where most of the pieces ran, and Collier Brown of *The Od Review*, I had complete control over my pieces, choosing the photobooks I wanted to write about and writing about them exactly as I saw fit. I almost always went for books that raised larger questions about photobooks, such as what makes a photobook approach art and literature, how do so-called street photographers transcend the street, how do photobooks create their own unique experience. I then used the review to examine those questions.

A couple personal essays start off the book: "Why I Love Photobooks," and, from 2016, "Why I Take Photographs." Then will come the reviews of fine photobooks, in the order I wrote them, and then another piece on my own work, Rules of Street Photography (2020), a piece I wrote for *Photobookstore Magazine* after writing about a book by Jeff Mermelstein, rules extrapolated from his work, and those I've learned on my own. In the pieces I talk in a wide-ranging way about my own work as a photographer out on the street; though if I had to boil it down, I'd go with the title on one of my own photobooks, *I Was Just Wondering Around.* The title comes from the mistranslation of a phrase Daido Moriyama says in a documentary on him, but isn't that what all great photographers do? Take their camera and just *wonder* around. What's more delightful than that: a good walk lifted by a higher, enrapturing purpose.

Well, maybe hunting out rare photobooks. I end the book with a three-part piece on my first trip to Tokyo (in 2018) combing the shops of that city for classic books I could afford.

Mysteries of Light covers all aspects of photobooks, and along the way helps define what makes up photobooks that will endure, as well as all the different forms photobooks can take. I discuss artists like Daido Moriyama and other Japanese masters such as Issei Suda and Masahisa Fukase, as well as well-known photographers like Alec Soth, Vanessa Winship, Boris Mihailov, Jim Goldberg, and Christer Strömholm, and fascinating newer artists like Jason Eskenazi, Laura El-Tantawy, Igor Posner, and Takahiro Kaneyama.

I also repeat myself a bit, since each piece was written on its own, to stand on its own. If you read straight through, you'll discover some of my photographic tics: I love Japanese Provoke work. I don't like the term "street photographer." I see no reason to take pictures of people looking at cellphones (their souls melt away). There are more favorite themes, and to the extent there's some redundancy, I apologize. Think of it this way: Each piece is one more blow as I hammer out an aesthetic of photobooks.

Reading over the pieces for this book, I also note my growing confidence, both as a writer on photobooks, and as a photographer. As I was writing away, my own photobooks made it into the permanent libraries of the Museum of Modern Art, ICP, and the New York Public Library. They've also sold well at significant shops such as PS1 MoMA, Dashwood, Printed Matter, the Strand Rare Book Room, and numerous other places worldwide. Hence there's more talk about my own photo work as the book moves along.

Still, at bottom the point of each piece, and of *Mysteries of Light* as a whole, is simply to get at the heart of what a great photobook is, and all the ways that photobooks become powerful works of art.

Enjoy.

Why I Love Photobooks

And some of the ones I love

1 – The Radiant Jukebox

IT ALL STARTS WITH one photo. The jukebox in the New York City bar in Robert Frank's *The Americans*, by my count, the fourth jukebox pictured in the book, the one that's pure light, glowing top and middle and bottom-sides, its no-doubt candy-colored exuberance turned into simple black and white, highly contrasted, the light framing a man's arm thrusting into the photo from the right, a bar sign also reduced to pure light floating above a couple at a checkered-cloth table, nursing their beers ... but of course it's the jukebox that's the star of the photo, holding center stage, broadcasting its glow, embodying every promise and joy of a record machine, kicking out tunes to dance to, fall in love to, or as the couple in the picture are surely doing, simply talking, drinking, maybe humming along to Sinatra or Elvis as he sings up a storm.

If at some holy center of art every medium melts down into another, then this photo is music is visual art is structure and intent, is deliverance and relief—is Rembrandt and Kerouac (obviously) and Mark Rothko and Buddy Holly and (of course) the Big Bopper, even if "Chantilly Lace" was still a couple years away from spinning majestically on this particular reverent machine.

Yes, the New York City bar jukebox is the *fourth* one in *The Americans*, which is why this is a piece on why I love photobooks. Because the jukebox is, as the art teachers would say, a motif. It's an image of import to Frank and to his vision of us, and it's the fourth because I'm looking at this photo (over and over, in the same way I re-spin a great Beatles LP, each time hearing it both fresh and new, yet old and familiar and deep) in a book.

A book. A series of photos. A photobook.

Definition here: By a serious photobook, I do not mean a simple collection of a photographers' snaps, a travel book, a museum catalogue, or any sub-form of the ostensibly uplifting *Family of Man* (except in exceptional cases); I mean a book comprised of photographs (words wholly optional; to my taste, best left out) that becomes a work of literature; the equivalent of a novel, a story collection, a book of poems (or all of the above)—works of words that hold together through one (however complex) vision, one idea, one compelling force.

So one of the joys of *The Americans* are the photos Frank chose, the order he put them in, the motifs he repeated. Think of this: The book is dotted with photos with flags in them, and each one works as a chapter beginning. *The Americans* is a novel, an epic of America, and though Jack Kerouac probably tossed off his intro with a bottle of Jack on the table and his trusty Underwood underhand, a road-whispering tire riff in his brain as the book at hand stood in for the trip he wished he were on, he was still the best choice for a preface: His fame got the book attention, his *On the Road* mimicry suits the shots (and takes nothing from them), and if we're going to put the *On the Road* scroll in the rotunda of the main New York Public Library fifty years after Kerouac pounded it out in three weeks, well, we're also going to fill up galleries at the Metropolitan Museum of Art with photos and outtakes from Frank's book.

I was there at the Met, taking in *The Americans* exhibition. The photos were stately on the walls, the light, well, art(museum)ful, the text informative, the museum-goers hushed and appreciative. Did the New York City jukebox radiate light? Of course it did, it's the same photo—an artist's print—but in the book it radiates more intensely. Because it's me alone holding the book the way I want to. Because of the other jukebox photos, and the flags, the lost black soul on the New Orleans trolley, the serene black soul in South Carolina, the angry black soul in San Francisco, the dead soul in his coffin back in South Carolina, the memorial crosses lining the road in Idaho, the two proceeding crosses, the shrouded body outside of Winslow, Arizona ... it's as Kerouac says, "you end up finally not knowing anymore whether a jukebox is sadder than a coffin."

There's a depth of sadness in Frank's America to rival Faulkner's South or Melville's star-crossed seamen or Gatsby's green light or Springsteen's Jersey losers ... it's all there, you can read and reread *The Americans* over and over, and it always pays off. It's never one photo or even any grouping, it's all of them together, and the stories they tell.

That's a great photobook: photobook as book, photobook as novel, photobook as singular work of art.

What's not to love?

2 – The Looming Tricycle

TAKE ANOTHER PHOTO. A key one for me is William Eggleston's tricycle, on the cover of his *Guide*. I still can't get over the angle at which the trike is shot; Eggleston presumably flat on the ground, hugging it, the little kids' bike the most important thing in this suburban ranch-house world.

It is also in color.

I can't recall exactly whether *William Eggleston's Guide* was the first photobook I bought, or whether it was Bill Burke's *I Want to Take Picture*. I was working at *The New Yorker* magazine in the mid-'70s and early '80s, then pushing along as a short story writer and novelist, that's pretty much all I was, but I'd been to Thailand and was fascinated by the ICP show in 1987 of Burke's work. I can remember wondering if I could afford the book, deciding I couldn't—I was truly struggling back then, living in a $90-a-month East Village tenement on next to nothing—and buying it anyway. *I Want to Take Picture* made me, well, want to take pictures, which I did assiduously for a couple years with my cheap Nikon EM (all I could afford), and scaring up money for film processing and dreaming of being able to pay for high-quality prints.

Back in those wholly predigital days, I could be a writer with the occasional ream of paper, my trusty Selectric typewriter, and enough postage to put on the self-addressed-stamped-envelope to bring back my submissions. Photography turned out to be just too much rich.

Still, I loved it, and I did pick up a handful of photobooks, including the Burke one and, now that I just pulled it off my shelves, my 1976 edition of *Guide*, which I must've bought earlier. So when I plunged wholeheartedly back into taking pictures and collecting photobooks a decade ago, I took some comfort from thinking I'd had good taste: The few books I'd bought new back in the day were classics.

I digress. I always wanted to shoot color, only color, and there was Eggleston, doing it better than anyone. And making a brilliant book out of it.

That was the thing about *Guide*, it was another great story, welcoming us with its first picture, a white door festooned with a basket of blue flowers. Come on in … maybe. Ease past the dog lapping the gray-blue rain puddle and the scattered puzzle pieces waiting for us on a living room card table—looks like fun … maybe. Of course there's a man strolling a grave yard, and a naked man in an orange-glowing room with spooky graffiti spray-painted on the walls ("Talley Ho," "God," "Mona"), and even further along an elder gent languid in his bedroom, grasping a pistol, an unreadable expression on his face.

Each photo, Eggleston's genius, is ideally composed, nothing obvious, just right. If photographers sometimes work to center subjects, or dally with the Rule of Thirds, Eggleston works by his own rules of composition—rules broken but always in just the best way. Everything, in composition and subject matter, is off-center enough to catch our eye, make us speculate as to what's going on, and draw us into Eggleston's world. He more than most photographers has what we prize in literature: a voice.

Now that Steidl seems in the process of putting out nearly every good photo Eggleston ever took, it's remarkable how all-present his voice is. Butt him up against his Southern contemporary, William Christenberry, and you can well see how voice works. Christenberry has one, too, a way of depicting roadside buildings and signs in a way all his. Eggleston trumps him, of course. He can shoot a building and make it his own, but he can also, as he does in his *Guide*, shoot a green shower or an open-door oven and make that his own, too. Try that: Pick the most banal, everyday thing you can find, and invest it with grace and significance.

That's the great power of *Guide*, how common nearly all the subjects are, yet how rich and meaningful and perfect they loom. I can recall spending long amounts of time looking at the shot of the lit-briquette barbecue, placed between the right wheel of an old car and a man with a clenched fist, placed just right with another tricycle, this one with streamers attached to the handlebars.

Why do I get so lost in this shot? It has fire, a burst of energy and light not that far from Frank's radiant jukebox, and somehow every object and line of the concrete is ... right. I keep using that word, *right*, because I can't, and am not sure anyone can, explain why all these photos work, just that they do. The photos work. The book works. Sometimes that's all that need be said. Further words can diminish the impact, the purity of the ever-rich experience of a great photobook.

And in *Guide*, all the shots are in color.

Justly famous is the shot of a distant female relative in her flowered dress, smoking, and sitting on a crazily-floral outdoor porch glider. As Eggleston puts it, "I remember I found the color of her dress and the chair very exciting, and everything worked out instantly.... I don't think I would have moved her in any way. I'm still very pleased with the photograph." Add that to what makes a great photobook: a gathering of instants that work out just that fast, that need not be changed in any way.

What make this photo of Eggleston's relative (her name's Devoe Money) work for us is the crazy contrast of flowered dress and cushions, the jumble of colors and shapes, almost too much, but of course not too much. It's a photo that could only work in color, and so it's good to recall that back in the 1960s and '70s, when Eggleston started working in color, how radical a move it was.

I don't think there's a photo in *Guide* that would work half as well in black and white. The way the colors fall, their extreme, at times Gothic qualities, and the way color itself becomes such a vivid compositional effect ... no, there's no other way the book can be. Color, when taken seriously, adds a whole new dimension to photography, makes it a geometric chess game, a Ginger Rogers in heels doing everything the classic black-and-white photographers did, but in a more difficult way. That challenge of making shots work in color inspired my own work, and countless others. And of course now black and white seems a little quaint, a clearly "artistic" choice. One piece in this volume, about *Astres Noirs*, even talks about how photos made on smartphones in 2016 have been bled of color and rendered in black and white—in ways, a radical return to the world Eggleston (and compatriots such as Stephen Shore and Joel Sternfeld) blew up all those years ago.

3 – The Nothing Photographs

HERE'S A STORY I love to tell about how photobooks have worked on me.

Back in the late 1960s, when I was a teenager, I used to spend a lot of time at the L.A. Free Press Bookstore, Los Angeles's counterculture book emporium on Fairfax Blvd., and I have a clear memory of seeing a small white book with a bunch of pictures of gas stations, then another, a similar-looking one, that folded open and showed every building on the Sunset Strip—and I thought they were the stupidest thing I'd ever seen.

The Strip, where as a music-loving, *Riot on the Sunset Strip*-type denizen, was a place I spent a lot of time; there were some great clubs, but there were an awful lot of boring buildings, too, and this guy, whoever he was, had photographed every one. Boring? Yes. Way boring.

And gas stations? In L.A. back then they were everywhere. So what?

The thing is, I remember vividly thinking that: How stupid, how boring. So now I own copies of all of Ed Ruscha's plain-white-covered books, *Twentysix Gasoline Stations, Various Small Fires, Some Los Angeles Apartments, Every Building on the Sunset Strip, Thirtyfour Parking Lots, Nine Swimming Pool and a Broken Glass,* and *Real Estate Opportunities.* Back at the Free Press Bookstore they cost $2.00 or so. Seemed like a fortune. Needless to say, I've paid a bit more for copies in the last ten years.

The thing is, though there's really nothing much to look at in Ruscha's "White Album" books, each volume emits an unwavering power and compelling interest. Like many of the photobooks I love, I can't explain what makes them so magical; or at least, I don't want to sully the books with too many or the wrong words.

But each Ruscha white book has enormous presence. They've been called the first artist's books that are more works of art than books, and it's hard to argue with that (the much older me says). The size is right, the paper, the minimalist printing, the almost silky glassine wrappers, the purposefully blank pages, the perfect banality of most of the shots, and yet the occasional surprise, such as the glass of milk following the Small Fires ... yes, it's all just right.

The remarkable thing about Ruscha's books is how many rip-offs they've inspired. I own a book that's nothing but takes on his White Album: *None of the Buildings on Sunset Strip, 17 Parked Cars in Various Parking Lots Along Pacific Coast Highway Between My House and Ed Ruscha's,* even the most perfect rip-off, *Various Blank Pages.* There are dozens, perhaps hundreds, and they keep coming.

So Ruscha's White Album books have had more direct effect on the world than any other artist's book or photobook. I guess there's something in the essential nothingness that makes people think they can make something artful out of riffing on Ruscha's initial ideas. They've persuaded printers, maybe publishers, possibly their friends ... and the books keep coming.

You've got to give the imitators props for being so brazen, but none of their books work anything close to Ruscha's originals. The originals ... they hold their power, their perfection, and though I don't get all that much from actually "reading" them, I always know where they are in my office, and simply having them there makes the room richer, fuller, more artful. Nothingness as compelling presence ... a nifty trick, indeed.

4 – The Inexplicable, Transcendent Glow

ONE OF MY earliest serious photobook purchases (circa 2012) was a book in a tattered plastic bag thumbtacked to a corkboard in a used bookstore in New York's East Village. It was a lot of money, but as I looked through it I saw something I'd never seen before, and haven't since: mostly night shots in black and white in which light appeared to rise off the page. That is, whatever is a light source on the page, bulbs strung along the tents of an outdoor circus, a cooking fire under a bridge, the light inside a trolley car, the window of a restaurant called Suzy, even whatever catches illumination glistening along a cobblestone street ... in this photobook, all light is so intense that the photographs don't simply depict light, they truly glow.

Glow as if actual bulbs are implanted in the aged paper!

The book, of course, is Brassai's *Paris du Nuit*, and the reason it was pricey (but, fortunately, not that pricey) was that it was the original iteration from 1933, in purest gravure. I've just been looking at my copy, went to get a cup of tea, and thought I'd better wash my hands before squeezing the teabag, lest I get ink all over it—even though the ink dried well over eighty years ago. (It's rumored that printers of the book died from too much gravure, however that might work.)

What is true is that although all further printings of *Paris by Night* (and its more disreputable cousin, *The Secret Paris of the Thirties*) show us excellent photographs with strong angles, memorable composition—there's a shot toward the end with four people inside a cab that Woody Allen cribbed for *Midnight in Paris*—and a vivid near chiaroscuro, there is no actual book like its first printing in 1933. All the others show us a master photographer; the original offers us light itself.

Is there a story to *Paris du Nuit*? I believe that *story*, if nothing else, a synonym for a cohering principle, is essential to a good photobook. By story I by no means expect an actual plot or characters or anything, just an idea that holds it all together, gives the book shape. Brassai's book has a rudimentary "story," but one that's powered other great photobooks such as Cartier-Bresson's defining *Decisive Moment*. I'll call this story the notings of a serious *flaneur* with a perfect eye. That is, is it enough to shape a book by sending out a photographer possessing this great eye to walk around a city, see what he or she sees, and capture what they can?

I believe so, with the codicil that even if the photos come from simply walking about, the book itself takes place in editing, the choosing and ordering. Note that *Paris du Nuit* is comprised only of photos shot at night. Follow its rhythms, from the mostly distant shots that open the book, to the excitements and gaieties of people toward the end. You know it's a great photobook because no photograph in it feels misplaced or wrong. Because it's as seamless an experience as a powerful novel. Because like any work of literature, the great photobook invites you in, takes you somewhere, leaves you changed by the end.

All of which Brassai's masterpiece does.

And, oh, yeah ... that enrapturing light.

It should be clear by now that I adore light, especially as it appears in photographs and certainly in photobooks.

And it could be argued that putting light (and dark) on a page is at bottom all black-and-white photography actually does.

What's indisputable is that no book does that more powerfully, magically than the original *Paris du Nuit*.

5 – The Rain-Streaked Window

AND THEN THERE'S color ... again.

Long before color was a glint in Eggleston's eye, color photos crept into mass magazines, around the time Dorothy in

The Wizard of Oz got swept up in a tornado and wasn't in Kansas any longer, but it really wasn't till the Eggleston-Shore-Sternfeld 1970s that it was taken seriously in art photography. This doesn't mean great photographers weren't shooting color before, just that it was still an outlier. Artists such as Paul Outerbridge played around with color in his studio-shot still lifes. The Danish photographer Keld Helmer-Petersen got even more ambitious in 1948, devoting a whole large-sized book, *122 Colour Photographs*, to shots he believed could only work in color. The photos are not wildly adventurous, but they have an originality and stiff beauty as Helmer-Petersen shows us commonplaces such as a stack of bricks, red-fingernailed hands, a locomotive engine, red tanks against a blue sky.

Then there's Saul Leiter.

His book *Early Color* is one of the great, enduring photobooks. It's comprised of shots from 1949 to '70, though the book itself wasn't published until 2006. Leiter was a painter, a black-and-white photographer, a denizen of New York's East Village (evidently he lived around the corner from me when I first moved to the city), and he was never hugely successful till the end of his life. He worked as a fashion photographer, explored the city, and along the way created a unique body of work.

What is a Leiter color photo? It's quiet, even in the hurly-burly of New York City. It's complexly framed, people often shot through windows or as in the cover shot of *Early Color*, an open slat in a Mondrian-painted billboard. A Leiter color photo can blend people with signage in a way that doubles, triples the meaning, as in the photograph of the smoking black gentleman beneath the bold, white-type awning spelling out HOUSE and BAR, behind which is the tail of a truck carrying WALKER'S GIN (MADE WITH IMPORTED BOTANICALS).

And most interesting to me and my own work, Leiter can double, triple, quadruple the layers of the city by shooting passersby through windows, naturally cloudy and a little out of focus, or truly at the mercy of the elements, rain-streaked, snow-flurried, even paint-gobbed. His most interesting photos exist on different planes, the here, the there, the far, the near. These of course are all just one snap of the shutter, but look at the shots, there's foreground, background, middle-ground, people-ground.

Leiter's also a master of slices and corners of life. Half a foot of leg and shoes atop three visible rungs of a ladder—it's enough for a picture, anything more would be extraneous. Or two hands and five inches of coat sleeve, one hand flourishing an artist's paint brush. Or a left foot tipped against the edge of a train seat across from the sitter. Or umbrellas ... just umbrellas, graceful arcs, safety from the rain, floating or bunching up down the street; or in one memorable shot, just the trace of a red curve on the edge of a snow-mushy road.

Shots patterned or broken up or refracted or reflected or mosaicked (in one of his few explanations, Leiter titles one shot "Times Square Mosaic") or abstracted (some reminiscent of Helmer-Petersen, just a lot more complex and interesting) or blurred into what could be paint strokes and dabs.

These are the photographs of a painter, which leads to two shots from Paris in 1959 that could have been painted by Renoir. Presumably that's intentional, the prints just a brief step beyond representational into a look that can only be called impressionistic, but the astonishment is that Leiter pulls it off. These are photos that don't look like photos but instead like paintings. There's a painterlike quality to all of Leiter's color work, as if somehow he can manipulate lens and film like a fine brush. Is there any other photographer so good at this, making unique photos that look like that whole other discipline? It's no doubt a credit to his darkroom skills, choice of film, etc., but really it's the singular quality of his eye.

The eye of an artist.

The photos in *Early Color* are the work of a man who seems to love art first, photography second, and yet has found his inimitable way to make his pictures glow as works of hand-created art. There's a joy, a bounty in each picture. His photos are a little like Beatles' tunes, they always make you feel happy even when they have dark depths, such as songs like "Nowhere Man" or "We Can Work It Out." Leiter's complex colors, his perfect form, the sly, slant, sexy way he sneaks up on a shot ... it's hard to think of another photographer who makes you feel so good.

A final personal note. I was fortunate to get my copy of *Early Color* signed by Leiter the year before he died. He was at his longtime gallery, Howard Greenberg, sitting at a small table, grinning hugely. After signing my book, he picked up a couple of small rubber stamps by his side, and plunging them into a red-ink pad, he gleefully stamped my book.

I'm looking at it now. There's a circle with the initials SL inside it. Then there are two red hearts.

Joyful indeed.

6 – Enough ... Too Much

THEN THERE'S Daido Moriyama.

What if you get sick of what you're doing? You've done art, invented new ways to make books—Xerox machines in rented storefronts, perhaps the original pop-up show—and become a preeminent photographer ... and then you get sick of it. Do you stop, or do you go so totally over the top in your rejection of your life's work that you make arguably your best book, and then propel a further life of work that seems to get richer and more intense as the artist moves through his eighth decade.

I'm talking about Daido's 1972 book, *Shashin Yo Sayonara*, translated most often as *Bye-Bye Photography*. It's a thick book, a dump of photos with negatives blurred, scratched, light-bled in development, some keeping their sprockets, photos hyper-exposed, cast off ... every possible thing you can do to film and photographs when you're furious with them and no longer give a damn ... all coming together in one of the most beautiful, powerful photobooks ever. (For someone's who is ostensibly giving up photography, given the number of shots in the book, he sure wants to go out with a big bang.)

I'm lucky enough to own an original, but the first copy I got was the excellent reproduction from Steidl's *Japanese Box*. There they were, the three Provoke books, Araki's *Sentimental Journey*, Takuma Nakahira's *For a Language to Come*, and then *Bye-Bye*

Photography. I pretty much knew what I was getting into, but let's say you're mostly familiar with the Western canon and thought Daido's book might be a somewhat normal photobook, the kind you see in stacks on a table in a Barnes and Noble. You pick it up expecting a collection of pictures that will take you some place, show you hopefully decisive moments, give you a glimpse into a world you might someday want to travel to ... and it's not till the fifth picture in the book that you can even kind of make out something recognizable: fish and/or dolphins in an aquarium.

Even this photo's mostly a blur and wash of light, but there, clearly, is a long fishlike entity; so, yes, it's representational, if that's what you need. So, you're thinking, these actually are pictures of real things ... and you go back two photos and finally figure out that the white thing that fills most of the frame is a close-up of a pair of briefs, on a male body (Daido's? probably), wrinkles and seams clearly denoting that.

O.K. It's going to be *that* kind of book. A book whose reigning principle is that there are no principles or rules or anything else in photography. I don't know how the book was taken in Japan in 1972, but it's not hard to imagine that anyone who thinks of photography as actual pictures is confused, angry, disgusted. *Bye-Bye Photography* is the premiere of Stravinsky's *Sacre du Printemps*, it's Picasso's *Demoiselles d'Avignon*, it's Dylan going electric at Newport, it's the Sex Pistols banging away in 1977 ... loud and raucous and assaultive and the beginning of a new way to take in and understand the world.

Moriyama back then is surely confused, angry, disgusted, too, and this inner state has found a rare shape in his "mess" of a book. If some of the best things art can do are to start to fly off the rails, and yet not; to break down boundaries nobody else knows are there; to assault us with a pure chaos that as we begin to understand its underlying rationale becomes a whole new way to order experience ... *Bye Bye Photography* accomplishes this in spades.

Daido himself calls the book one of "pure sensation without meaning," also saying it's the book closest to his heart. He asks, "Could one give meaning to the meaningless act of printing a simple black and white of a frame that by accident recorded nothing?"

Except it's hardly nothing. *Bye Bye Photography* captures the edges of sight, the far boundaries of the world as we take it in. Here's how Daido puts it: "We perceive countless images all day long and do not always focus on them. Sometimes they are blurry, or fleeting, or just glimpsed out of the corner of the eye. Our sense of sight, which is active all day long, cannot be constantly coming to rest."

So everything Daido's masterpiece shows us is there in the world. We just haven't seen it before. Now we do.

And these edges, once seen, can never be unseen. The photobook as world-expander, as guide to the barely known, as celebration of empty walls, blown-out faces, a sea of rooftops, a vague line on a city street.

What I—what we all—learn from Moriyama's work is that we can photograph anything, and our worst, least-understood photos might be our best.

Of course it helps that it's Moriyama's eye and unshakable editorial coherence at work. There are countless billions of bad photos out there these days, just poke around Facebook or Instagram, but only genius can put them together into a book that not only makes these nothing photos make sense, it also changes the world.

7 – Punks on the Boardwalk, Guns in the Streets

As Daido demonstrates so well, a photobook can ignore all interest in depicting a graspable world—showing us people doing what they do, probing society—and get away with it. But a great photobook can also go right into a world, the characters who inhabit it, and bring back not only enduring shots but also clear understanding. I'm thinking about documentary photobooks in which the quality of the shots lifts the book beyond just telling us what's going on. I'm thinking in particular about Bruce Davidson's *Brooklyn Gang* and Susan Meiselas's *Nicaragua*.

Brooklyn Gang is the record of Davidson's hanging out with a Brooklyn gang called The Jokers. Straight society got all worked up about juvenile delinquents (JDs in parlance) back in the 1950s, witness such flicks as James Dean's *Rebel Without a Cause*, and in 1959 Davidson reached out to a social worker to make contact with The Jokers. (The book itself hails from 1998, one of the last gravure print books ever, beautifully put together by Twin Palms.)

I'm writing about *Brooklyn Gang* specifically because it took almost forty years for Davidson's shots to make it into a book (though on my desk right now I have a copy of the Summer 1962 issue of *Contemporary Photographer*, the "Bruce Davidson Issue," with a number of the Brooklyn photographs in it). That's hardly because JDs were still news in 1998. Indeed, few things in our current world are more amusingly quaint than straight 1950s America getting all bent out of shape by teenagers with slightly long greasy hair who smoked cigarettes, drank from the bottle, and danced to that wild rock and roll music. (Davidson tells us that a few years after the photos were taken, drugs ravaged the gang members; a far more serious situation.)

No, the photos in *Brooklyn Gang* were collected because 1) they're all wonderful, moody, evocative, enduring shots; and 2) because they continue to tell a powerful, personal story. It's the same reason we still read James Agee's *Let Us Now Praise Famous Men* about tenant farmers in the Depression, or Tom Wolfe's *Electric Kool-Aid Acid Test* and Joan Didion's *Slouching Toward Bethlehem* about the California '60s. These books aren't merely sociology or even history, they're literary works worth reading in their own right.

The characters in *Brooklyn Gang*, like characters in a great novel, slowly take shape for us. Davidson captures such telling moments in their daily lives that we begin to know them. It's only in an afterword circa 1998 that we learn some of the characters' names and personal fates, but knowing any of that's hardly important to what we get simply from the shots in the book. Davidson captures anxiety, anguish, confusion, toughness, kids posing as tough, loneliness, flirting, the joys of dancing, the stirrings of teenage sex (a particularly evocative shot, a shirtless boy and a girl necking in the back seat of a car, turned up as the cover shot of Bob Dylan's 2009 album, *Together Through Life*), moments of teenage braggadocio followed by uncertainty and despair, fights, tenement gymnastics, cool ways to smoke cigarettes, showing off a new tattoo, a tender moment in a nighttime park, and the pure pleasure of, as the Drifters put it a few years later in 1964, life under the boardwalk: *Out of the sun, having some fun, people walking above, falling in love....*

Here's the basic test for a great photobook: Is there one shot in the book that is weak and doesn't belong? The answer in *Brooklyn Gang*: not a one.

And some, such as the famous shots of a girl combing her hair in the mirror of a Coney Island cigarette machine and another girl pinning up her hair in the glow of a jukebox, are as good as photography's ever gotten.

The same applies to Meiselas's 1981 book, *Nicaragua*. Meiselas, a Magnum photographer, went to Nicaragua to cover the end of the Somoza regime and the Sandinista revolution, which she does brilliantly; but she also made an enduring book of enduring photos. As with a reportorial book such as Orwell's *Homage to Catalonia* on the Spanish Civil War, Meiselas's book is not simply a record of what happened but a work of literature. It's history—and it's the history of the war that shapes the book—but it's far more than that. Meiselas has captured a deeply felt human story, a unique take on the violence of civil war (the equal of Robert Capa, also in the Spanish war), and photos with a power to move us no matter what they were about.

Particular standouts include a yellow-glare of triumphant, Sandinista-flag-waving motorcyclists running toward us; a dark silhouetted gunman standing guard at a corner of a burned-out town; a fighter teaching a cock-eyed woman to shoot a pistol; and the startling cover shot of masked revolutionaries behind a row of sandbags. Meiselas is so close to the fighting, the violence—she's so damn *present*—that her fearlessness and bravery are hardly noticed. She's just there. Right in the middle of it. Capturing the war and making photos that would be great in any context.

The Mysteries of Light

And she did it in color.

In 1981, color was still relatively new, somewhat suspect, for serious photography. Perhaps Meiselas needed to shoot color to get her photography into magazines around the world, but for that purpose she hardly needed to shoot it so well. Take one shot: a row of rebel soldiers with heads stuck out of a school bus, a Sandinista flag flowing along the bus's side. The top third of the shot is a bar of school-bus yellow and the gun- and fist-flourishing soldiers. The second third is the bold red of the flag, the bottom third the black of the flag. It's a perfectly composed shot, presumably grabbed split-second as the bus ran by. In *Nicaragua*, we're not just getting timeless war reportage, neither are we simply getting decisive, telling moments that make a long-ago civil war fresh to us. What we're getting are photos fiercely composed in color, taking full advantage of an artist's wide pallet, making strong statements just in the way the colors fall on the page.

I again can't resist the old Ginger Rogers riff: How she did everything Astaire did, but backward in heels. That's Susan Meiselas shooting color in the dead center of a violent war, in 1981, when serious color photography was so new that that year it got its first book, Sally Euclair's *The New Color Photography*. Nobody in this landmark collection was shooting war photographs, and curiously Meiselas didn't make it into any of Euclair's collections. But along with Eggleston, Stephen Shore, Joel Sternfeld, and Helen Levitt, Meiselas's color work helps define the advent of color as a serious medium.

I love color. I shoot only color. And I can still remember the thrill of the photos in that first edition of *Nicaragua* I bought when it came out. Last year, I met Meiselas and asked her to sign my copy of her book. She did: "To Bob, from long ago."

Yep, long ago in years, but in the timeline of enduring art, just the other day ... and all days to come.

8 – Over, Under, Sideways, Down

I LIVE IN New York, so I shoot mostly in New York. Yet I hesitate to call myself a "street photographer" because it sounds dated, as if I wanted to hang out on the corner of Fifth Avenue and 57th Street along with Garry Winogrand and Joel Meyerowitz, in the same way I might want to play guitar down in a folk club in the Village so I can be Bob Dylan or thrash away at CBGB's before it became a trendy clothing store. All that *was* a long time ago.

But still the streets, especially of New York, with its incessant jumble, parade of characters, ever-pulsing energy … you can still get strong photographs on the streets of New York.

But will anyone ever again make a book that shouts and cries, pulses and leaps, with the energy and abandon of William Klein's *Life Is Good and Good For You in New York*?

When the Beatles hit America in 1964 and "I Want to Hold Your Hand" was the No. 1 record everywhere, folksingers took up electric instruments, kids who never gave music a thought learned guitar, and everyone grew out their hair. The world changed—and fifty years later, the Beatles can still change the world.

So can Klein's *New York*, now sixty years on. Boom, you see the book—especially a first-edition gravure copy, though Errata's version can stand in—and it can make you change the way you shoot, haunt street corners, then yearn to put everything you have into books that desire to be livelier and crazier than anything else out there.

There are pictures I love in *New York*, but the greatness of the work is how as a book it skirts the border of New York madness. It's subtitled *Trance Witness Revels*, and that's the deal: *New York* as psychedelic experience a decade before LSD took off. The book's a phantasmagoria of city life … and yet it *is* city life. Again, that's the astonishment of photography: You gotta be there to take the pictures. Klein was there. Got all the shots, from the pre-Provoke masterpieces of blur and indefiniteness, to the straight-up shots of guys walking around with signs, crowds pressed together, Brooklyn Dodgers fans in the stands, to the general weirdness of our streets, the dwarf held high on a man's shoulders, the famous shot of the boy shoving his toy gun into our faces, the huge, mysterious question mark drawn on the rear door of a delivery truck stopped on a cobblestoned street.

New York rattles, pulses, nearly explodes with its energy, and all that's in how it works as a book: photos all different sizes, collaged or alone, one per spread, almost a dozen per spread, loosely themed but not burdened by the rough breakdown into chapters, faces mute, faces overexpressive, parts of the city you barely notice, people way in your face in classic New York City style.

It's all here, the whole city, circa 1954 and '55, for sure, yet as with any of these photobooks I'm treating as enduring literature, Klein's *New York* is as alive today as when the book was first conceived. The movies on the marquees change, Daido Moriyama found different ones during his first visit to NYC in '71, and Robert DeNiro as Travis Bickle walked beneath other marquees in '76's *Taxi Driver*, but the city—the irreducibly pounding and ecstatic city (trance reveling indeed) doesn't change. It's Klein's, it's ours, and it's here forever in his book.

9 – How Close Can You Get?

THE PHOTOS IN my books are all taken on the street or under it, mostly in my home of New York City; and I shoot with a 23-mm Fuji X100F, so if I want an intimate picture, I simply follow the fixed-lens mantra: If you want to zoom in, just get closer.

As I walk about with my Fuji, I have a few rules, one of which is that I don't talk up anyone who's picture I take, I just take it. So sometimes I can get close, in a crowd, say, where my camera flies up and captures somebody's face inches from where I am. And I like close, like the intimacy a photograph can bring, but I also need my anonymity. I don't go so far as a Walker Evans to grab my subway photos—Evans painted his Contax camera black and hid its body under his coat—but I also don't have to.

A lot of people on the NY subway have cameras these days, I'm just one of them. But I also agree with Evans when he wrote about the book of his subway shots, *Many Are Called*: "The guard is down and the mask is off."

Stripping away the mask, getting as close to human truth as you can, is one of photography's highest aims.

Evans certainly got close, but there was still the width of a subway aisle between him and his subjects. A photographer who really gets close, in every possible way, is the masterful Swedish photographer Anders Petersen, an artist for whom I have the purest admiration.

I'm flipping through his *City Diary* now. Close for Petersen is: a plump nude woman on her bed, a *Nosferatu* tattoo on her shoulder; a man with a heavily bandaged right eye talking on his cell phone; a bride with a bouquet juxtaposed with a close-up of a surgeon's hand going into a body; an odd-looking balding gentleman, his comb-over curling curiously between eye and ear; and, oh, right next to him, a spare tire leaning against a building wall.

A *City Diary* indeed, Petersen walking about camera in hand, grabbing whatever's interesting, but also pushing in ... talking to subjects, getting them to pose, getting involved ... really involved. Look, a few pages later, a picture of Petersen himself looking beat-up, blood dripping down his chin.

Petersen's known for full immersion. His best-known book, *Café Lehmitz*, is Petersen learning his craft by spending a lot of time in a bar in Hamburg in the late 1960s, heading home only to process his film. He tells us that he slept in the kitchen, no doubt drank as heavily as the café's regulars, and ended up publishing a book that basically forevermore makes further bar photography redundant. We get incipient brawls, a woman raising her top and squeezing her naked breasts, some slinky dancing, breast nuzzling, a hand up a woman's skirt as another woman delightedly leans around a post, and finally the last shot, an empty table, beer bottle coasters and a sparsely filled ashtray on it, as a few feet back a jukebox nearly as radiant as Robert Frank's glows over two men's legs. Other photographers have tried to capture bar culture, but nobody will do it as well, as completely, as timelessly as Petersen did.

And that's the thing, at bottom *he was there*. Living there. Hanging out. No doubt drinking, maybe hitting on women. Getting ragged on for always taking pictures, but never an interloper, a dispassionate observer. *He was there.*

In his photobooks, Petersen continues to be there, fully there, wherever he is. He always passes the basic test: Every photo in every book is interesting, revealing, vital. You have to admire his unerring eye, his quick shutter finger, the extremes (and sometimes banalities) of his subject matter, his heavy-contrast black-and-white shots, his always-right editing in his photobooks.

But most of all Petersen goes places, places I don't go (and I bet, most of you reading this also don't go); and if you do hang out in such disreputable joints, think about how difficult it be to photograph anything coherent, let alone artful. I mean, Petersen gets the shit beat out of him and still takes powerful shots!

But that's only one reason Petersen's great. Every shot he brings back from his sojourns tells us something nobody else can, and also makes it clear that what he's discovered are things we need to know. It's kind of a miracle, isn't it?

10 – Theaters of the Mind

A WHILE BACK I went to a talk with Hiroshi Sugimoto in honor of the latest issue of his *Theaters* photobook series. He talked about sleeping in cheap motels, having to stand in theaters for two hours at a time while a movie played and he captured its passage on his eight-by-ten camera, then going back to his cheap motel, developing the negative, realizing he hadn't gotten what he wanted, then going back the next day to do it all over again—dedication.

But what caught me was one of the last exchanges, about how Sugimoto has these visions in his inner mind that he uses his camera to try to capture in the real world; to, as he put it, "Let everyone see what I see."

What intrigued me was this question of the balance between

inner vision and the outside world, and how photography can bridge the two. And what really grabs me is the question of how much the camera isn't simply a tool to make manifest on paper what one wants or hopes to see, but is an actual actor in that process; that is, how much the camera itself enters into the magical melding of inner intent and external, real world.

I think about this because in my own work with my Fuji X100 I let the camera have its way as much as it wants. Sometimes I just fling it about. The second day I owned the camera I trained it on a copper sculpture inside a pop-up gallery in Soho a friend and I had wandered into, and when I looked at the pictures I took I saw nothing but shards of light flying off abstract copper-colored shapes.

My mind was blown. I didn't intend these pictures, I just pointed this camera I barely knew how to operate at the sculptures. (Again, this was my first day of shooting with the camera I'd scrambled to purchase the day before; at first issue, the Fuji X100 was as hard to get as a new iPhone.) Some of the shots show the copper plates hanging from the ceiling just as they were, but the next few photos were nothing but bursts of brilliant light and abstract shape. I didn't create these, the camera did. And yet it's my camera, and I pushed the shutter button.

So whose photos are they? And where did they come from?

Yes, they're my photos, since I did the bare minimum of effort to get them. (And, no, I have never taken a photo that demanded I spend a week watching movies unspool one after another in a dark theater. And, no, my photos don't yet fetch tens of thousands at auction houses.)

Where did my shots come from? That's the truly intriguing question, perhaps in all artful photography. We rarely call a photographer an artist who is sent out by a publication (or even themselves) to capture an actual image and bring it back for some useful purpose. That's just work.

And we may not call a photographer an artist when he or she has a vivid inner vision that they painstakingly work to realize in a print we call can look at—if that's all they do.

No, the art comes in when the mystery and magic also come in. When the photographer is surprised, either by the moment they've captured on the street, or, say, the heaven-glowing movie theater screen put perfectly onto a print. The unknowable mind and soul of the camera have to be involved in the art. Of course it's the person working the camera who takes the credit, but the camera often times does just what the camera wants. At best, all we may do is simply set it loose.

Which is as it should be.

At his talk, Sugimoto waved his hands, smiled, and said, "Yes, it's all there in a relationship between what I see in my head and what's out there in the real world and what the camera itself does." He laughed. "The exact nature of that relationship is always changing, never certain."

So that's why I love photography, and why I love a good photobook. Because photography is such a perfect medium for inner vision made manifest. Because it's so full of serendipity, the kind of serendipity implied in the famous Cartier-Bresson "decisive moment" quote: the unexpected instant of revelation that a great photographer can grab because they're inside that moment; more, that they're inside the whole flow of moments—inside time itself—that lead to the actual picture we're looking at.

Photographers grab lots of moments, then choose which ones work. Spending time with *Looking In*, the essential companion to *The Americans*, is hugely instructive. In *Looking In* we can study Frank's proof sheets. Look at them. Sometimes there are three shots of any given subject, of which two of them are duds but one has everything going for it and ends up in his masterpiece. But quite often there are two snaps, sometimes only one. These photos in *The Americans*, so present to me that they often pop into my head at random, as familiar as an old Beatles song, are one of three, two, sometimes the only take.

Here's the question: Would it make a difference if the shots of Frank's we know so well were the product of dozens of attempts at that photo?

I think it would. One, if it took so many tries, what're the chances Frank would have gotten just the right arrangement of heads inside the New Orleans trolley, just the right glimpse of the bald gentleman between two wide-shouldered gents on the club car to Washington, just the right puckered lips on one of the top-hatted politicians in Hoboken, New Jersey?

No, too many tries means you're at best guessing, at worst foundering about. A gazillion smartphone snappers can shoot all day and post like mad to Pinterest and not come close to a great photo. No, you have to be fully in the moment, flowing with it, seeing not simply the world around you but the world organizing itself into possible photographs. Look, there's one. You anticipate it electrically, then flick down your finger on the shutter at just the … right … moment—and hope that what you end up looking at (on the screen on a digital camera, in the darkroom) has, well, let's say that mysterious quality that simply blows your mind. Something moving, telling, ineffable.…

Humbly knowing that you didn't really choose what the photograph ends up to be, you were there, the camera was there, the outside world was there … and the photograph happened.

It's this mechanical necessity of having to have a camera turned out in some factory to make a photo (how crude compared with Michelangelo's hands!), along with the uncertain relationships of intention and result, thought and practice, and the long unrecognized—and basically inexplicable—desires of the camera itself that made it take so long to treat photography as an art form.

That's because in photography, personal agency—the toiling work of the artist—is at best ambiguous.

Photography is not a ballet, shaped and endlessly rehearsed. It's not a painting, oils scraped off and reapplied to get what the painter wants. It's not a novel with draft after draft filling up files on your computer. (It's not even this paragraph, which I've been retooling for the last hour.) And it's certainly not a movie with a script written, then rewritten, again and again; producers butting heads in; actors cast, fired, new actors hired; a whole army of camera- and soundmen working to shoot dailies; and finally scenes cut and reshaped and moved around, followed by test screenings and box office obsessing. It took a long while for movies to be considered art because so many people were involved, and they were a big business, and who was really the artist anyway? (Turns out it was John Ford and Alfred Hitchcock and Martin Scorsese, directors with manifest and inescapable vision.)

The Mysteries of Light 41

It took photography a long time to be seen as art because wasn't it just somebody out there pushing a shutter button? And what did a photographer do but just that?

No, you can't repaint a portion of a photograph, you can't rewrite it or edit it in a new way. The photograph is a record of an instant (or with Sugimoto, a stream of instances). Nonetheless, it is what it is.

But then there are photobooks. It's in a serious photobook that you can find an artist's thought and intention and purpose. To make a book, you have to edit and move around photographs. You rework it. You can bring all your subtle intentionality and instinct toward the project ... your personal agency. You can guess and second guess a book in the way you can't when making anything but the most studio-bound photograph.

Simply, you can make a photobook say a lot more than any one shot. You can orchestrate it, play with a reader's focus, their engagement, even their emotions, humor and sadness, delight or confusion (or both together, as in my Provoke heroes) ... you can make a photobook a true theater or museum of the mind.

One glowing Sugimoto theater screen is a lovely thing. Thumbing through a book of them is a near hypnotic experience. The sameness of the eternal white screens, the differences in each theater. The thrilling leap to drive-ins, then the unsettling return to actual indoor theaters toward the end of the new book, this time the glorious theater palaces in ruin, the movie-going public in multiplexes or at home with their huge Samsungs and Netflix.

I'm sure Sugimoto, with his joking asides about being a poor artist and even now staying in cheap motels, will understand another great thing about photobooks: While it's now understood a great photobook is a work of art in its own way, even the most collectible ones are far less expensive than an original Sugimoto or Diane Arbus or Robert Frank print.

Which is great for me, and for all of us who love photobooks.

But the key point is that a print of a photograph is a whole other thing from any photobook that intends to be more than just a catalogue of shots.

That's what I'm getting at in this piece, in this book. That photobooks are not a new artistic discipline, they're just a somewhat newly recognized discipline. The Badger and Parr history of photobooks has helped a lot in letting us all see this. The flood of new books each year (a number of which I've written about in the rest of *Mysteries of Light*) testifies to how essential this new art form is.

You of course can't have a photobook without photographs, though it's my argument here that there's a huge difference between the two. A straight-up photographer tries to shoot the best photos they can. A photobook artist may or may not be interested in "good" photographs, but the final intent is to make the best book possible: either one composed of nothing but strong shots, such as *The Americans*, or one put together with nothing but nothing shots like Ruscha's white books, or even John Gossage's aptly titled (and fascinating) 2016 book, *A Dozen Failures*.

The book is all. The order of the photos, the way they're laid out, the paper, the cover, the overall tactile experience, the size, the binding, the elements laid in, the surprises (think Warhol's *Index*, with its fold-out castle, Velvet Underground flexi-disc, and that damn red balloon that glues two pages of all extant books together), the way each photobook tells us how it should be read. (My own *Angel Parade* series puts two books back to back, the same way 1950s paperbacks often contained two separate novels; and it burns me no end to have someone stand there in front of me looking at the book, and just keep going forward, not even noticing the pictures have suddenly flipped upside down.)

At bottom, there are near infinite choices in putting together a photobook, and artists today are exploring them all as never before.

But of course, even taking into account the manifest power of the book as a book, it still all comes down to the photos inside the books, the strength, surprise, and mystery of the range of shots, the themes that hold them together, the order they're in, the way one photo plays off the next, building to the best cumulative experience.

An intriguing conundrum, what comes first, the photo or the book, the chicken or the proverbial egg?

The Mysteries of Light

The Mysteries of Light is a book on photobooks, and clearly I have my own ideas. Simply, a great photobook is far more than the photos within. A great photobook is a form of literature. Why not?

As I first wrote this, Bob Dylan had just won the Nobel Prize for literature. Some carping voices say he's just a rock and roll musician, what does that have to do with literature? But anyone who knows his work understands he's sui generis, that his songs possess the weight, complexity, and sheer brilliance of the best literature.

So why not photobooks? The best are analogues to a novel, say, or maybe a collection of poems. Frank's *Americans* is at the least a collection of short stories, part Sherwood Anderson, part Faulkner (not to mention the obvious comparison to his pal Jack Kerouac's *On the Road*). Ruscha's *Twentysix Gas Stations* is a collection of short, demotic poems, if not Walt Whitman, certainly William Carlos Williams. Klein's *New York* is a big, galloping novel of the city, part John Dos Passos, part Hubert Selby's *Last Exit to Brooklyn*. Daido's books howl like Allen Ginsberg's poems and Dylan's coruscating songs.

I love and cherish my favorite photobooks as I do the novels that first blew open the world for me, the poems that showed every twist and turn of consciousness, the songs I hum when I'm at my most expansive.

A great photo lifts me ... and I hope in *Mysteries of Light* to begin to get at the power putting a lot of them together in one book, in the right way, can capture.

So let's let one of these estimable novelists, Jack Kerouac, coming up with a few pages to introduce *The Americans* over sixty years ago, have the last word:

"What a poem this [book] is, what poems can be written about this book of pictures some day by some young new writer high by candlelight bending over them describing every gray mysterious detail, the gray film that caught the actual pink juice of human kind. Whether 't is the milk of human-kindness, Shakespeare meant, makes no different when you look at these pictures....

"Anybody doesn't like these pitchers don't like potry, see?"

See.

Why I Take Photographs

It all begins with a long breath, *whssssped* in as soon as I hit the street. A deep inhalation, air lifting my nostrils, tilting back my head, focusing my eyes—my eyes zeroing in on everything in front of me. My head clears and I start to not simply see the street in front of me, I see a flow of shapes, forms, colors—I begin to see possible photographs.

There's not going to be a good photo between me and the subway a block away, well, there almost never is, but as boy scouts still tell us, preparation is all—and I'm prepared. I pull my camera from its bag, drape its leather strap over my neck, take off the black lens cap, turn it on, check a few settings ... and then I start looking even harder.

"Camera-seeing," is one way I describe it, and being in camera-seeing mode is a main reason I take photos: to have a good reason to slip into this heightened, focused, eyes-swinging-side-to-side, nothing-gets-by-me (I hope), all-consuming mental state. I'm no longer just a regular person walking down the street, I'm all in the street ... and yet I'm not. It's a funny presence, you're walking—and dodging passersby, missing dog leashes, avoiding broken sidewalk—but you're also floating above the actual street life, that buzz and thrust, enveloped in an artful nonparticipation participating, watching the street, pushing consciousness out into it, and of course waiting ... always waiting. The point is to be out there in the street, yet not fully part of it; aware enough of what you're doing, where you're going, but even more aware of possible photos. When everything's working, I'm all eyes (and let's hope quick reflexes), and if I Zen-out into the sunlit morning just right, that's all I am. I see just what's in front of me, what my camera might capture; the rest of the world—personal worries, what to have for lunch, all the quotidian pleasures and trials—is ignored.

The Mysteries of Light

I've written novels what seems like all my life, so I'm pretty good at both being fully in a moment and yet away from it. When writing, you have to follow the flow of the story, typing like mad, yet also always asking if what your fingers are getting down is right, belongs. As I tell my writing students, you have to be like a hummingbird's wings, one wing creating, the other wing cutting back what you've just written; and you have to do this so fast it's not just a blur, it's invisible.

Taking photos is similar: I have to see something, judge whether it might make a photo, try to grab the flow of the street-moment so the shutter pops at just the right millisecond, then ask myself if there's another photo about to come. (A few quiet moments later, I look at the shots on the back of my Fuji, and mostly call myself an idiot and delete a bunch—or now and then say to myself, *Hmnn, that one could work*, and keep it till later. More on this to come.)

The point for now is that for me the greatest pleasure of photography is slipping into this heightened state, this artistic high, and being lost to it. I like it there. When I have my camera around my neck, almost every day I do, I'm in this special place. I don't take drugs, haven't since when as a kid I gave being a hippie a go, so my high is this heightened state of photographic possibility. It works. It's fun—and pretty damn cool, too.

Yet I'm not taking pictures just to get a buzz on. I'm after something bigger, grander, more startling. I'm chasing art.

So, contra social media, and maybe a little old-fashioned (and yet as new and cool as the vinyl record resurgence), I'm working to accumulate a body of photos that will end up in a book. They'll be offloaded from my Fuji, then edited in Lightroom and Photoshop, dragged into folders, pulled up again in Lightroom in potential book groupings, and then chosen and unchosen, ordered and reordered, as I work toward the string of shots that will make up a physical book.

I've always thought any art (paintings, books, music, etc.) was special, and took a lot of time and work. I'm wary of the seriousness of anyone simply feeding their Instagram account, though I'm also open to a strong body of work coming from anywhere, any which way.

Still, I have my way of working—don't we all—and I believe it works for me. The start is taking pictures on the street, the ending is a physical book somebody can enjoy and appreciate.

So how do I get there?

Often before a day's camera-wandering, I pull a photobook from my shelves, not really to learn anything further from it, really just to use it as a touchstone, the way a sports team will all pass hands over a totemic bat or helmet on their way to the field, to orient myself, get focused, tell myself I'm on my way out the door to do *serious* play, not of sport but taking pictures.

One photobook I'll look at is a big, fat glob of Daido Moriyama. I look at his photos for a few reasons. One, they tell me anything's possible; and two, they suggest that an awful lot of photos can pile up and still make a great photobook. Not all of his shots are gems, but all of them are all his.

Not mine, his. All his.

Daido always reminds me: Be true to yourself, your own vision. Make every shot you take your own.

Another totemic book, perhaps my most often touched on my way out the door, is *Photographing America*, a collection of shots by Henri Cartier-Bresson and Walker Evans of just that: America. The book is literally a touchstone: I run my hands through its pages, look at some of the photos I know so well, using them to jog my mind just a little—to get me thinking, These are good photos, deeply telling, well-composed, and ultimately America-defining.

Indeed, much of what I've done, in photography as well as my fiction, is to capture America; and many of the artists I like best are those who, in their singular ways, have done just that: Walt Whitman, Herman Melville, William Faulkner, Bob Dylan, Jackson Pollock, Edward Hopper, Emily Dickinson, Bruce Springsteen; and photographers such as Robert Frank, William Klein, Walker Evans, Helen Levitt, and Saul Leiter.

Of course most of these are white men, but they're also indisputably our forefathers, and if what I'm after as I head out on the streets is to take my photos in the first portion of the 21st Century, these souls create a solid grounding (as well as,

The Mysteries of Light

I hope, deep inspiration). If Dylan is inspired still by Woody Guthrie and Child ballads and the old Testament and Homer, well, you take your strength from wherever it comes.

Again, it's not that any one photo in *Photographing America* directly inspires me, it's just a head-turn, a way to set each step from that moment on toward the point of adding to that photographic canon: Photographing America.

And also to get me out into the street. To take street photos.

When I first got excited about taking photos, I realized I wanted to do what historically has been called street photography, so I read *Bystander: A History of Street Photography* by Joel Meyerowitz and Colin Westerbeck. I wanted to know where the work I was interested in taking on had been, so I could figure out where I could help make it go.

I learned a lot, got a lot of ideas, but the more I looked into the whole idea of being a street photographer in our decade, the less I liked the sound of it. It was like trying to be a rockabilly artist, say, a doowop group or a synth band: Years back it had been discovered as something fresh and new, moved the world, and now it was close to nostalgia.

Which posed a challenge. I wanted to take photos as I *flaneured* around the city, camera in hand, but I didn't really want to be a street photographer. I mean, I'd love to have been Garry Winogrand, Lee Friedlander, Bruce Gilden, or Meyerowitz when they were the only guys standing out on Fifth Avenue waiting for photos to stroll on by. But that was fifty years ago. And as another great (if unreadable) American writer put it, You can't go home again.

The thing is, Fifth Avenue is still there, bustling, teeming, and there are still good pictures to be pried from its wide sidewalks. Indeed, the other week, as I was talking past the corner of Fifth and 42nd—OK, lingering there, camera ready, for five, ten minutes—I saw another guy with his camera doing the same thing. What did I think? Garry Winogrand is dead, dude! What did he think of me? I didn't stick around to ask.

You can't go back ... but again, the streets of New York are still pulsing with new life, new drama, and photographs eager to be taken.

So I wouldn't think of myself as a "street photographer." I'd just go out on the street and take photos.

Aside: I'm not alone. Here's Winogrand on being a street photographer: "I hate the term. I think it's a stupid term, street photography. I don't think it tells you anything about a photographer or their work." Also from Winogrand, always a fount of photographic wisdom: "I don't think about pictures. When I photograph I see life. That's all there is."

Truth is, I also couldn't do it the way it had been done before. No one's ever going to top the Cartier-Bresson photo of the man behind the Gare St. Lazare in Paris, leaping past a ladder floating in shallow water, his reflection perfect below him, the leaping dancer on the sign behind him a true mirror image; or Winogrand's shot outside an American Legion convention in Dallas, a legless man pulling himself along by his hands as Legionnaires stand by indifferent ... those perfect moments of composition and magic somehow put onto film by the fastest, best eyes in the biz.

I can think of dozens more street shots never to be excelled. But I wanted to at least try. But I also do not want to take those photos again—they've been done.

*****

So how to do it? What can I add to the canon? What at bottom am I up to?

Large questions, and if for starters I didn't have that much of an idea, I found I did intuitively discover some dos and don'ts.

For one, I'd shoot in only in color. Why? I love black-and-white photography, Atget, Brassai, Cartier-Bresson, Frank, Klein, et al, but for my own work I like color best. I think it adds another dimension, or at least another challenge: If at times, it's a climb to make a shot work in color, well, start climbing. Make any photo I take work in color. On the other hand, I'm interested in the play of colors. I like Mark Rothko a lot, and mostly what he does is drop two or three blobs of color on a canvas ... and the whole room glows. That's a game, the way colors interact in a rectangle, I want to play. Plus, it's a lot easier to do color work than it used to be. Shooting digital, you don't have to go into the darkroom; owning a decent Epson or Canon printer, you don't have to pay through the nose for high-quality prints.

In a piece on William Eggleston in *Aperture*, John Jeremiah Sullivan talks about the advantage that Eggleston's wealth brought to his photography: Simply put, once Eggleston discovered the beauties of dye-transfer color prints, he was fortunate enough to afford them. Not a small advantage, as I recall my first serious work in photography back in the all-analogue days, and as I lived my starving-novelist life in my East Village tenement, quailing at the cost of even a barely adequate large color print.

With digital, shooting color is as easy—way easier—than old-school film black and white. An interesting fact: The classic black-and-white film photographers out on the street, Winogrand, Friedlander, Bruce Davidson, et al, reportedly shot lots of color film, they just couldn't afford to print it. (That was Eggleston's great patrimony as an artist: Not just artistic genius and a nonpareil eye, but enough bucks to print those color photos any way he wanted.) Now we see books of their color shots, and a magnificent show of Winogrand color slides recently at the Brooklyn Museum, pictures in ways as striking as the '50s, '60s black-and-white work. But they—and certainly I—couldn't get good color prints back in the Kodak days.

Now I can ... and that's what I shoot. Black and white? Somehow for me flipping a switch in Lightroom to make my digital color shot black and white seems too easy, though Lightroom makes everything pretty easy anyway. So maybe it's mostly a question of what kind of photos I want to take, and which photos I love most of all.

※ ※ ※ ※ ※

Another intention for me: Don't be noticed. As I go out walking with my camera, I'm not an Anders Petersen or Bruce Gilden; I don't feel comfortable talking to strangers, asking if I can take their picture. I like to shoot on the fly, often with my camera only hip-high, grabbing shots as they come, whoever's in the frame (I hope) oblivious to what I'm up to.

I'm pretty good at picking up on what people on the street are paying attention to. Anyone on a smartphone is not paying attention to anything but their own digital daze, and as I said above, that makes them fundamentally uninteresting. I find it's a fairly rare person who even knows I'm looking at them, thinking about taking a picture. But I do occasionally find truly street-smart folk who know exactly what I'm thinking, what I'm up to. I can tell, read it in their eyes, their gestures.

It's that awareness, that consciousness that I'm there that I don't really want ... unless it makes for a good picture.

I think of Robert Frank's shot of the couple in Dolores Park in San Francisco as one of the strongest in *The Americans*, the man in the picture looking back and glowering furiously at the photographer. Did Frank expect that? Probably not. Did the man say anything? And how fast did the photographer get out of there?

I've only gotten yelled at, "Hey, what're you doing, don't take my picture!" a few times over the years, so I think I'm pretty good at slipping about unnoticed. Only once did somebody actually start after me, shouting, "What are you doing? Are you taking pictures?" but things were busy and I scooted away. Don't look back, as Dylan's movie has it, and I didn't.

I've also taken pictures where it looks as if somebody is gazing right down the barrel of my camera, even though as I took the shot I was sure they had no idea I was there. Who knows what was going on with that? But ideally, to quote another Dylan song, when I take a street picture, *I'm not there.*

At bottom, all that should be present is a human consciousness, a soul, in concert with a camera, ready to be arranged into a composition resonant and telling, with a quick-enough spark of energy to bring all meaning, implication and metaphor together in a telling visual moment, one that becomes fixed as an image, then edited, printed on paper, put into a book.

What does the prosaic *I* have to do with that?

✳ ✳ ✳ ✳ ✳

Do I HAVE rules for what I do? Well, I talk about a bunch of them in a piece later in this book, written four years after this essay, so I won't go on much here. Let's say that instead of rules I have intentions, and ideas, things I've thought up over the years.

The Mysteries of Light 51

The most important: Always take along a camera. Everywhere. You can't take photos without having a camera. I know, Duh.

More ideas. A few don'ts, for starters. As I said, no shots of people on their phones, if I can help it. I'm wandering the streets to capture (at best) people's souls. Look around, it doesn't take much to discover that anyone peering deep into their smartphones is, at least in that moment, essentially soulless.

Another don't: no panhandlers or homeless people. At least not straight up, as in taking advantage of anyone's misery.

But other than that, subject matter is wide open. It's simply what catches my eye, and that which I in turn can capture in my camera. Essential subjects can be people, lights, patterns, striking details, or redolent cryptic blurs—or a mixture of all the above ... in essence, any photo that captures, or at least teases, the idea behind the title of this volume: The Mysteries of Light.

The eye is all. The seeing. The awareness. The floating along both in the world and outside it.

Oh, and one more absolute rule: Always be interesting.

This is what I go for in the novels I write, and what I always tell my students. You're not really writing for yourself, you're writing for others.

So, be interesting.

How does that work in my picture taking? Interestingly (I hope), it's tied in with the kind of Zen state of walking down the street ready to take pictures, flashing the shutter button, then ... well, pictures are immediate these days, they turn up on the back of my camera after pushing a button, so I can see how well I did.

Idiot! Loser! Fool! I've shouted these imprecations at myself, coming so close to a good picture but just not getting it. If I'd just been a millisecond faster, got my camera down a few fractions of an inch, not simply seen the picture, but as a pitcher eyeing the strike zone, actually delivering the ball where it had to go ... that could be me, going all Mark Fidrych on myself, screaming in my head at my camera for having thrown a dead-on strike.

But the above paragraph is just the harsh editing part of my brain, the one that's always alongside the blithely creative one, both working simultaneously. I'm taking the picture, then judging it, all at the same time. I'm creating and devouring. I'm attempting something and failing ... or maybe coming through.

It's a curious mix of consciousness, being psyched up one second, then seriously frustrated the next. But for me it's part of taking pictures, and in the search for the perfect shot, an uplifting part at that.

Because if I'm trying to be the best photographer I can, I can only be that if I easily and casually condemn any work that falls short.

Inside the work and outside it. You have to be both, in the same microsecond, success and failure flapping as fast as that hummingbird's wings.

Then one way or another, for better or worse, what I just snapped is what it is ... and I'm on to the next shot.

✳ ✳ ✳ ✳ ✳

THE MORE I take pictures, the more interested I become in capturing a kind of magical realism, the sort of thing Gabriel Garcia Marquez did in his novels so wonderfully a number of decades back. As I see magical realism in photography, it's imbuing a photo taken on the street (reality) with qualities far beyond what we think of as real. I have various techniques I've stumbled upon, often using purposeful mis-focusing, sometimes using reflections off of buildings, sometimes using forms of glass before the lens, sometimes doing things with my Fuji camera I can't even explain. (As I've said, often that ol' Fuji has a mind of its own; I'm constantly surprised by what it decides to do with whatever I thought I was up to.)

The results are to make street photographs that don't at all look as if they were taken on the street, or at least any street anybody knows. It's my own private place, somehow rendered through a camera.

Sometimes I call what I come up with Impressionistic, sometimes Expressionistic, sometimes stream of consciousness ... well, I really don't put any labels on my work, these are just words and phrases that sometimes flit through my mind. It will be interesting to see what critics will come up with to explain what I do. I'm sure it'll be something. And then I'll have to disown whatever phrase or allusion they endow me with.

Because whatever it is, it's not what I'm thinking when I hit the street. Usually what I'm thinking first is, Where do I want to go for lunch? That quotidian question often determines where I go out shooting each day. Yep, just that. That's the secret to my work: Where to have lunch. Oh, and my other secret: I don't know anything about cameras, can't begin to compare lenses or aperture settings or anything like that. I'm a novelist, not a trained photographer. I use one camera. It does weird stuff all the time.

And yet somehow it all comes together in the flow and flitter of my photobooks, the images cascading upon each other, the colors flying, the magic (I hope, I pray) rising off the pages.

That's why at bottom I take pictures. I do it to capture a whiff, a slant of light, an emanation of magic.

The novelist John Irving once told me that one had to do something each day to "redeem the day." He said that writing well would do that for him (and it's done it for me, too), but if the writing didn't go well, he'd make a good meal ... yes, a simple but loving meal could redeem the day.

So can taking a good picture or two. Capturing an image no one has ever captured. Building a book not like anybody else's.

At bottom that's what it's all about: a way to redeem each and every day.

Book Reviews

Daisuke Yokota, *Taratine*

October 2015

TARATINE, THE WILDLY TALENTED and experimental young Japanese photographer Daisuke Yokota's latest book (unless he's whipped up something quick and newsprint-dirty in the last few minutes, which is entirely possible), may be his most accomplished one yet. Said to be his most personal work to date—more photographic novel than photo collection—*Taratine* takes its title from a gingko tree Yokota saw during travels to Japan's north in 2007, yet is equally filled with far more recent shots of his longtime girlfriend in the throes of ecstasy and devotion.

The book, beautifully produced by the New York City–based Session Press, is also a mix of black and white and color, as well as different papers and printing processes. The good news: The book works wonderfully as a whole, even with all its disparate sections and production techniques.

The way the book is made feels very personal and yet magically abstract, qualities all Yokota's best books have. His first, *Backyard*, is, well, his backyard, though the photos are all blurry, a canvas of gray tonalities with faint hoverings of trees and people. *Taratine* follows Yokota's usual methods, torturing already murky prints with scratches, hot water, and god knows what else to create near mystical visions. We know what each photo shows us, but never clearly; our imaginations are always fully engaged, senses alive. We see all through a murky scrim that simply delivers the truth—and surprises abound.

If *Taratine* is a novel, it's a highly plotted one, with neck-whipping twists. We're looking at the sky, some out-of-focus buildings, and then a naked woman alone on a mattress appears. Soon she's up, walking toward us, then we're in the woods (those Gingko trees), then she's back, in intense facial close-up, till her image blurs away simply into shapes and forms, ending on stubby fingers. Color returns, blurry color, for sure, and there she is asleep, in repose. Then she's up again, in the highest-contrast prints in the book—ones printed thermographically—and these are the most original, the ones I like best.

With the thermographic prints the ink is thick (reminiscent of classic gravure), though in this case shiny and tactile. Dots of ink are either all black or all white, so the contrast is as intense as it can get. (*Taratine*, short-listed for this year's Aperture photobook of the year, reminds me of another shortlisted "book," Anthony Cairns *LDN EI*, in which the whole work is enclosed in a hacked early-generation Kindle, taking full advantage of the device's minute balls, which are, again, either all black or all white.) The *feel* of these thermographic pages is almost as delightful as the photos themselves; there's an unexpected texture to excite our fingertips. Yokota is clearly interested in the physical properties of photographs and books, and Session Press publisher Miwa Susuda and the designer, Geoff Han, have brilliantly assisted him with the way they've produced *Taratine*.

The book—the story—ends with a series of photos of the sea and disturbing black birds. This portion recalls Masahisa Fukase's classic *Solitude of Ravens*, but as always with Yokota—one aspect of his genius, in fact—is how he embraces the Japanese tradition of *are, bure, boke* (Daido Moriyama and Nakahira Takuma come to mind) yet moves that tradition powerfully forward.

Yokota *is* the future, yet *Taratine* is also perfectly of the moment—of his own most private and revealing moments, too. In its complex production, the photos of breathtaking abstraction yet secret personal truths, all laid out in an always intriguing and magical sequence and printed on the right paper with the right tonalities, *Taratine* is a masterpiece. As simple—yet powerfully complex—as that.

Time Ravages the Photobook: Huger Foote, *Now Here Then*

February 2016

Although in most ways I'm an analog kind of guy, when I shoot for my photobooks, I shoot digital, unapologetically. Since I'm coming to my photo work after years of writing novels, digital work is almost all I've known. (Back in the nothing-but-analog days, I could kind of afford color film but not making prints; as a writer all I needed was to boost a ream of paper from my job at *The New Yorker* magazine—hence I stayed a writer.)

So let's say I want to show the effects of time passing on my photos. I could hunt around the Web and perhaps come up with a Lightroom plug-in to add scratches and creases and emulsion spots to the images on my computer. I could, say, print out the photos on my Epson and stick them somewhere where time and the elements would have their way with them. But anything I did would be self-conscious, a bit affected, certainly anachronistic, a little like the way kids are embracing cassettes for music mix-tapes—hoping to capture a lost era.

With the photos in Huger Foote's brilliant new book, *Now Here Then*, the passing—no, the inescapable effects, the ravages—of time is central to the meaning of the book. These thirty-six photos were taken decades ago, initially shot with a sense of serendipity, of letting fate help Foote capture the strongest images possible; then time stepped in, the prints messed-up back then while being edited, tossed into drawers, nearly forgotten, then pulled forth three years ago and carefully turned into the stirring work under review here.

Time is Foote's friend. He speaks of his love for the "element of time and decay" and its role in the beauty of images, and it's certainly both beauty and complexity that the passing of time has brought to these already strong shots. As Foote gladly admits, these are *damaged* photos, all the more lovely for it.

The Mysteries of Light 57

Take for instance the image of an unlit light bulb hanging in front of a daylit window. The photo itself is a nice, Eggleston-like shot of a common, not always noticed corner of our daily world. But what's this laid over the photo, a weird bright-yellow, lopsided-trapezoid emanation jutting off from the bulb? Is it an emulsion spill? Another print that stuck to the one in the book? Hard to tell, but it renders the commonplace scene almost abstract, and shimmeringly lovely. Magic.

Another photo, one of the three different covers: two face-unseen women wrestling with each other on a chair, their clothes coming off. What could in 2016 be an iPhone party shot posted on Instagram is instead a cracked, white- and red-stained print that has a patina like a Matthew Brady Civil War photo. More magic.

Then there's a portrait of William Eggleston, a personal friend of Foote's. In this photo the circular lamp over Eggleston's head reads as a halo, though in the book it's been tarnished with black schmutz, perhaps time's sly comment.

Which leads to the essence of *Now Here Then*: the way that time has simply made things right. Take one of the already complex shots, a flurry of leaves and flowers before a red bench (another of the three covers), which is turned almost unearthly by whatever fluid has washed over the print, and stuck. A black-and-white nude of a woman (with hints of a dancing Isadora Duncan) is blurred, cracked, washed out by the visitation of time upon the print, and thus seemingly more ethereal and evocative than the original shot.

"Every single one of these images has a story," Foote says. The earliest picture is one Foote took of his mother in his backyard when he was 13 or 14. Old friends pass through, there are trips to faraway lands, a flash-burst, light-concealing self-portrait in a spotted, antique mirror—in a way this book must feel to Foote like his autobiography.

Photos with stories, photos lyrical and lovely, all that is in *Now Here Then*. But what I keep coming back to is how time has simply made the pictures *better*. It's as if Foote's gift isn't just taking the shots but being possessed with just enough distraction and carelessness—and, perhaps, Prospero-like sorcery—to let the elements work with him to make the prints the best they can be. Time, what does it do but make us older, less vital, more damaged? Beauty in this damage? Vitality in desuetude? That's the province of high art—and dreams.

Which leads to the final joy of *Now Here Then*: That the photos Foote chose, old, physical prints begrimed by time, damaged by indifference, could easily feel elegiac, too much like history; but instead the book is surprisingly fresh, with its blooms of color, fascinating concatenations of objects, alive and of the moment.

That's true photo magic.

The World in the Photobook: Jacob Sobol, *By the River of Kings*

February 2016

JACOB AUE SOBOL'S NEW book, *By the River of Kings*, plants him in Bangkok. Last year he put out a Leica tie-in book called *Arrivals and Departures*, composed of shots from his travels across Asia. Sobol's an impressive photographer, and his work is always strong and vivid. But the books that count are the ones in which Sobol lives in a place, romantically involved or not, and truly gets to know it: He digs deep, finds its curious corners, develops a vision of the city. That's what he did in his first book, *Sabine*, living with his then girlfriend in Greenland, and that's what he did in *I, Tokyo*, moving there with another girlfriend in 2006. In *I, Tokyo*, he speaks about how hard it was to begin to know the city, and how taking his shots brought understanding.

So in this new book, what do we understand about Bangkok, this city along the banks of the Chao Phraya river? The more I stare at that question, the less of an answer I have. We see interesting faces, contorted pets, some nude women, lots of old people, a snake in a pudgy man's hand, a twine-tied beetle crawling over a man's naked torso. Glimpses of the city, nothing straight on.

Which is fine. Travelogue-style subject matter rarely makes for a good photobook. Instead, what counts is a photographer's style, vision, sense of discovery—at bottom the power of the photography itself. Understanding becomes a way of seeing (the Helen Levitt reference is not misplaced). And Sobol's way of seeing—what he chooses to shoot, his tight focus on faces, the odd corners of experience he grabs, the textures of his imagery—all add up to one of his strongest books yet.

When I first saw Sobol's books, I wondered what they added to the work of photographers we already know. Sure, *Sabine*, his first, had the adventure of his life in Greenland, and many strong, Araki-like photos of his girlfriend, but it occasionally wobbled into the diaristic. With *I, Tokyo*, he found his next task: to carve out his own space between the intense, high-contrast blur of the Japanese masters Daido Moriyama and Takuma Nakahira, and the heavy, close-up, saturated-black visions of fellow Scandinavians Christer Stromhölm and Anders Petersen.

At first look Sobol seemed too much like Petersen, but that's a worry I no longer have. The book they put out together in 2013, *Veins*, is instructive. There's a generational tussle at work, yet in *Veins*, Sobol begins to pull away from his brilliant forebear. Put side-by-side, there's a similar sharp vision and hyperfocus to the photos, yet there's a difference, too. Petersen's work feels closer to Stromhölm's, and their strengths come from a certain coolness and distance amid the close-up intimacy of their shots.

Sobol is just as close-up and intimate (perhaps more so), but in his new work I find more heart—and mercy. Perhaps that's the understanding of Bangkok Sobol comes to: the human predicament, comprised of lost souls, aging flesh, glimpses of terror, faces of fierce determination. This greater empathy doesn't make his work better than his elders', but it does begin to make it his own. In *By the River of Kings* in particular we watch him continue to define his place in the canon.

To Sobol's credit, as he follows this task of refining his vision and creating unique work, he never denies his masters. *By the River of Kings*, in particular, is subtly allusive. In one picture he nails the impossible: He's made a photo of a boy with a toy gun pointed straight at the photographer. The shot works! (Tip of the lens cap to William Klein.) He's caught children at play (thanks Ms. Levitt). He brings us a scurvy dog reminiscent of Daido's famous glancing-back-at-us devil mutt (Sobol's dog at least as tormented).

But with *By the River of Kings* Sobol also stakes out his own turf. There is an unforgettable photo of wizened hands embracing an equally wizened tree trunk; a small, light-colored image of a boy clutching a bouquet in the center of a huge dark pool of floating flowers; two near toe-less feet hovering above empty sandals. I can't find a weak photo in the book, nor one that doesn't manifestly belong.

It makes perfect sense that *By the River of Kings* is put out by

Super Labo, the exceptional Japanese publisher whose recent books include ones by Moriyama, Araki, Kitajima, and Fukase, and the company has done a superlative job with Sobol's book. It's one of Super Labo's best-produced works yet. The inks are an ideal black, the contrast epic, the editing superb. The photos live in a way they don't quite in the Leica book.

By the River of Kings lets Sobol acknowledge tradition but never be boxed in by it. To the photographer's great credit he lets his forebears lift his work, move it forward. Sobol's gone far in this book on Bangkok, and it's exciting to anticipate the cities—the worlds—he, and we, will come to understand next.

Fiction and Metaphor in the Photobook: Marcelo Greco, *Sombras Secas*

April 2016

Marcelo Greco's Sombras Secas (*Dry Shadows*, from the Portuguese) is a black-and-white Provoke-era-style photobook comprised of 35 recent shots from Greco's home city of São Paulo, Brazil. The Provoke influence intrigues. *Sombras Secas* successfully captures the *are-bure-boke* visions of early-'70s Japanese masters such as Daido Moriyama and Takuma Nakahira, yet Greco transports the visual approach across decades and continents, and in doing so keeps the aesthetic fresh and enlightening. In *Sombras Secas*, Greco's blurry, out-of-focus city is *not* Tokyo, but it's not demonstrably anywhere else, either. As with the best of the Provoke masters, the landscape is more dream and metaphor than physical space.

There are strong photos in *Sombras Secas*, but they don't leap out from the book ... because here the book is everything. Spend time among Greco's shadows and you begin to sense the book's a journey, a narrative, possibly even a novel.

The journey is set up in the first photo as we meet our guide: a ghost image of a middle-aged man (our Virgil?), hand to chin, pondering, about to lead us into his half-world. Where does he take us? Past high-towered apartment buildings, melting into the sky. Past graffitied walls and stark black trees. We hop on the subway, a figure in huge sunglasses indifferent above us. Further along we come upon a lonely-hearted streetlight; in another shot, a tarp twisted over two strings of barbed wire. Those further photos, what are they? No way to know, the blur, as intense as anything in Moriyama's nihilistic masterpiece, *Bye Bye Photography*, reveals nothing but a cruel beauty.

The story's overall meaning? Implicit, never articulated, but still satisfying.

Again, *the book* is all ... which leads to a slight digression.

A few weeks back I picked up a copy of Chris Killip's far

different photobook *In Flagrante* (the first edition, not the forthcoming version two), and a line from his short intro hit me hard: "The book is a fiction about metaphor."

That line seems key to any great photobook. Even though by definition comprised of actual photographs created through a camera lens, the great photobook is invented, the same way fiction (even if "based on real events") has to at bottom simply be made up. The great photobook also tells a story. Even though, curiously, casual lookers at photobooks tend to flip around from page to page or even to start from the back—I've seen this time after time when proffering my own photobooks to interested souls—I like to think that if a reader begins to cherish a photobook, they'll read it from cover to cover, the way the photographer/author intended. And when they do, they'll discover "a fiction about metaphor."

Metaphor is key. In the great photobook, images stand for other things. Pictures talk to each other, the discussion is always about more than what's depicted. Themes abound. Meaning lurks in shadows, whether wet or dry.

Time will tell if Marcelo Greco's *Sombras Secas* is a great photobook, but it undeniably does what great photobooks do. It sweeps us up into a story, carries us through its haunted landscape, surprises us, challenges us to find understanding, yet ultimately leaves us as uncertain as the guide we met in the first shot in the book.

Look, here he is again, four photos from the end: a black silhouette shot from the back, atop a flight of darkened city stairs. The next photo is comprised of three layers—bricks, violent graffiti scribbles, rusty corrugated metal wall. The penultimate shot: Our guide again? Hard to be sure, a lovely blur of what looks to be a man slipping away from us in the lower righthand corner. Then the final image: A deserted interior, an inexplicable free-standing concrete wall, a pointless window in the wall's center.

It's an ending for sure, though I won't speculate on where we've ended up, and what it all means. What I know without doubt is that *Sombras Secas* is a journey well worth taking.

Provoke: Between Protest and Performance

May 2016

IF YOU LOVE JAPANESE PHOTOGRAPHY, as I do, the new book *Provoke: Between Protest and Performance* is essential—and a godsend. The thick, black tome is many things: a catalogue with copious reproductions of pages from pre-Provoke protest books, the actual works that make up the Provoke canon, and important works that followed in the Provoke spirit; useful essays (read: very little pretentious academic twaddle); numerous historical documents translated into English for the first time; and current interviews with some of the major players such as Daido Moriyama and the late Takuma Nakahira. (Quick note: Shomei Tomatsu's shots from 1975 capturing Daido being transformed from a hipster kid to a geisha are worth the full price of admission.)

The best news is that the book's component parts are in ideal proportions. You can pick up *Provoke* simply as you might one of Jeffrey Ladd's fine Errata: Books on Books series; as a way to actually look at books you'll never see anywhere else. (At a show on Provoke-era photography at the Japan Center in NYC there were numerous great books, but all under lock and key in vitrines. Though on a recent class visit to the Museum of Modern Art library, the first edition *Provoke* books were brought out for the students to look at. As the helpful librarian Philip Parente said, "We're a library. Our books are meant for people to touch and enjoy.")

Still, in *Provoke: Between Protest and Performance* all the books live.

The next best news is that you'll learn much about the Provoke era. It's the editors' contention that Provoke itself followed from a flurry of black-and-white photobooks produced to commemorate and inspire further protests in the streets of Tokyo. As the introduction has it: "The present volume treats photography in Japan of the 1960s as a pivot between protest

The Mysteries of Light

and performance, politics and art." The key word seems to be *pivot*, where disruptions and excitations in the culture fed—and were fed by—photography. (One fascinating tidbit: If you're shooting political demonstrations, it seems wise to blur your photos so none of the participants can be hauled into court and your photos used to prosecute them—hence a damn good practical reason to come up with a "rough, blurred, and out of focus" aesthetic.)

I came of age at the same time as Provoke, though in Berkeley, Calif., where I went to university (and got tear-gassed in the streets). I actually remember the '60s fairly well (and, as the joke has it, I *was* there), and I know that protests in the street went hand in hand with eruptions in the culture. That's the thesis of the book here—that politics and culture were one big stew—and that made me think of the first time I met Daido.

I'm standing before the master, and spontaneously I burst out, "I think you're the Bob Dylan of photography."

What did I mean? Not all that sure then, but after reading the book before us, I see how through Dylan's genius the political impulses that founded his career ("Blowing in the Wind," "Masters of War") inexorably moved his poetic vision to rough, blurry, out of focus songs such as "Desolation Row" and "Visions of Johanna"—in effect, allowing 1960s political revolution to inspire, even demand, a revolution in consciousness.

Dylan has said many times that he was never that political, and in their interviews in *Provoke*, Daido and his cohorts say much the same. Makes sense. The job of the artist, at least in those years, was to bring forth visions and worlds theretofore unknown. From *Provoke 1* (before Daido's contributions): "We as photographers must capture with our own eyes fragments of reality that can no longer be grasped through existing language." How thrilling that in Japan, when language breaks down, the form the culture finds to reimagine itself is ... the photobook.

And that essential thrill is what makes *Provoke: Between Protest and Performance* such a great work. Big props to Steidl for logically and vividly laying the book out, and its usual exemplary reproduction of some of the best and most important photographs ever. Big thanks to the editors who put the photographs first, then let us know so much of what was going on in the world around them. And of course thanks to Daido, Nakahira, Tomatsu, Kazuo Kitai, Eiko Hosoe, Nobuyoshi Araki (who intriguingly wanted to join Provoke but couldn't, and still feels "torn and jealous"), and all the other photographers who, as with Dylan, changed not just the world of their art but the consciousness of the world at large.

A "Storytelling" of Ravens: An Appreciation of Masahisa Fukase's Masterpiece

June 2016

THE AFTERLIFE OF MASAHISA FUKASE continues apace. In the last year I've picked up *Slaughter* (staged shots of his first wife, Yoko, posing in a slaughterhouse in 1962) and *Wonderful Days* (cat photos), and now from Mack comes a new book, *Hibi*.

Fukase died in 2012, but twenty years earlier, after tumbling down steps at his favorite Shinjuku bar, he suffered a brain injury that left him in a coma. Any works we see now are from before 1992.

It was that year that Fukase finished work on what Mack delightedly calls "literal" street photography—shots of actual roads, with a particular fascination with dark fissures cracking along the concrete or asphalt, and forming not wholly uninteresting abstract patterns. Sometimes we get a passerby, a child's chalk scrawl, and so memorably that the shot is on the book's cover, what's presumably the photographer's shoe. So much for a major plot turn.

Perhaps knowing that nothing but shots in which you point your camera at the street wasn't quite enough, Fukase went on, as the publisher puts it, to overlay "a set of bromide prints with fluid drawings in brightly colored inks, and on every image the physical presence of the artist is traced, a shadow-presence which seems to offer a reading, an interpretation but one that can never be fully resolved." Well, perhaps, though without the lines, dabs, smears, and washes of color, the run of black-and-white shots of cracking street surfaces (there are 111 in the book) would in essence demonstrate not much more than a truly gifted artist obsessively following an idea much further than it should go.

Of course, the reason *Hibi* is of great interest is because it is the work of an artist who obsessively followed an idea, a brilliant one, much further than it ever should have gone.

I'm talking of *Ravens*, Fukase's masterpiece from 1986.

Ravens, that most haunting and literary of photobooks, was deemed in 2010 by *The Guardian* to be the best photobook of the last 20 years. No argument here. If a primary job of a great book is to take you far into another world, and along with that the author's deepest consciousness, then *Ravens* does just that.

Curiously enough, there are two English phrases specific to a flock of ravens: *storytelling* and *unkindness*. Consider that. What words could better encapsulate Fukase's book, for in *Ravens* there are, in the majority of shots, lots of unkind ravens—storytellings of them, perched on stark, bare trees or darkening the daylight sky. In Japan, I'm told, ravens are symbols of menace, of somber failure, and they sure connote that here. Most of the photos were taken just after Yoko, his first wife so memorably portrayed in *Slaughter* and, from 1978, *Yokoh*, had left him; and many were shot during train trips home. Powerful, compulsive thoughts made manifest on film—can photography do anything more? Even the pictures without a raven in them seem possessed by the birds' dark spirits. In one a woman's hair is flying out wildly on a boat trip like a wild bird gone berserk. The famous cat shot in the book shows an animal just as feral and nightmarish as any shadowy, preying raven perched on a power line.

What makes *Ravens* so stunning? Certainly, the black-and-white, post-Provoke-style shots, blurry, like shadows of dreams. Then there's the wealth of composition, no picture even close to conventional. But perhaps *Ravens*' greatest power comes from Fukase's obsessive chasing of these dark, hovering presences.

Ponder this:

"Aside from those more obvious considerations touching Moby Dick, which could not but occasionally awaken in any man's soul some alarm, there was another thought, or rather vague, nameless horror concerning him, which at times by its intensity completely overpowered all the rest; and yet so mystical and well nigh ineffable was it, that I almost despair of putting it in a comprehensible form. It was the whiteness of the whale that above all things appalled me."

That's Herman Melville in that greatest of all turn-a-creature-into-a-symbol books, *Moby Dick*. Fukase's *Ravens* has a similar resonance: his birds "so mystical and well-nigh ineffable" that they can mean anything and everything to us. The numerous photos with smudges of bird shapes, what are they but the flitting, wingy shadow play of nightmare. The murky gray sky studded with a boundless flock—a darkness that will never end. One winged shape against a long smear of smokestack smoke—evil in its proper element. That feral cat—perhaps it's hunting its own dream of a raven, to who knows what kind of success. The naked corpulent woman in bed like an inscrutable Buddha ... I won't even hazard a guess as to what she means.

But I can't turn away.

The above are just photos I flipped to randomly. There's not a shot in *Ravens* that isn't enigmatic, compelling, the very trigger of our deepest, most haunted intuitions and visions.

Hibi is with us now because Fukase, our photographic Ahab, is an artist of singular value, and Mack should be commended for bringing any work of his to us. Still, the book that should be coming out again is *Ravens*. Copies on the open market run from $400 to $2,000, and those are just for reprints. If you want to meet Melville's white whale, you can download *Moby Dick* for free from the Gutenberg project. It's time for a high-quality, celebratory reprinting of "the best photobook of the last 20 years," Masahisa Fukase's work of stunning, inscrutable genius, *Ravens*.

When Once Isn't Enough: Chris Killip, *In Flagrante Two*

July 2016

IT'S ONE THING SIMPLY to reissue a classic photobook, as Steidl did recently—and exemplarily—with Cartier-Bresson's *Decisive Moment*, but it's a bit more to put out a great book in a new, amended edition, as the same publisher did this year with Chris Killip's *In Flagrante Two*.

In both *In Flagrante One* and *Two*, we get a powerful social examination of England in photos taken between 1973 and 1985, when manufacturing in the north, in Killip's words, "quickly fell apart." The book is a social document, but what makes it endure, as with any great photobook, is the originality and power of the photos. So we get almost none of men on the dole and in welfare offices (as Paul Graham shot so effectively in *Beyond Caring*), but instead vivid, dramatic compositions of people weathering the elements (the very world itself?), making do in a landscape harsh in nature (and no doubt made worse by the collapse of the economic base). But tell me, what does the unforgettable photo of a black-cowl-clad young woman atop a white horse, looking hindward, tell us about Thatcher's England? What I get from it is: This is one of the most powerful photos I know, something Thomas Hardy might have shot had he a Leica back in the late 19th century.

So one way or another, *In Flagrante* is a great photobook. There's a reason it was among the first four chosen by Errata for its celebrated Books on Books series. But what interests me in this piece is what happens when a new edition of a photobook is released years after the original in "a radically updated presentation," as the publisher puts it.

In an interview with Martin Parr for *Time*'s *Lightbox*, Killip talks about how the Errata edition got him thinking about *In Flagrante*, and how his book could be produced anew, addressing some of the things that always bothered him about the first incarnation, especially all the shots spread across the gutter and the not-great quality of 1988 British printing.

Now I'm always a little suspect of new, rethought editions of work in any medium. Great recordings come out with a remastered CD, but also outtakes and contemporaneous live tracks and anything to make the whole thing a grand box set and charge more money. If it's the Beach Boys' *Pet Sounds*, I'll get the box (the first time; there's a new forthcoming edition I think I'll pass on), be happy for the remastering, maybe listen to some of the early versions of songs, then let it live on my shelves. Still, when I want to listen to *Pet Sounds* on CD again, I'll play the cleaned-up, remastered version—why not? It simply sounds better, richer, more alive.

With books, though, photographers can go all Walt Whitman or Henry James on their work: rethinking the photos in the book, adding a bunch, changing the order ... in effect, making a whole new thing. Is this redoing better? Depends, of course, but there's a lot to be said for trusting youth and initial impulses and just the way it all first came out.

With *In Fragrante Two*, we're getting not so much a rethinking as a remastering of the original, though there is a little reediting. Some photos have been dropped, others added. For instance, following the immensely powerful shot of a boy squinched-in on a brick wall, his grimacing head buried in tight fists, there's now a wide industrial landscape centering on kids playing on a jail-cell-like climbing apparatus. The two photos work together. The all-important story of the book is enhanced.

But it's clear that what attracted Killip to a new edition is the way they are positioned ("If I was to do anything ... I wouldn't put the images across the gutter") and that they now sit one per page, with a white facing page. Also, that the photos be well-reproduced.

Well, Steidl's putting out the new book, so the reproduction is unparalleled. The blacks and grays are lighter, there's more tonal range in each shot, more details, too. Intriguingly, each shot is more delicate, more pristine on the page.

Is this right for *In Flagrante*? If it were a remastered CD, of course it would be: more information, more detail, more depth. Go listen to the Beatles' first appearance on CD back in the '80s then compare it to the current digital versions: no mud, little blur, crisp guitars, distinct voices ... indisputably an improvement.

But then play the original LPs. *Hmnnn*. I don't want to get too deep into the vinyl versus digital music argument, but vinyl simply sounds better. Does this apply to analogue reproduction (all there was in 1988 for books) versus digital printing? In some cases: No book I've ever seen has as rich black and whites as the original photogravures of Brassai's 1933 *Paris du Nuit*. Even later analogue editions lose much of the magic.

So each iteration of a book is different. I own all the versions of Robert Frank's *Americans* except the French original. Which one do I prefer? Sometimes the Grove—it's the first. At other times, the lovely, current Steidl book. I imagine Frank sitting in Göttingen getting each photo just to his taste. But sometimes I like the 1969 Grossman edition, with its strong, blurrier blacks and ominously dark reproductions.

I go on about this here because the 1988 *In Flagrante* is closer in spirit to the Grossman *Americans*: It's overall darker, heavier on the page, always murkier, but also more emotional. In the shot of tweed-coated workers before a barbed-wire fence in the original, the man on the left has only a black blob for his cap and hair. In the new version you can see the strands of his hair, the nap of his coat.

But also in the new version there's far less of the barbed-wire strands dangling over these men. So which reproduction is truer to the emotions of the shot? I go back and forth, greater detail and finesse from Steidl, stronger yet blotchier blacks from the original. In the case of the men before the fence, though, I think I'll go with the original book and its far more pronounced barbed-wire fence. I am a sucker for a good symbol, as my recent piece on Fukase's *Ravens* will attest.

But my preferences are truly photo by photo. Look at the shot of a boy sitting on a heap of sod carefully holding what appears to be a young chick in his hands. That photo gains nothing from being black and blurry, and is far more moving with Steidl's delicate touch.

The new version of *In Flagrante* is terrific. The intensity of Killip's vision comes through, the slight editing of photos makes for a flowing, still moving experience, and for most photos the greater clarity enhances them. But for others the heaviness in the original increases a shot's power.

Bottom line: *In Flagrante Two* is easily available, the original is not. *Two* may be a bit more like going to a museum show and looking at photos on walls rather than seeing them in the down-and-dirty paperback I own, but that's the way it is. I also think for the majority of shots, the new book makes the photos stronger.

The good news is that no matter which edition you go with, the power of Chris Killip's photos hasn't diminished, and the book remains one of the best ever at taking a socially aware vision of a country and time, and lifting it to the level of enduring art.

Beyond Black and White: Katrin Koenning and Sarker Protick, *Astres Noirs*

July 2016

WHAT DO WE DO with black and white these days? Photographers can of course still shoot film, process it, print it; they can chase masters such as Garry Winogrand and Bruce Davidson as if it's still forty, fifty years ago. But if a photographer wants to bring black and white into the current century—modernize it, exploit all the current possibilities—then what to do?

One approach that caught me at last year's New York Art Book Fair was Antony Cairns's *LDN EI*, in which he put his high-contrast black-and-white images on a hacked Kindle. Clicking through the "book," you saw less a photo and more an arrangement of tones. I bought the Kindle version of *LDN EI* (still available), yet passed on the printed version—it wasn't as interesting, not as pure an experience.

One exciting thing about Katrin Koenning and Sarker Protick's *Astres Noirs* is that it brings experiment and new technology in black and white back into a physical, bound book—indeed, one of those photobooks that could only be an actual book. But what intrigues me most about *Astres Noirs* is that in a way it understands that it's *not* black-and-white photography at all, but something else instead.

You get a clue to what's going on as you open the book and find the words "All colours ... within black." Then you realize that half-hidden under a folded sheet is the word *disappear*, so the phrase reads, "All colours disappear within black." And that's what *Astres Noirs* is: a book of photos in which the colors have been removed. We call it black and white (or, as we'll see, more accurately black and silver) because that's what we're used to, but in truth the book is onto something else. Just look at the title: In English, *Black Stars*. This book is not called *Black Holes*.

The Mysteries of Light

Light and form do not disappear but instead shine forth, but mysteriously, ambiguously, contradictorily.

Astres Noirs was conceived, edited, and published by Chose Commune out of Paris. Cécile Poimboeuf-Koizumi and Vasantha Yogananthan had been following two photographers on Instagram, liked their work, saw similarities, and asked them for a Dropbox account's worth of photos to be made into a book.

For their part, Koenning and Protick had been shooting on their smartphones (presumably in color, shots then drained of color), Koenning from Australia, Protick from Bangladesh. Many of their photos are of commonplace things, a puddle, a horse, a bird. Some are more mysterious, more telling: a soft ball of light, a floating body, specks through an airplane window, faces nearly lost to the shiny blur.

Now I'm always keen on photographs—by definition, representational art, since a person has to actually be somewhere and record a picture with some form of device—that do not reveal exactly what they are. Such uncertainty is often the case here, but I'll also suggest that what the photos are literally depicting, even if clear, is of minimal interest. What truly matters is the way the shots come to us—the way the work's been constructed.

The book itself is a standard size, six-by-nine inches, and is comprised of black sheets of paper, each of which is folded at the top. Thus, a page is closed at the top and at the book's center, where it's bound in; but each sheet is also open at the far edge and the bottom, which gives each page both the thickness of two sheets, and, more important, a hidden area between, which by judicious lifting can be looked at. These semi-hidden pages are put to intriguing use; photos are sneaked in from time to time. Separate a folded page, there might be a glimpse of a transitional shot, a kind of harmony note.

What else is singular in *Astres Noirs* is the way the printing technique (from Cassochrome, in Belgium) paints each black sheet of paper with silver ink. The effect is nothing like a black-and-white darkroom print. Indeed, the intensity of light on the page reminds me of the original 1933 gravure printing of Brassai's *Paris du Nuit*, in which the pages truly glow. (Get yourself to a library with a first-edition copy; you won't believe it.)

Pages light up in *Astres Noirs*, too; some more than others, but that's good. At times the book wants the subtlety of a classic print and its near infinite range of tones, and Cassochrome pretty much delivers. But when the book wants the image on the page to simply shine, it does that also. The printing is always interesting, always alive. And the photos, even if just a flickering of light spots across the black page, all hold together. The experience of the book is a unity, one thing.

A photobook that truly works should be as captivating as a fine piece of music—a triumph of form, theme, movement, instrumental coloration, and, of course, the passion of the playing.

What we have here reminds me most of a late Beethoven string quartet: dark, intense, moody, powerful, and all of a piece. So large credit to the quartet behind *Astres Noirs*: two photographers, two editor/publishers (and a masterful print shop) who have all come together to perform this photobook so well.

Too Many Palm Trees
Intentionality and the Photobook:
Renato D'Agostin, *Archaeologies: Los Angeles*

September 2016

I WANTED TO WRITE about Renato D'Agostin's new book *Archaelogies: Los Angeles* because I was born and raised in L.A., and on trips back to the city I'm always trying to find the best way to shoot it. My own photo work is mostly based on my perambulations around my longtime home of New York City (see especially my photobook *New York Street*), where I have a tight city to shoot, with an abundance of unexpected subject matter. Shooting New York allows me to constantly go after texture, surprise, the concatenations of pedestrian energy and concentrated color leading to bursts of startlement and magic. When I'm in L.A., I'm also out and about, no plan in my head other than to hope for more surprise; but surprise is a lot harder to find in the endless roads and empty sidewalks.

I've never set out simply to capture a city, but in *Archaeologies*, that's what D'Agostin appears to be after: a determined investigation of Los Angeles, a way to understand the city through his photographs. I think of this as the top-down, intentional way of getting shots. You don't go out hoping to be see something you've never seen, a moment that will crystallize a truth you might not even have been aware of till you saw (and with luck, captured) it. Instead, you go out with pretty strong ideas in your head about what you'll shoot.

In D'Agostin's case, this means a lot of conventional L.A. imagery: palm trees, surfers, Watts Towers. Doubt his intentionality? Then how else to account for all the overhead shots of freeways and urban sprawl. D'Agostin clearly had to go up in a helicopter to get those shots, hardly an *Oh, wow, look at that; hope I can catch it* approach.

So given his intentions, what has he come up with? A book of many strong black-and-white shots, with high contrast and lots of negative- versus positive-space compositions. D'Agostin worked as Ralph Gibson's assistant, and it shows. If we do have to see a photo of surfboards and their fins, at least the angle of the shot is not straight on, and the image is paired with a far more mysterious one of sharp-pointed lights stretching feather-like across a totally black space.

Which *is* a strength of the book: Thought has gone into how to match up photos, to make the most of patterns and the play of dark and light. And there are many striking shots: a woman's wedge heels shuffling off an Escher-like patterned floor; what looks to be a burlesque dancer's corset floating over her white skin; the back of a platinum blonde wearing a shaggy jacket and snuggling a furry pooch; and even a mysterious blurry smear of palm trees against the smog-bound sky.

That blurry shot of a palm tree works, but the first one in the book, a chiaroscuro of palm fronds, isn't very interesting. The next one, palm trees reflected in one lens of a pair of sunglasses, should have been cut for being too L.A. sun-worshipy obvious, as should both its neighbor, silhouetted palm trees shot through an airplane window as another plane passes by, and three pages later, a shot of another copse of palms before the gradations of a gray sky.

That's a problem with the book: shots that startle and intrigue mixed in with too many tourist snaps. (O.K., often the tourist shots are imaginatively taken, but still.) The book isn't a travelogue, per se, but D'Agostin's desire to take in the city as a whole ends up too close to a standard coffee table book.

I do have to stress, though, that there are a lot of fine photographs here. Another one I like a lot is a floating large white V hung on cables against a grainy backdrop. This shot has the feel of Ed Ruscha's powerful L.A. signage paintings, and of course it was Ruscha who also got into a helicopter for one of his notable photobooks, *Thirtyfour Parking Lots*. But thinking about Ruscha and Los Angeles can also help us see what goes well, and less well, in D'Agostin's book.

In his classic white-covered books from the 1960s and early '70s, Ruscha was consciously fulfilling one simple idea: shoot every building on the Sunset Strip, fly over thirty-four random

The Mysteries of Light

parking lots, show us some swimming pools. There's also no conscious artiness to Ruscha's shots, they're flat, demotic portraits of unexpected and banal parts of the city—yet these books capture the true archeology of Los Angeles better than anyone ever has, and the books themselves retain a totemic magic (just look at the vast hordes of imitators).

In D'Agostin's *Archaeologies* too many of the L.A. shots are either clichéd or try too hard. They don't honestly surprise us, in the way truly great photos can and do.

Here's another way to look at the problem.

There's a long interview with Garry Winogrand, at Rice University—he couldn't look more relaxed, slouched down, feet sprawling over some desk chairs—that's well worth taking a look at. In the video, easily found on Youtube, he speaks of a statue of St. Augustine at the very end of Sunset Boulevard in L.A. Winogrand says: "I shot that goddamn statue and made a reasonably good picture of it. Then I saw the Frank book [*The Americans*, with Robert Frank's picture of the exact same statue], and it killed it; it put me away six ways.... The picture I made was *made*. The picture he made *happened*.... He didn't make any attempt at making any points.... And it taught me a hell of a lot."

That's what ultimately sinks D'Agostin's *Archaeologies*. Too many shots feel made, they don't appear to just happen. No question D'Agostin brings vivid composition and a talented eye to his shots, but at bottom that's technique—a way to make reasonably good pictures—not the true magic the best photobooks evoke.

True Intentionality:
Arthur Bondar, *Shadows of Wormwood*

October 2016

IN MY LAST REVIEW for *Photobookstore Magazine*, I looked at Renato D'Agostin's *Archaeologies: Los Angeles*, and took it to task for the limitations of its intentionality: How it set out on purpose to capture the city of Los Angeles in photographs and ended up with a book notable for its lack of surprise and abundance of shots of typical L.A. totems: palm trees, freeways, car fins, etc.

Well, I'm reviewing now a book even more intentional, Arthur Bondar's *Shadows of Wormwood*, photographs both taken and found of the so-called exclusion zone around the Chernobyl reactor, which melted down—and shocked the world—thirty years ago, and Bondar's book could not be more different from D'Agostin's. This book *is* a true archaeology—a deep examination of a place that tells us as much about it as we could dare to want to know.

Bondar's book opens (and often works) like a movie. We get a stark forest, black-and-white stripes of trees crowded together, followed by a blurry shot of wiry towers, as if from a moving car; then a hand reaching in from the right and pointing at a haphazard barb-wire fence. Then, faint type on a black background, the title: *Shadows of Wormwood*. (The Wormwood Forest is also known as the Red Forest, which, as Wikipedia tells us, is "the four-square-mile area surrounding the Chernobyl Nuclear Power Plant within the Exclusion zone. The name 'Red Forest' comes from the ginger-brown color of the pine trees after they died following the absorption of high levels of radiation.")

Bondar spent eight years photographing the exclusion zone, and the book is a special kind of photobook: a "memorial book" to human disaster. Though Chernobyl was an accident (or, less charitably, a failure of Soviet technological safeguards, then its bureaucracy) and not a planned attack like the U.S. atomic

The Mysteries of Light

bombings of Hiroshima and Nagasaki, it also looms large in the course of human tragedy. (One can argue that Chernobyl stopped the building of most new nuclear energy plants, thus boosting coal-fired ones, thus speeding up climate change.)

The parallels between the nuclear meltdown and the atomic bomb seem clear to Bondar. His book has a similar look and feel to Kikuji Kawada's classic *The Map*, Kawada's book on Hiroshima published twenty years to the day after the bomb fell. What do we see in *The Map*? Mostly the stains and scars left on Hiroshima's Atomic Bomb Dome, these stunning abstractions of what an agent of human death can write on unforgetting stone. Kawada also intersperses left-behind war detritus and even advertising posters into a powerful dialogue of then and now.

Bondar also captures a then and now, though for Chernobyl, the death the meltdown brought will never be replaced by any vital present. We won't be making metaphoric correspondences between the horror of the meltdown and what's going wrong with Chernobyl today because there *is* no meaningful Chernobyl today, barely any society at all in the exclusion zone. There is only what follows an eternal poisoning of the land.

Both Bondar's book and Kawada's are made up of high-contrast black-and-white shots. Instead of Kawada's scarred stone, Bondar finds his overriding motif in the lost pine forest. Even though the photos are stark black and white, not color (which would show off "the ginger-brown"), the trees look damaged, not of our world. It's with the line of pines that the book begins, and that's how it ends. In between are Bondar's own photos mixed powerfully with artifacts of a pre-disaster Chernobyl he picked up along the way.

We can tell which photos are found ones because they're framed in black. (Bondar's own are full-bleed.) But what he shoots is *also* what's left behind—everything at Chernobyl is left behind, even the people still there. The whole book is haunted by what took place those thirty years ago. Yet there are signs of life. A pool of fish—are they alive or dead?—is followed by a boat in dry dock, hoisted feet above a forest floor, but that shot is followed a net full of fresh-caught fish, food, sustenance, life.

The next clip—yes, the book does read like a movie—is a

solitary biker scooting across a wide white expanse, and then we're on to those souls still in the exclusionary zone: a crusty old peasant woman, a yapping dog. Life is with us, but not for long. Here's an abandoned train track, there a stately building (empty, crumbling) and an empty window in it, surrounded by faded scribblings.

There's nothing unknowable in *Shadows of Wormwood*. Bondar's chosen to remind us of exactly what happened. At the center of the book, on thin, yellowish paper, are documents, a report in Russian, a London *Times* headline, a map. A quick historical jolt, then we're back in the zone, looking at people gathered with candles, then more people, in perfect blurred Provoke style, looks of horror on their faces.

Further along, a found photograph of the plant being built, followed by those dark, bare-treed, haunted grounds. There is no escape, not for the drunk-looking man reaching out for help, and not for those endless scarecrow-stark blighted pines that opened the book. As I said, that's also how *Shadows of Wormwood* ends: more trees, more blur, more confusion, no possible hope.

In Ryuichi Kaneko and Ivan Vartanian's indispensable book on Japanese photobooks of the '60s and '70s, they end the piece on *The Map* with these words: "Needless to say, this book was quite challenging for readers when it was first published; though it received critical praise, the general public found it overly abstruse, and at the time of its release, it sold poorly."

To that small slice of the general public who cherishes powerful, artful photobooks: Don't make the same mistake with Bondar's *Shadows of Wormwood*.

Photobooks in Concert: Daido Moriyama's Never-Ending Tour

November 2016

THE MOST FUN I'VE had with photobooks was five years back when Daido Moriyama re-created a 1974 Tokyo "Printing Show" at New York's Aperture Gallery, in an event called "Printing Show—TKY."

What made it so great?

The photobooks I love most are the ones that come off as a complete work—as a *book*—rather than just a collection of photos. To this end, the order of the shots, how they fall on the pages—their ebb and flow, the way one photo talks to the rest—is key.

With my own photobooks I spend hours and hours sorting photos, looking for connections, digging for a theme, then ordering and reordering the shots to tell a kind of story—to make up a book. When is it finished? When it feels finished. It sits for weeks or months, gets revamped, feels done again, then sits for longer, and finally, with luck (or exhaustion), truly feels finished. When a new book is ready to go to press, every part of it simply *snaps* into place.

So there I am at Aperture on a chilly November day in 2011, gathered with a few hundred other photobook-loving souls, as well as the master Moriyama himself. The northern wall of the gallery is festooned with double-sided spreads of his photos. We're all handed a pencil and a card with 20 empty boxes for the spreads we want and their order. (There are also two choices for cover.) Then we're turned loose to stalk up and back along the wall, ponder the photos, start to take them all in—there are so many, they're all brilliant—and when we begin to feel comfortable with our choices, begin to scratch their numbers into the box grid.

This ain't checkers. It may not even be chess, but closer to Go. For we're not just looking at single photos but these dang double-sided spreads, which means we're not simply choosing pictures we like, we're choosing what we'll see first on a page, then the picture or pictures when we open the spread, then the back of the spread, and how that sits next to the opening shot on the next spread ... and on and on.

Basically, it's amazing. I'm in a blissful creative fog, choosing this, unchoosing that, putting them all in this order, no, wait, *that* order—all the while working with some of Daido's best photos, in both black and white and color, knowing that what I end up with might demand to be wholly different later in the day, that it certainly would reconfigure itself tomorrow ... and yet when I go back to that book I made nearly five years ago, it still looks pretty strong to me. I think it's one of Moriyama's best! (Of course, my version of *TKY* is the only one of his works I got to personally edit myself.)

Side note: When I received my *TKY* in the mail, the order of the pages was not at all what I'd chosen; the busy minions manning the stapling stations had gotten almost everything wrong. I hied myself back to West 27th Street and insisted Aperture remake my book. Without hesitation they did.

I'm going on about this because I just picked up Moriyama's À la Carte, from his latest Printing Show, this one at the Fondation Cartier in Paris in February. (He did one at the Tate in 2012.) Alas, I wasn't in Paris, so this copy is an artist proof put together by somebody else. The book is comprised not only of spreads but single sheets. And all the shots are black and white.

So, O.K., I like my *TKY* book better—it's full of my choices, my ordering, my story. I also like the flash of color among the heavy, contrast-rich black-and-white shots. And of course I have my memories of that November day, not to mention the photo Daido kindly snapped of me with my camera.

But I cherish À la Carte, too, because apart from the early Daido masterpieces such as *Japan a Photo Theater* and the nonpareil *Bye Bye Photography*, his Printing Show books seem his most personal, even as they're records of a public performance. He puts his best shots on the wall, and those lucky enough to be there get a handmade book (those intrepid, if sometimes confused helpers!) stapled together with an on-site silk-screened cover. I'm such a fan of these performance pieces that I picked up the still-available (and somewhat pricey) reprint of his first Printing Show, from 1974, *Another Country in New York*. That book proves, if nothing else, that copy machines sure have improved; though in a way, the really blurry crap reproduction suits Daido's shots well. (At TKY, Aperture had an original *Another Country* locked away under glass.)

It's wonderful that Daido's keeping on doing these shows. In a recent piece here I talked about how I think of Moriyama as the Bob Dylan of photography; and much as in July I went to see the latest local stop on Dylan's Never-Ending Tour, let's hope that this perhaps purest expression of Moriyama's art, the Printing Show, is also never-ending—that it, too, will go on forever.

Words and Photos:
Mikiko Hara and Stephen Dixon, *Change*

November 2016

THE FIRST QUESTION WITH Mikiko Hara's and Stephen Dixon's *Change* is how to read it. The photobook, the first published by the Gould Collection, interleaves Hara's photographs with a short fiction by the novelist Stephen Dixon. The photos are printed on a fine white semi-gloss paper; the pages of the story are on a blue rag paper and an inch shorter on the far side than the rest of the book. The two papers keep words and pictures nicely distinct.

Which is good. Even though I'm both a novelist and photographer, I like my disciplines separate, and I'm hardly alone. In a recent interview William Eggleston says, "It's tricky. Words and pictures don't—they're like two different animals. They don't particularly like each other." Of course Eggleston isn't talking about a book like *Changes* as much as what his interviewer wants from him, to comment on his own work; though he probably also is talking a bit about what I'm doing here, writing words about photobooks ... but still.

So, again, how to read *Changes*? I chose to take it first as a photobook, looking only at the shots, in order, moving through the book. Hara's photos, her in-book bio tells us, "capture the random people and places of her daily existence," and that's what they seem to do. There's nothing self-consciously arty here, nothing particularly dramatic, just somewhat washed-out, seemingly casual shots of those daily people and places. (The work of Masafumi Sanai comes to mind.) Yet there's not a weak photo in the bunch, and even if the photos are intentionally random, the power of their being in a book comes through: The photos begin to imply a small, secret, but telling story.

I can't tell you what Hara's story is, at least not yet. So now it's time to read Stephen Dixon's actual story, "Change."

Whew, good job! Short, intense, focused on a random man

and his daily dayness, exhorted at the beginning by a woman in his life to change, to lose his "cynicism, scorn, arrogant egotism and unsociability, and overall unfriendliness." Fair enough, right?

The nameless man has a plan. He'll start "from the most elementary human intercommunication and gradually [work himself] up to the most complex."

How hard can this be? He'll simply start saying "Good morning" to everyone he meets.

And here's where Dixon's story lays down a deep floor of meaning under Hara's own daily dayness. In the story "Change" the nameless man's effort to be welcoming and friendly to everyone at first simply annoys people, then really upsets a boy, who threatens to call the police, which brings a crowd, and suddenly our narrator is in jeopardy. So much for good will. Turns out everybody on the street is too busy to make too much of him, so he's off the hook, only to keep crying out "Good morning" loudly enough to draw the ire of a man in an apartment who thinks this ostensible civility is all way too early in the day and tosses a bag of garbage at the narrator.

So underlying our most casual, well-intentioned daily civility lies anxiety, indifference, fear, and anger? And our hopes of changing for the better? How quickly do you want a bag of garbage thrown your way?

Hmnn, good to know.

And I sense that Hara knows all this, too.

The photos in *Change* are deep in emotion. The young woman gazing wistfully out a subway window; faded not-quite-golden straw windblown before a train track; a woman, palm forward, lost behind a gauzy curtain; a stern-faced woman at a bus stop; lychees in a metal bowl; a woman's blurry bare shoulder; even what's probably a self-portrait, a woman, features unclear under her straw hat, holding a child to her, camera pointing into a bathroom mirror.

Daily shots. Nothing-special shots. Some focused, some (like the woman with the bare shoulder) easy to toss aside. Whether it's actually there or not, it's not hard to read into Hara's photos a quotidian disquiet, traces of anomie, anxiety.

Emotions certainly amped up by Dixon's always in-focus, never ambiguous short story.

So this is how I read the photobook *Changes*, and how it works. What's implicit in the photos is drawn out by the vivid message of the short fiction. Images and words mix, and meaning is turned, amplified, and, yes, *changed* by putting the two together.

Credit to Russet Lederman, Laurence Vecten, and Yoko Sawada, the editors of the book, as well as Tadao Kawamura, its designer. *Changes* is expected to be the first of a series of blendings of photobook and short fiction from The Gould Collection, which has been established in honor of Christophe Crison, a Parisian photobook collector who died recently at forty-five. Crison's online moniker was Gould Bookbinder, the protagonist in two of Dixon's novels, so it's particularly appropriate that Dixon let "Changes" be attached to this book.

Changes indeed. It turns out that a photobook paired with a short fiction can work as long as the integrity of both forms is respected, and extreme care is taken to make sure the photos set up the fiction, and the story in turn enlarges implication and deep meaning in the photos.

Maybe not the first of its genre, a photobook paired with literature, but one that definitely makes welcome more to come. We should all look forward to further works from The Gould Collection.

Autobiography and the Photobook: Takahiro Kaneyama, *While Leaves Are Falling*

January 2017

WHAT IS AUTOBIOGRAPHY IN a photobook? On one level all photobooks are autobiographical, since a photographer has to be there to take a shot, thus has to have lived the moment in some way. But most photobooks tell us how a photographer *sees*, how they understand their art and pursue it. A true autobiography—a work set out to capture actual events in a photographer's life—is much rarer than you might think. Consider Robert Frank's classic *The Americans*. When we get to the final photo, of his wife and two children in their car (I recently learned it's the back of Frank's daughter's head in the foreground), the shot is a startlement. We've been looking at America, or at least Frank's profound story about the nation—how he *sees* it—and are not prepared to drop into his personal story, all those endless days and hours driving no-count back roads, sometimes with family in tow.

There are a few classic out and out autobiographies. Perhaps the most famous are Araki's *Sentimental Journey*, the visual story of his honeymoon with his wife, Yoko, and Nan Goldin's *Ballad of Sexual Dependency*, the self-revealing record of her wild 1980s (and recently a powerful audio-visual exhibition at the Museum of Modern Art). Both works are wholly revealing (Yoko post-coitus, Goldin herself black-eyed and battered), and both are unflinching autobiographies, there not only to reveal the photographer's life but to tell an essential part of his or her story.

These days it seems everyone's documenting their lives with cameras (phones, throwaways, what have you), even if it's just spur-of-the-moment selfies up on Facebook or Instagram. Is this autobiography? Of a sort, but more like a diary, though possibly a whole new form that will be codified in the future. But it's not yet serious, committed, artistic autobiographical photography. To achieve that you need that personal story to tell and an unhesitating desire to tell it in full ... as painful as that may be to do.

Which brings us to a new work that does both: Takahiro Kaneyama's *While Leaves Are Falling*, the powerful story of his mother and her two sisters, a book both revealing and disturbing.

What do we see? At first read, Kaneyama's mother looks to be a proud woman, a strong one, a sad one, and from the pained lines on her face and haunted eyes, perhaps a soul not wholly well. We see her holding her beloved tawny Yorkie, out with her sisters behind a cloud of blown bubbles, the three women along a balcony before a gentle hill, stolid, posed, unrevealing. So what is the story here?

You only have to turn to the afterword to find out. There we learn the mother was diagnosed with schizophrenia when Kaneyama was in his teens ... *oh!* Look back through the photos. Now the storyline is clearer: The family does its best to hold the disintegrating woman together, but from the expressions on the mother's face, we can see every step of how she falls apart—and how her son's world falls apart around her.

Kaneyama intersperses other photos, mostly of landscapes. These shots, taken, he tells us, on short trips around Japan, mostly to places his mother always wanted to visit, both lighten the book (pulling it away from the familial intensity) and demonstrate a fine and subtle eye for nature. As the book's story pulses along you get the notion that some of these photos—a blue mountain shrouded in a blue cloud, the end of a pier—might have even more significance. They could reflect Kaneyama's mother's disintegrating mind, or his own distress.

Then our hearts break. We come upon a full spread of five old-school snapshots, a lovely young woman and her newborn son, her white dog, her infant in a traditional Japanese robe. Happy, healthy, their whole lives before them ... till the disease wipes it all away.

The next photos are in a hospital, a stark bed, a woman whose crumpled face betrays little yet expresses all the sadness in the world.

One final spread toward the end brings this soul-stripping book to poignant art. The mother sitting on the floor, before a set of windows, staring at the camera, her eyes telling us now of unfathomable anger and loss. She looks present ... too present. There's a message there she needs for us to know, and she knows we don't want to know it. You can't take your eyes off this face even as your gaze drifts to the photo next to it: three furry toy chicks, white, yellow, pink, the kind you buy as cheer-up presents in a hospital gift shop.

There is no cheer. Just a final shot of the courtyard of the hospital, followed by a reprise of the cover shot, the three damaged women, the sweater-bound Yorkie, the ever-haunted expressions, the unhelpful sea.

Is *While Leaves Are Falling* a true autobiography? Even though it's more directly a portrait of the artist's mother, I believe it is. Araki's *Sentimental Journey* was mostly photos of his newlywed wife, yet he was there, experiencing it all as closely as a human can. So, too, is Kaneyama *there*. The questions we might ask only make this more apparent. Why does he take this shot of his mother? Why juxtapose it with a jumble of apartment buildings? What's the effect of her disintegration upon him? How does the face of chaos and terror affect you when it's your own flesh and blood? The way he chooses his shots, breaks up the portraits with the travel shots (metaphors?), drops in the historical family snapshots, it's not hard to feel what Kaneyama is feeling. There's no way around it: This is his *mother*, as heartrending as that fact may be.

The afterword and a guide to when each photo was taken help us. As a rule I think photobooks should tell their stories just through their photos, but with *While Leaves Are Falling*, because the story is so personal, and the histories behind the photos essential, we need this supplemental info; it expands the power and meaning of the book. That *"oh!"* again. Now we know what's going on. Now we know how we got here, and what we're looking at. There's no way to get Kaneyama's story wrong, not take it seriously enough. It's all there in front of us.

Revealing. Upsetting. Heartbreaking. And a worthy successor to *Sentimental Journey*.

The book itself is impressively made, with fine details. There are two choices of cover shot, both photos laid into the front and framed nicely with an inset indentation. (I do question running the black title over the very darkest part of the cover photo, at least on the version I have.) There's a faint ghostly impression of the cover picture on a thin leaf before the title page. A handy job all around.

But the real value of Kaneyama's *While Leaves Are Falling* is the subtly powerful tale of this young man and his burdened, shattered mother and family. It's not an easy tale, but this is not a normal photobook. It's overtly personal, and a great example of how the photobook can expand, like written literature, to encompass all types of stories and approaches, even the most harrowing.

My True Story:
Jim Goldberg, *The Last Son*

January 2017

IN MY LAST REVIEW for *Photobookstore Magazine*, I talked about autobiography in photobooks, how all photobooks in a way chart a photographer's life, since he or she physically takes the pictures, but how an actual autobiographical photobook is rare, because it demands an intention to deeply examine one's own life, then to tell that story, and well. I also talked about the specific problem of photobook autobiography: Because the photographer is *taking* the picture, he or she can't usually be *in* the photo. (I don't think of Lee Friedlander's *Self-Portrait* as a genuine autobiography, more just his having fun snapping his shadow.) In a photobook of autobiographical intent there's an inevitable reflected quality: This is my story because I'm taking the pictures of a story around me that matters.

Well, now we have Jim Goldberg's *The Last Son*, the inimitable photobook maker's own story that really *is* his own story.

We know Goldberg's style, from 1995's *Raised by Wolves* to 2013's redo of *Rich and Poor*. (Actually, 2016 brought us a repurposed version of *Raised by Wolves*, done in the form of Xeroxed pages, as the book was first designed, and in the street spirit of the kids who populated it, especially Tweeky Dave.) Goldberg takes deeply personal photos of folks willing to tell their stories, souls wealthy, impoverished, feral, and then lets them scribble essential messages about themselves near their portraits. He also collages a lot, throwing in, in *Raised by Wolves*, random found snapshots, film strips of a snowy-screened TV, even a Carl's Jr. advertisement backed by a long personal confession by one of his street urchins. He's an anthropologist of sorts, printing in set type long interviews with his subjects.

Turn the page on a Goldberg masterwork, you don't know what you're going to find: the bottom of a well-decorated skateboard, a letter from a physician throwing up his hands at the unresponsiveness of one street kid, a map with felt-tip-pen markings of where one of the subjects had been.

And always brilliant, raw, revealing photographs taken by Goldberg of at least Danny Lyon intensity: A boy with a throw-away needle between his teeth. The most squalid of crash pads. A gun barrel used as a pointer finger.

Raised by Wolves, in particular, reads like the most complex and powerful of social-realist novels. The stark, powerful photos tell stories, but the added subject comments, interviews, and the unexpected visual leaps (you won't forget the open drawer with stilettos and a pistol among a lot of rechargeable batteries; the childish pen drawing by Ronda of "Daddy fucking me") that twist and turn the story, making it nearly inexhaustible. This is an incomparably rich book.

And now, in *The Last Son*, Goldberg directly tells his own story. (It's the second of three planned autobiographical works with the estimable Japanese bookmaker Super Labo.)

The Goldberg style I've painstakingly cataloged above applies fully in *The Last Son*. There are a lot of self-taken shots, but since this is an out-and-out autobiography, there are also numerous historical Kodak snaps; a personal history typed out on cut-up slips of paper; contact-sheet shots marked up with yellow and red grease pencil; random-seeming, nonidentified portraits; a running motif of big white circles taken from sprockets of old home movies; even a full-bleed color spread of a huge gas-guzzler outside a farmhouse, the whole photo chemically damaged, those white circles strewn about, the image itself almost melted away.

As expected with Jim Goldberg, surprises on every page.

But at bottom Goldberg is telling his personal story, as clearly as he can, and pretty much chronologically. This is a book you can—and should—read straight through from beginning to end.

We open with the family: labeled photos of Dad, Brother, Mother, Sister, Me. We then get a typescript explanation of Goldberg's place in the family: "I was always told the story that the reason I was born so long after my brother and sister was because my mother refused to have another child until there was an extra bathroom in the house…. I don't think that this story was true." (Indeed, elsewhere Goldberg talks about feeling unwanted, a mistake.)

But think about the prose. It's a huge strength of the book. The writing is perfectly straightforward, the history is clear, and Goldberg wryly tells us just what we need to know to understand his life.

Of course Goldberg didn't become a writer but instead a photographer (initially, as he tells us, to get into special places and to pick up girls)—and he *is* a photographer—so it feels right that a lot of his story is comprised of shots he's taken, either one per page or in clusters throughout the book. We're not always able to discern the meaning of these photos to his own personal life, other than that he took them—and that they're strong, revealing shots—but his storyline is always clear because he quickly returns to those typed slips of paper telling us what happened to him next.

An overall theme develops: To become who he was fated to be, Goldberg "photographed everything and anything."

What specifically does this mean? Well, one rainy afternoon he follows an old man who reminds him of his father to Georgia's Rooming House, a fleabag joint in Bellingham, Washington. There he goes door to door, introducing himself, and for months gets involved with the rooming house denizens—and of course takes their pictures. It's implied that this is where his singular photographic practice begins: put himself in a strange demiworld and record, in photos and interviews, just what goes on.

He was also a good son, and in the way of the book, we make a leap from one theme to another by a page of photos, followed by a written explanation. So we get a page of sunny snaps of what we can guess are his parents on vacation. The slips of paper on the next page tell us it's a trip to Florida to check out the state as a retirement move. His father's health is deteriorating. "Jimmy" is pained but has his own troubles, "an ex-girlfriend beating her head against the wall because we had broken up," "a bad mushroom trip."

Goldberg does have his photography, though, and in 1974 moves to Philadelphia to be with a photographer he'd met,

John Bundsen, who turns out to be "less the mentor I had hoped for and more just a sad alcoholic." Still, "the good part was I could go out during those winter days happy to wander and take pictures."

Always taking photos. It's an astonishment to me how, in my own work, taking photos, especially stumbling upon a good one, can redeem the day. My guess is that Goldberg knows this truth more than most.

Back to his story.

On to California in early 1974, crashing with a friend in Santa Monica. There's a fascinating handwritten sheet of what Goldberg saw his first month there, including: "the special quality of light," "Chandra the tantric dancer," "the Santa Monica Blvd. bus stop," "a very drunk man who threw up on me," and " 'luck in the air.' "

Goldberg was ambitious; he was determined to photograph the nascent glam scene at Rodney Bingenheimer's English Disco. He finally gets invited to shoot there but doesn't have a flash. In a hilarious passage he tells us about hitching to Westwood to get a rig, getting picked up by a guy named Mark, who takes him home, gives him a joint laced with angel dust, comes on to him. Goldberg somehow makes it out but ends up at the English Disco with a too bright strobe and very little film. For his troubles he does get a picture of an epicene dude in sunglasses flipping him off. Maybe not so much luck in the air that day.

On to 1975, Goldberg calling his folks, now in Florida. All seems well. He's going to go to school and study photography. Then his father says, "Let's tell Jim the good news."

Jim: "Good news?"

And that's it, the book's perfect inscrutable ending, except for a couple shots of his aging parents and a full page filled with a Bazooka bubblegum wrapper.

Overall, *The Last Son* is an astonishment. You can curl up with it, read it like a book; indeed, I'd call it simply "a good read." The story it tells, Goldberg's coming of age, is plainly told and engrossing in its forthright honesty, and yet this is a serious *photobook*. The photos don't just illustrate his life (though they do some of that, too) but enlarge upon it. The editing is inspired.

The Mysteries of Light

Not a bad shot in the book, and with every one, if we can't immediately place who or what it's about, we inevitably wonder how it fits into Goldberg's story—who is this, why do we care, why put this shot into the book, what does it mean?

Answers hover but never fully resolve. Goldberg has found inspired, original ways to blend words and images. The photos make this autobiography a meta-experience. It's Goldberg's life ... but much larger than that, too.

We're Not in Japan Anymore
Politics and the Photobook: Fyodor Telkov, *36 Views*

February 2017

We open the new book *36 Views*, by Russian photographer Fyodor Telkov, to find a shot of a Soviet Realist painting depicting heroic miners deep underground, followed by a historical photo of the pride of young Soviet womanhood parading with flags through the small mining town of Degtyarsk, no doubt celebrating those heroic miners. There's a gray, barren lump of a hill behind the parading girls, and as nonvisual as that round, featureless hill is as a subject, that's just what we're here to look at.

Thirty-six times, in Telkov's subtle and powerful photobook.

Inspired directly by Japanese artist Katsushika Hokusai's famous early 19th-century series *Thirty-six Views of Mount Fuji*, comprised of lovely, delicate, and most carefully rendered color prints of people doing this and that, always with Mount Fuji in the distance, Telkov has come up with his thirty-six photos of Degtyarsk from all kinds of angles and focal distances, with different foregrounds, compositions, and reflections, but always with one of the two huge lumps of mining waste somewhere in the picture.

Hokusai's series, among other things, is a fun game of Where's Mount Fuji? It's in every drawing, sometimes just a single line, other times a tiny bump in the distance. You feel good whenever you spot it.

In *36 Views* the response is exactly the opposite: *Oh, no, there's that sullen, soulless lump again. We cannot escape it.*

Still, the variety of ways Telkov places one of the hills in his pictures is impressive. I particularly like two shots that are mostly close-ups of barren trees, a faint line demarcating a darker shape from lighter sky deep in the background. It's an elemental Hokusai gesture—whoosh, and there's your Mount

The Mysteries of Light 99

Fuji. For Telkov in Degtyarsk, it doesn't take much to place this ever-present pile of sludge in any landscape around the town.

Telkov is an accomplished photographic storyteller, which, among other things, means he lets us know right off just what's going on. The book's first shot is of a hill in all its bare, ugly glory. The next photo, an overhead view of the town itself, has the hill popping up in the distance like a pimple. The third shows tracks through the snow for the train hauling the valuable copper out and leaving the sludge behind.

Then Telkov's story gets more complex. The next shot is the first of foregrounded trees with only a hint of a shape behind it; if we didn't know we were looking for the waste heap, we could be looking at a Robert Adams forest.

Which brings up a couple of interesting questions. First, are these photographs beautiful? Well, some are; and all are accomplished. Second, is beauty a problem when you're depicting environmental waste? My thought: It's a delicate balance, you don't want single photos to be too beautiful, and none of Felkov's are; you just want them to be powerful (even if lovely) in their own right. You don't want the meaning subsumed by aesthetics, but neither do you want photos without any good reason to look at them. In *36 Views*, I think Felkov hits the balance very well. These are strong photographs, every last one of them, but none are so fine that they get in the way of what the book is about, which is life amidst environmental waste.

Which leads to what else we find in the book: the Degtyarsk townsfolk. Oh, yes, people live under these barren hills. (Which makes it not as bad as the other recent Russian book I reviewed for *PhotobookStore Magazine*, *Shadows of Wormwood*, about the dead zone around Chernobyl.) Thanks for small blessings; the copper sludge doesn't poison you, at least not as quickly as radiation. The first two souls we encounter in the book are a couple boys in knit caps walking past a junked car, the hill perfectly framed above their oblivious stroll. A few pages on, another Adams-y shot of bare tree branches, these almost concealing some kind of march, mostly women, some carrying balloons. Celebrating something? No way to tell, but of course there it is, that gray arc of the looming hill above them.

Telkov's photos start getting more inventive here, now that we know the story, what's going on. There's a fine shot of a barnyard, a baby goat and some ducks going about their business, unaware of that gray dome in the distance. There are a number of snowy landscape shots in which the white of the snow almost—*almost*—wipes away the white hill. Even with the overall gloom, we come upon the first out and out beautiful photograph, this a fine chiaroscuro of light and dark, a woman carrying two pails down a sunlit road on the left, and almost nothing but black ink on the right ... except that, yes, there's that inescapable trace of the hill. Another shot, dare I say, is almost a devil-world Ansel Adams, the hill now glowing white in moonlight, standing out vividly in the gray town. (Wonder how much photos of mining sludge will someday go for at auction?)

Yes, a book of photos of mining sludge, with a clear message, subtle but inescapable: *Just look what we've done.*

To Telkov's credit he doesn't hit us over the head with this idea. Indeed, even in two more explicit sequential shots—one with the hill reflected in a pool, cast-off bottles next to the water; the next a wash of timber waste and an abandoned tire in a stream flowing under the hill—the environmental message isn't hit too hard. It's just there, a part of things. Simply: *We cannot escape it.* And, again: *Just look what we've done.*

Which leads to a striking, up-to-the-moment political meaning to the book, even beyond the environmental.

Here in the U.S. (not to mention everywhere else) we're contemplating whether Trumpism might make America more like Russia; *New York* magazine devoted a whole cover story to that worry a few issues back.

In *36 Views*, we get a good idea where unbridled commerce and no regulations can lead us. I have no doubt books similar to *36 Views* could be done now about coal mining in Appalachia or Scotland, but these days we're all worrying about this in a new way. Indeed, photographers everywhere are also trying to work out fresh ways to capture the new political moment, what's going on in the streets and everywhere else.

36 Views, in its quiet, subtle, innovative way of observing the dark fruits of a political system, gives us ideas.

The Mysteries of Light

First off, like Telkov, you have to be clear in what you're about. You have to say directly what you mean, and each photo has to elaborate on that meaning.

But then you have to find those new angles, new approaches. Maybe instead of shooting in the heat of a demonstration, you could capture people, say, dining al fresco while somewhere in the distance a protest march passes by. (That single fine Hokusai line.) Or maybe the protest is just a distant smudge on a city's landscape? I don't know. I only know that finding fresh ways to capture what's going on, and make its import felt anew, is essential.

And to not lose hope. Felkov's final shot ... well, it says mountains. There's the back of a solitary person at the very top of the snow-covered waste heap, a small, dark figure amidst all the whiteness, in a full-length black coat, arms stretched out—an undeniable image of victory, of triumph.

Can we save things? Will we turn around the world that leaves sludge heaps, literal and figurative, carelessly in its wake?

With books like *36 Views*, and millions more ways of direct protest, we can certainly try.

Disparate Harmonies, Tall Climbs: Shane Lavalette, *One Sun, One Shadow*

March 2017

Photographer Shane Lavalette had the good fortune (and as we'll see, the tough climb) to be commissioned by the High Museum of Art in Atlanta do a study of America's South. (He's from upstate New York.) The book that resulted is *One Sun, One Shadow*, published by Lavalette's own publishing house.

Photos in the book alternate between black-and-white shots and color ones; between portraits, landscapes, and abstractions; between crisp images and the murk of heavy Southern air. We get a lot of different pictures: a couple kids making out, a shot of praying hands stenciled on a wall, balloons against a clouded sky, a model of a church in a sweep of meadow grass, a pair of binoculars on a green table surrounded by cherry tomatoes.

For a theme to hold the book together, Lavalette says he chose music. Makes sense. Certainly music is central to the South, what with blues and jazz and country music emanating from there, not to mention rock and roll. He also chose not to shoot anything as obvious as only musicians. There are some photos of instruments and even a moody green-fog landscape with a barefoot boy holding a banjo, but if there is a true music to the book, it has to lie beneath the wide array of different kinds of pictures, and the photo-rhythms they try to capture. (Perhaps something in line with Walker Evans's vaunted comment about his work being "lyric documentary"?)

So how well does music hold *One Sun* together? Do all the photos flow together to make up a book? Long breath. I can't say they don't, but I also feel flung around an awful lot. If the book's a musical composition, it's less Brahms and more late Schoenberg, with the disparate pictures testing tonality. Take five photos I turned to randomly from the middle of the book. We jump from a large black-and-white two-page shot of a hill, dried flowers in the foreground; to a color shot of a middle-aged African-American with a couple dollar bills stuck to his uniform shirt; to a Stephen Shore–like rainy traffic intersection; to an elegant, almost Walker Evans–esque curved outdoor staircase, to that same black-and-white staircase printed in reverse on the next spread. Again, five shots in a row, not much in common. Tonality ... or atonality? Music ... or noise?

The two allusions just above point to another concern with *One Sun*: the looming presence of other photographers. Consider two of the photos I mentioned a few paragraphs back, the model of a church, the binoculars with the cherry tomatoes. Here's how the Southern fiction writer (and, not incidentally, photographer) Eudora Welty spoke of a similar concern. Regarding William Faulkner, the great novelist (and her friend), Welty said that being a Mississippi writer along with him was like living under a huge mountain.

Well, that model church shot lurks under a small hill of Southern photography: William Christenberry. The binoculars on the green lace tablecloth? A photo inescapably underneath the towering photographic peaks of William Eggleston. And for a quick side trip, two shots, of a black guy with binoculars before a wall of bricks, followed immediately by a distant shot of what looks like the same guy entering a discount clothing store, call to mind the sequential-photograph path Paul Graham walks in *A Shimmer of Possibility*. Oh, and Evans again? A bare brick wall almost cries out for the torn scraps of an old minstrel show bill.

Influences? Perhaps. Or maybe it's just the way certain photographers take over a landscape, a people, a scene—a way of shooting—until not much is left. I can't quite say Lavalette's photos are simply derivative, it's just that he hasn't been able to escape some pretty well trod ground.

Can anyone? How does any photographer replenish a world in 2017 so well-scoured? Is it possible to make a photo of an American flag fresh after Robert Frank? (I'll admit I've tried, in my book *Flags* playing off the red-white-and-blues rather than the flag itself, but who knows?)

Yet that's our job as photographers. If we have to climb looming mountains, we need new, original paths up them. And if we have to venture deep into land previously so thoroughly staked out, well, isn't there new land we can discover if we tread past the well-known?

I don't think Lavalette set out simply to tramp around over such well-trod ground (though I just looked at the next photo after my five-shot sequence above, and see a shot of a bearded guy before a table on a porch, gazing wistfully off; I can't help but wonder if Alex Soth's *Sleeping by the Mississippi* is looming over that one, too). But it's also hard to see how he found a wholly original way to capture the South.

One photo that doesn't immediately call up other influences is one clearly important to Lavalette. It's a black-and-white snap of a totally ripped-apart tire on a stretch of pavement, the rubber and its shreds weaving and circling through the picture. The photo opens *One Sun*, a similar one backs the first, and a third version is the last shot in the book. I've driven Southern highways; destroyed tires is as good a central image as any. (Though of course shredded tires turn up on any highway anywhere.)

Still, that photo is a potentially strong motif for the book, this ripped-apart rubber, highway detritus, not to mention the rubber circles and flung-off rough strips, and yet I don't see these initial notes repeated in the rest of the shots in the book. Music? Good music states its theme, then plays around it; it harmonizes, reveals inner connections, sums up into a work of perceptible power. Is there enough music here? Turning the pages, I don't feel that inevitable flow, each photo belonging to the whole, and being in the right place.

So what are we left with in *One Sun, One Shadow*? A book of disparate photos, black-and-white and color, portraits, moody landscapes, and those trashed tires, many that call up allusions (probably not intended) to other photographers, and an underlying run of notes that, as they leap and turn, don't build to any perceptible climax.

Still, *One Sun* is an honorable piece of work, and you can almost feel Lavalette on his assignment, down from the north, working to discover his own version of the American South … and almost getting there. But as Faulkner also famously said, in the South "the past is never dead. It's not even past."

The Mysteries of Light

All of us as photographers are burdened by our glorious photographic past each time we shoot. Is that street photo too much like Garry Winogrand, that American-vernacular one too Evans-y or Stephen Shore–like, and why does Eggleston loom above almost any richly-saturated color shot of banality? It ain't easy finding our own way, but it's always worth the effort.

Loving the Life:
Mao Ishikawa, *Red Flower:*
The Women of Okinawa

April 2017

O<small>NE OF THE RAREST</small>, most interesting of photobook genres: I'm a talented young photographer, I'm doing wild, socially deviant stuff, throwing myself all the way into a crazy scene, and I'm taking my camera along.

You know the classics: Danny Lyon's *Bikeriders*, Larry Clarke's *Tulsa*, Nan Goldin's *The Ballad of Sexual Dependency*. (Hunter Thompson, of course, made a career of this in letters.) In the immortal words of Muddy Waters, these photographers lived the life they loved, and loved the life they lived.

Add to their joyful, complex ranks the Okinawan photographer Mao Ishikawa, celebrating again just that well-loved life of outlawdom and thrills in her latest book, *Red Flowers*, based on her years from 1975 to '77 as a bar girl in Okinawa, hanging with all the other girls servicing African-American sailors, loving the men, laughing and playing with their fellow bar girls, and rising and falling through the full parade of human emotions.

Mao worked in a black district in the entertainment district, which in an intriguing interview she explains this way: "Black soldiers and white soldiers wore the same uniforms and worked together, but once they changed into their civilian clothes and went out into town, there was trouble and endless fights. I have heard that that is why the entertainment districts for U.S. troops were segregated into white and black districts. However, I don't really know if that is true."

True or not, in *Red Flower* we see a lot of young Okinawan women making the scene, cavorting, diving deep into sexual escapades, even sharing children with African-American soldiers out of uniform. Some of the women working the clubs were Okinawan, but many, Mao tells us, were "women from mainland Japan who liked black music from when they were little, found a lover at a club that black soldiers frequented, followed them to Okinawa when they were deployed and lived there. They broke up with their boyfriends but would stay in Okinawa and work at a black bar. There were many such cases."

How deeply was Mao involved? "I too worked at a bar, and lived with a black soldier that I met there and loved him."

She wasn't alone. Here's how she explains her friends' thinking (probably disgraceful back then, now wondrously liberated): " 'What's wrong with loving black people? What's wrong with working at a bar? What's wrong with enjoying sex?' they asked, and lived their lives freely and openly. Those women were very cool."

There's also something very cool about a photobook of full immersion in a fascinating world long gone. The key phrase above: "full immersion." Mao was there, her friends were there, the soldiers were there, and they all were living it up and carrying on: sex, drugs, pleasure, freedom. Mao's wholly uninhibited photos capture it all.

More history. Okinawa was annexed by Japan, and by force, in 1879; Okinawans still think of the country as occupied. As Mao puts it, "The history, the relations between Okinawans and the Japanese, the history of black people and their relations with white people; I think they are very similar. I think that sympathy is a big reason I liked black people more and more."

That "liking" is manifest in *Red Flowers*. Women drape themselves over the soldiers, make love to them on camera, hang with them wholly naked, even look through one guy's Afro presumably checking for nits. There's an abundance of laughter, huge smiles, joy. Liking? More like out and out love. It's clear these women loved their men, no matter what other arrangements (business, companionship) were in play. That love, that joy, comes through throughout the book.

Red Flowers is also a vivid reminder of that simple photobook fact: Put the right person in the right world at the right time, let her snap away without inhibition, and a powerful photobook can result.

On to the book itself. The black-and-white photos are touching and revealing, full of secret glimpses of lives as well as brazen displays. The book is brilliantly edited by Session Press publisher Miwa Susuda, and she's ordered the book in a very telling way. We start with all the women on their own, their daily lives, proud and cheery. (Mao admits she found the bar girls more interesting than the men.) More than one woman sports her own primo Afro. There are also a number of bare breasts, often just one squeezed out from a jersey. One woman demurely shows off the arrow-pierced-heart tattoo on her left tit. What else do we see? The scatter of their lives: packs of Kool cigarettes. Hair curlers and lipstick, and of course a Bruce Lee poster on the wall.

Then on to the sailors. Lots of hugging, squeezing, sex. Beautiful young nude bodies, black men and Asian women. A big transistor radio, you can just hear Gamble and Huff tunes pulsing through the dingy rooms.

Three quarters through *Red Flowers* the girls go on a beach trip, all the young dudettes disporting nude in waves and on sand. And finally, far more serious, family life. More than one sailor has had a child with one of the Okinawan women, and there they are, seemingly happy families ... until the sailors are called home.

It is interesting how time works on photos like this. Fortysome years later, there's of course no current news in *Red Flowers*, though there is the discovery (once again, since an earlier version of this book came out in 1982) that such an unprecedented world existed. But as a look at a unique time and place, never to be repeated, and so thoroughly cataloged by Mao's touching photos, *Red Flowers* shimmers as a distant dream—of making the best out of a form of military occupation, of a true occurrence of a startling racial harmony, and of course the presence of so many original, powerful photographs. To my eye, a lot of the shots have a Rasta vibe, like snaps from Kingston when Bob Marley was just getting going. *That* kind of unique world.

The book, from Session Press, is beautiful in an edgy way. The size is grand (9.5 by 13 inches), and the silk-screen cover powerful. Recent Daido Moriyama books have used silk-screen covers to great effect (imitating his groundbreaking 1970s "performance," Printing Show, where he made *Another Country—New York* in a Xerox store, then covered it with a silk-screen cover), and *Red Flowers* has a similar physical presence.

But it's the sweet forbidden world inside the book that resonates most.

Back to Muddy Waters:
> *So if you see me and think I'm wrong*
> *Don't worry 'bout me, just let me go*
> *My sweet life ain't nothing but a thrill*
> *I live the life I love and I love the life I live*

That's Mao Ishikawa's *Red Flowers*: A photobook of living and loving, strong pictures of daring, bold certainty, ultimate heartbreak.

A photobook that is simply essential.

The Photobook as Literature:
Igor Posner, *Past Perfect*

May 2017

Perhaps it's because I'm a novelist, and studied lit in college, but what moves me most in a potentially great photobook is what moves me with a great novel or poetry collection (or even record album): shape, depth, coherence, narrative, flow … simply a reason for all the shots to be there other than that of a catalogue or some artist's current work gathered up. But of course more than that, too: vision, enlightenment, and emotions larger than we ourselves can imagine.

That is, the weight and richness of literature.

I'll be writing soon about the Mack reissue of Masahisa Fukase's *Ravens* (photography's own *Moby Dick*), but now I'm looking at Igor Posner's *Past Perfect*, and just a dozen photos in, I'm back on my thin, lumpy undergraduate mattress, my brain spinning all night through *Crime and Punishment* (one of a few novels I recall rereading immediately after first finishing it), following Raskolnikov down the murky streets and up the cramped stairways of St. Petersburg as murder and conscience bedevil him.

Past Perfect is set in St. Petersburg, but that's not why I think of Dostoevsky, it's the rich black-and-white tonality, the blurred figures in remarkable poses, the deep mystery to the art of Posner's photobook. There's also no crime at the center of *Past Perfect*, but it also isn't for any sort of murder mystery that we read *Crime and Punishment*. What sticks with us are lives tortured and unredeemed, and morality twisted until it bleeds.

Yet *Past Perfect* isn't really a novel at all (though the info included with the book does refer to its setting as "a fictional city"), but a photographic work of intentional memory, Posner's visits from 2006 to '09 to St. Petersburg, the place of his birth (then Leningrad); visits that appear to have stirred up the most extreme memories and emotions.

Past Perfect itself is full of beautiful, lush black-and-white printing, in high contrast, and with a definite Japanese Provoke blur and energy. If the book is predicated on Posner's remembrances of St. Petersburg, the way the photos are shot and printed invokes perfectly the essence of memory: clear moments, faded moments, true moments, reinvented ones. Each photo is just representative enough—we know what's going on, buses in the snow, a haunted woman crouched naked in the corner of a room—but always filtered through layers of murk and shadow, excrescences of the past overlaying the present.

Which makes the book truly powerful. We see both what's there, and see how Posner *sees* what's there, and what time passing has laid upon what may or may not ever have been there. In *Past Perfect*, the past is perfect only in the way the photographer has rendered it: true to memory if not to anything else.

The book's powerful underlying story: the way the past creeps inevitably into the present. Let me invoke another great novel, Proust's *Remembrance of Things Past*. For Proust, it's that infamous madeleine that sweeps him back into his lost world. For Posner, well, that's part of the intrigue of the book, what is his most vital touchstone? My first guess, the faded, speckled cameo of a woman, circled by a halo of light. Or maybe it's the evocative opening photo, a shroud-wrapped flower lady, offering up her winter blooms in sad-looking buckets. Perhaps it's the scarred wall with a crude invocation of eyes, nose, mouth. Or the work's inspiriting shot could just as easily be an ornate room further into the book, with vivid wallpaper, a candle and pen and writing paper—tools of nonphotographic recollection—on a checkered tablecloth. Presumably this is a room with powerful implications for Posner, else why would it be there.

The picture of the room is followed immediately by one of a woman, head tilted back, hands raised, a necklace on her neck, wearing what looks to be a somewhat see-through blouse ... and clearly lost to some form of rapture. That's the thing with great photobooks: We rarely know all the contexts behind the pictures. What is she feeling? What's inspiring, or terrifying, her? No way to know; we only see that this photo leads to a photo of a young man against a wall, holding a can, looking both resolute and dismayed. (Throughout *Past Perfect* emotions run high, always vividly expressed through Posner's camera.) The next picture is a man in a café, cigarette raised to his mouth, an indistinct woman in the foreground. Friends of Posner's ... old friends? We don't know, but it hardly hurts to imagine that these characters walked out of his own past into the book to proclaim their presence in the tortured present.

Nobody in *Past Perfect* appears calm or innocent, all seem riddled with streaks of rapture or despond. (Dostoevsky would know these people; perhaps he half-invented them.) Take the older man, standing blank-faced to the right of the photo of another woman, in an almost Caravaggio pose of religious exaltation. Two photos later we find a presumably naked man, on the page mostly a big splash of white against a mottled black background, his head clutched desperately in raised hands, an expression not quite blurry enough to conceal his absolute despair.

I'm not making Dostoevsky allusions lightly: The range of emotions in Posner's book is wider and richer than almost any other photobook I can think of. This is not a book for the fainthearted. Here lies a full expression of humankind, and if the photos in *Past Perfect* are merely shards of Igor Posner's memory reinvented through his camera, his vision is as wide as any artist working today—and at least as serious.

But what makes the book truly impressive is that Posner is somehow telling all our stories, at least those of our darkest dreams and broadest literary imagination.

Big props to Jason Eskenasi and his Red Hook editions for putting out *Past Perfect*, and printing it so brilliantly. (Eskenasi is the force behind the transcendent celebration of Robert Frank's *Americans*, *The Americans List: By the Glow of the Jukebox*, in which dozens of photographers comment on their favorite shot from Frank's book; not to mention an extraordinary chronicler of things Russian in his own photobooks.)

But of course *Past Perfect* is all Posner's vision. Doubt a photobook can read like literature? Then take up *The Americans* in the spirit of *On the Road*, *Ravens* while considering the obsessive drive of Ahab after that damn white whale, and *Past Perfect* as all your Dostoevskian hallucinations come to life.

That important, *that* essential.

The Darkening Sky:
Masahisa Fukase, *Ravens*, Part 1

May 2017

IMAGINE: THERE'S A NOVEL that towers over all of 19th-century American literature, there's a group of French poems that takes you where no other poetry book does, there's an album of dark tunes by Britain's (the world's?) second-greatest rock band at the height of their powers ... and you can't read or listen to any of it. Sure, there's a copy from years ago available of *Moby Dick*, but it costs minimum a few hundred dollars. Libraries don't have it. Your friends don't own it. You can't even really see it online. Same with *Une Saison en Enfer*. Same with the rock 'n' roll masterwork *Aftermath*. They're all out there somewhere, you've heard about their greatness, but there's no way you can even touch them.

Fortunately, with Melville, Rimbaud, and the Stones, that's not the case; their works—probably all their works—are now and forever in print. But what about Masahisa Fukase's superlative photobook, *Ravens*? Well, with Mack's excellent new edition, just like that, a world-class masterpiece is back in our hands. For most, this will be the first opportunity ever to actually see, let alone own, the book. And for that, the publishing company deserves all the plaudits possible.

In a second part of this review, I plan to write about the work itself, what makes *Ravens* so extraordinary that a panel of experts famously called it the "best photobook of the past 25 years" (no argument here), but first I want to compare the new Mack edition with the original. I happen to own the first Japanese printing, from 1986 (I know, I know ... and someday an heir can sell it and put somebody through coll—well, pay for at least a week or two at a top-drawer university).

I've just gone through both books closely. First impressions: Mack clearly worked from an original, coming up with a an almost exact nubby black cloth for the cover and embossing the solitary raven silhouette on the front just as in the original. (On the back of the book, the original publisher, Sōkyūsha, repeated the raven image; Mack goes with Fukase's signature in roman text.) They've also gone with an almost exact paper for the innards, what looks like a silk-coated ultrawhite.

Can you fault Mack for trying to re-create a masterpiece as closely as possible, especially for its first true reproduction? Should they have changed paper stocks to, say, mimic the creamier, thicker, uncoated stock of Roshin's recent book of Fukase's cat photos, *Afterword*? Or even the paper on Mack's earlier Fukase book, *Hibi*, which I reviewed here as a springboard to talking about … *Ravens*. My answer: *Afterword* and *Hibi* were original works, and since Fukase is no longer with us, you can't take much issue with what a publisher chooses. But for a re-creation of an original work that is also a towering work of art? I think the first duty is to be true to the original.

I do have to admit I kind of wish *Karasu* (*Ravens*' Japanese title) had originally been published back in the 1960s, when it would have been done up right in rich gravure. The photos in the book, all murky blacks and ominous forms, call out for thick slabs of ink, luminous whites, printing so rich you can almost smell it … but the original printing ain't that, looks like duotone offset to me, and though it's far more detailed and stronger than its only American edition, Bedford's *The Solitude of Ravens* from 1991, I can't say the original is better page by printed page than Mack's new version. (The only version of *Ravens* I don't own is Rat Hole's, from 2008.)

There are differences between the original and Mack's version. For one, the original puts page numbers below the images, in effect numbering them. Mack for some reason puts the page number on the facing page (on the left), which might be the correct page number but is confusing when talking about the actual photos. That is, photo number 75 in *Karasu*, an ominous sky of ravens, looks to be photo 74 in *Ravens*, since that's the number across from it. Does this matter? Well, the next photo in the sequence is another ominous sky of ravens, this one with dots of lens flare, which is photo 77 in the original, ostensibly 76 in the Mack edition. A possibility for scholarly confusion looks to exist.

The Mysteries of Light

Enough on page numbering, what about the printing? To my eye the Mack prints look slightly darker, with a touch more contrast. In some photos—for instance, another ominous sky of ravens (Mack page 81)—the contrast brightens the whites, makes the shot more dramatic. On another, the well-known snap of two women on a boat shot from the back, their hair flying wing-like into the sun, the printing feels more lively in the original but more dramatic in the new version. There is also an arguable greater degree of detail in most of the Mack book's prints. So the page 81 raven sky works better in the Mack book. But in others, *Karasu* has the slightly stronger print.

Here's another example. Take the stark opening shot, a raven in dark silhouette (the same image stamped in relief on the covers). Both photos are startling—look, this black-birded beast, looming on the first page like a wrong turn in a nightmare—but *Karasu* has a powerful but, in comparison, more muted print of this dream image. Mack's *Ravens* reproduces the stark form darker, and if darkness—boundless, literary darkness—is one of the chief points of Fukase's book, I have to here give Mack the edge: Their silhouette is simply a more powerful springboard into the place the book's about to take you ... and a warning that it could be a place you might not wish to go.

Indeed, if inducing a primal, symbolic terror is an intention of Fukase's work, the photos most powerful in taking us there are stronger in the Mack version. I'm thinking now about the feral cat across from page 43. In part two of this review I'll talk much more about cats in Fukase's work, but this striking photo raises lots of questions: Is this feline here to stalk ravens? Would she have a chance of catching one? Or is this cat simply a cognate for the featured bird, another whip turn on the book's shadowy carnival ride? I'll go for the latter explanation—an aspect of Fukase's genius, he spooks us no matter what he shoots—and if the darkling evocation is part of what he's up to, I think the higher-contrast printing of the cat hits us harder, takes us further ... except the longer I look at the Sōkyūsha print, the more I have to work to peer into the depths of this stalking cat, and in a way, the more I find. She's no longer right up in my face, but that doesn't make her diabolical purposes any less fearsome.

Then I turn the page. In part two of my review, I'll be talking a lot more about the photos in *Ravens* that *aren't* of ravens—the shots that pace the book, expand its meanings. And here's one of the main ones: a corpulent, sagged-teat nude woman on a light-blanketed bed. We're told this is a masseuse, and who's to know. One thing she isn't is a flock of whirling black birds in the sky.

Here Mack, as is customary, prints the woman with higher contrast. She's definitely more *there* ... but also less emotive and mysterious. In Mack she's a woman on a bed, in *Karasu* she's more human, and all invocation: of companionship for a lonely man, possible satisfaction (in a way Mick Jagger might've intended, though certainly not with a woman of her girth), even potential serenity; though of course in context, she's as spooky as the stalking cat, the lumpy fish head that follows her, and all the rapid flutter of ravens' wings gyring through the gray skies to come.

At bottom, though, I'd say that the Mack version available here is at least as good a book experience, and certainly no less true to Fukase's dark vision. The book is beyond recommended; it's essential.

And, yes, what of the photographer's vision?

Read on....

The Darkening Sky: Mashahisa Fukase, Ravens, Part 2

June 2017

TRUE STORY: I WAS twenty, on a beach in San Diego, California, reading *Moby-Dick*, Herman Melville's sprawling God/devil–bedizened tale of Ahab's obsession with his white whale, when I read a sentence so beautiful and powerful I pulled my gaze away from the page. My head lifted back, and a shaft of light beamed from the sky straight at me—a spectral vision manifestly created by Melville's dazzling prose. An unforgettable, transcendent moment; certainly one of the most powerful in creating me as a novelist and photographer, and for all of my life.

I bring up white whales and skies bright (and dark) with light and transcendence, and natural beasts manifest as symbols so powerful they still rock the heavens ... bring all this up because Masahisa Fukase's *Ravens* is exactly *that* kind of book, a tale of obsession finding focus on natural-world symbols, in this case profound heartbreak searching out possible solace (or ongoing despair?) in endlessly photographing ravens from a train window. The photographer Stacy Oborn, in an essay entitled *The Art of Losing Love*, explains well how *Ravens* came about: "Fukase's best-known work was made while reeling from loss of love [after his wife of 13 years left him]. While on a train returning to his hometown of Hokkaido, perhaps feeling unlucky and ominous, Fukase got off at stops and began to photograph something which in his culture and in others represents inauspicious feeling: ravens. He became obsessed with them, with their darkness and loneliness."

Darkness and loneliness. No question *Ravens* contains that. Inauspicious feeling? Ditto. Ominous? Oh, yeah, a whole lot of that, too. But what else does a reader find in the book? As with Melville's white whale, different projections of meaning onto the beast are manifold. Is *Ravens* a memory/comment on Japanese war planes coursing the skies? Is the line of birds on a sea-born concrete abutment hints of what awaits us all when *we* pass? Is the endless scatter of dark birds an expression of a soul exploding into pieces, then flying toward the aether? Or is the final shot, what looks like a homeless man plodding down a city street, a ripely-stained blanket over his shoulders, all that's left you after you've spent your hours—far too many hours—with the ravens?

And if instead of reading a sentence so perfect the heavens open ... if instead you feel a curse so dark and burdening that when you look skyward you see only wheeling ravens ... and if you *are* that dark and burdened, could you possibly care what those ravens represent; what symbology is manifest? My guess is that you're more concerned with whether your train gets to its station on time, and why your heart won't heal.

Train schedules and broken hearts were Fukase's burden; it's our blessing that he turned his life into astonishing art. With the new version of *Ravens* so widely available (thank you again, Mack!), I'm sure there will be countless exegeses and theses on the meanings of the book. If that's to happen, though, it's worth considering this passage from Ernest Hemingway, talking about his own beast-laden book, *The Old Man and the Sea*: "There isn't any symbolism. The sea is the sea. The old man is the old man. The boy is a boy and the fish is a fish. The sharks are sharks, no better, no worse." Perhaps Ernie's being a tad disingenuous, but his point's worth keeping in mind.

So no further here about an interpretation of Fukase's ravens; instead I'll talk about how he has created a work so *worthy* of interpretation, the power of his astonishing artistic vision, that quality that allows him to turn everything he photographs, with whatever intention, or none at all, into forceful and moving art.

First off, there's not a shot in the book that doesn't swell with dark feeling. I'm just randomly opening pages now: page 87, specks of ravens atop a thick sheath of winter trees, the photo all grays and smudges; page 37, a bird (raven? dead?) centered in a flood of snow on land; page 12, a photo bisected on the diagonal by a row of ravens at the top of a bramble of branches, their eyes unearthly glowing white dots; page 71, another twist of dark branches swelling with a flock of ravens, a shot very much

The Mysteries of Light 119

in the muted spirit of a Japanese watercolor; page 117, a raven, wings fully extended, flying only feet above a striped crosswalk on a road; and page 79, a smudgy scatter of ravens on telephone lines above a snowy landscape, clearly one more shot grabbed in a flash from the window of Fukase's train hurtling north.

I note all these photographs to show that there's not a banal shot in the book, each one—flocks of ravens streaming the sky, a solitary bird a bare speck above us—rich and evocative. The book is dark. Heck, *raven* means dark; raven-haired, raven-souled.

Which gets me thinking. In a way, we are what we shoot; what grabs us, draws our cameras, the subjects we give ourselves up to. But of course you or I could take pictures of ravens (if we could find some; last time I checked, not too many in New York City or London), and chances are what we'd come up with would just be pictures of birds, not shots redolent with mystery and implication. Still, *Moby-Dick* is about an eerie albino whale, not a guppy; and even the marlin in the *Old Man and the Sea* is a hoary one, a repository of countless years of struggle and determination. It matters what we choose to shoot (or what chooses us), of course it does.

It just matters more *how* we shoot it. A touch of the magic of photography is that there are a gazillion ways to shoot a subject, but perhaps only one or two that are the right way. The great photographer finds that correct one. He or she cannot, let's say, take a bad photo; or at least publish one that isn't worthy.

That is, great photography always comes down to how it's done; a mix of vision, determination, passion, and, yes, choice of subject. But vision is paramount, and in Fukase's case, his vision is so compelling and strong that everything he shoots, raven or not, is original, artful.

Which leads me back to his cat books.

In Part One of this review I mentioned the recent publication of *Afterword* (the new volume of Fukase's cat photos) and the way, as he shot his beloved Sasuke, Fukase invested the feline with metaphorical power. It's as if that's Fukase's gift/curse: whatever he touches reeks of meaning.

In *Afterword*, the publisher, Roshin, cleverly mimics the original printing of *Ravens*: There on the felt cover is an embossed image of the cat, Sasuke. The opening, title-page photo is an extreme close-up, eyes warm if wary, below which Sasuke's incisors look sharp and threatening. Ohhhh-kaayyyy, this cat ain't just a cheery little critter.

There's Sasuke out in a field as a kitten, already looking predatory. There's the cat flying through the air like a bat; there it is draped somnolently over a cathode-ray TV showing what looks like a Dickens' film; now the cat's using its paws to play Go—the range of what Fukase has Sasuke do in the book is astonishing; like Bach's *Goldberg Variations*, wringing every possible emotion from a small set of cat moves—and then, an extreme close-up again, Sasuke's eyes bright with the devil, mouth and fanglike teeth a vision out of a nightmare.

That's my point, of course: Fukase can shoot nothing but his beloved Sasuke and make the cat embody rich, full worlds, of both reality and spirit.

And that's just one (ostensibly) domesticated cat.

In *Ravens*, Fukase rings another world of variations on an essential theme: this time, the way these dark birds fill the sky, and our dreams and nightmares.

But the book is not all ravens, and that's an aspect that truly intrigues me. That is, with a book called *Ravens*, and obsessed with same, why and when does Fukase interrupt the raven shots with those of something else? (Sasuke is in every photo in *Afterword*.)

Here's a list, in order, of many of the photos clearly without ravens in them. (Some shots, especially of trees or fields, may not contain birds, but they're too indistinct to be certain.) Page 19: Three blurred figures under a black cloud-shaped blob. Page 20: Less-blurred figures on a snowy street. Page 21: Three schoolgirls at a rudimentary bus stop inside a wooden hut. Page 22: Another blur of snowy northern buildings. (Four linked photos, then … more ravens.) Page 31: A small boat on a sea scattered with what look like ducks (not ravens). Page 43: A stalking cat … a photo implying threat at least as deep as the birds themselves do. Page 44: A corpulent nude woman, a masseuse, we're told. Eyes closed, she doesn't promise much comfort, though a comfort-woman she may be. Page 47: What looks like a big, scaly fish, its tiny eye prominent (and spooky). Page 63: A flurry of white snow globs rushing the camera lens just like ... a flock of ravens. Page 93: A soaring flock of sea gulls ... flooding the frame like ravens. Page 95: Dead fish on a seashore. Page 103: Three girls' windblown black locks looking like ... raven wings. Page 105: A ship on a horizon, the sea filling one-fourth of the photo. Page 106: Beautiful shot of a calm sea, one person floating on their back, another striding to shore. Page 107: Ominous black bottom of a jet streaking the sky ... yes, like a raven.

Then the final four photos in the book, not an actual raven to be seen. Page 119: What looks to be an explosion blowing detritus off a railing, filling the air. Page 121: A seated man in a trash-bestrewn parking lot, can of soda or beer in his hand. Page 123: A pair of cloth gloves aflame in what looks like a camper's cookout. Page 124, the final photo in the book: A small picture, a beggar with a crumpled, dirty blanket on his back trudging down a city sidewalk.

There are sixty-some photos in *Ravens*, and by my count a little more than a third of them don't have a raven in it. This is both an astonishing concentration of subject matter, and, in the non-raven shots, different themes and imagery underlying the basic obsession. Remember: What makes *Moby-Dick* great isn't simply Ahab's obsessive quest, it's the microcosm of the world as embodied in the officers and mates and their own obsessions (nailed doubloons!) aboard the whaling ship Pequod.

Indeed, that's part of the genius of *Ravens* (and *Moby-Dick*): all the *other* stories they tell.

I keep likening Fukase's photobook to Melville's novel, and obsession is one thing that binds them. But obsession is not all. The photos, every last one of them, stir us. It's just that there are numerous photobooks with almost all stirring photos, but few that concentrate the attention, pull the reader so far out of themselves into another world, let us share—nigh, meld with— the furious mental typhoons and tornadoes ripping through the photographer's mind.

There is, of course, one profound difference between any novel and a photobook: The novelist scribbles or types away someplace inventing characters, and they act out their fates. The photographer has to *be there*, and the fate enacted has to be his or her own. I suppose in theory a photographer could shoot a whole book in character (might be interesting), but I can't think of one off hand. (Cindy Sherman's wide swarm of characters is something different.) In any case, the obsession at the heart of *Ravens* isn't that of an invented mad ship captain but instead Fukase's own.

It's always an interesting question how much a photographer actually shoots what's inside her- or himself. Some of the most interesting photographers (Arbus, Araki, even Cindy Sherman, perhaps) find a way to make images far more about their inner lives, their desires and despairs, than what the photo is ostensibly about. Count Fukase here as one of these tortured souls whose pictures clearly capture inner landscapes and voices. Storm-strewn towns? Flocks of black birds? Burning gloves? Shards and figments of his own inner life.

Would we wish that pain and torment on anyone? Probably not. But when that's the way the world works, and one man's dark visions become our own art, it's our job to celebrate the achievement.

Kudos again to Mack for bringing this towering photobook back to life.

Going Home Again:
Mike Mandel, *People in Cars*
Larry Sultan, *Pictures from Home*

July 2017

FUN TIMES! IN THIS PIECE, I'm looking at books from my own growing-up world, the celebrated/ridiculed San Fernando Valley suburbs north of Los Angeles/Beverly Hills proper. Turns out Mike Mandel, author of the recent *People in Cars*, was in my high school class! How do I know? Well, I didn't know him at all back then (big school, lots of cliques), but I picked up a copy of *Good 70s*, the reprints of first printings of a lot of his work from the 1970s, and when I got the orange box home, well, its contents looked awfully familiar, as in, *This could've been my life*. I reached out to Mandel and found out that, yep, it *was* my life; he'd caught that particular Valley ennui and pointlessness perfectly because we were in it together.

I got out of the Valley as soon as I could (I'd had enough of ennui and pointlessness; ended up in New York City), and so did Mandel, but the cultural afflatus remains. What's the Valley known for? Well, besides Moon Unit Zappa's '80s song "Valley Girls"—*gag me with a spoon*—pretty much car culture and porn. For porn, we'll talk about Mandel's friend Larry Sultan later in this piece, but for now, let's look at Mandel's *People in Cars*.

This *is* Valley life: driving everywhere, often for no reason; cruising Van Nuys Boulevard trying to pick up girls or not get into fights (don't think anybody does it now, but back in our high school days, it was a huge deal); parking up in the hills and trying to make it with your date ... life in the Valley *was* car life, and Mandel captures it perfectly.

His car-life story begins on the cover, one of those silver-ink-on-black-paper deals that seem in vogue these days. I like it. I also like the sultry, puffed-lips look and back-seat eyes of the blonde in the passenger seat. Did I lust after her in chemistry class at Grant High? Did Mandel steal her away? Damn good chances both.

So, again, I'm right at home in this book, but since Mandel's photos are so uniformly strong, you will be, too. *People in Cars* is not just a sociological examination, it's a beautifully printed, rich black-and-white deep look at all the ways people disport themselves in automobiles. There's grumpy granny, sunglassed, silver-haired, puffing away on her Kent cigarette. There's the paisley-shirted (and, of course, sunglassed) driver leaning over to flip off Mandel as he takes a snap, no doubt from his own car. There's I'm-gonna-whoop-your-ass goateed dude, with knife-fight-back-of-the-liquor-store eyes. And of course another smoker: glare-y high school girl just lit up, the glowing dashboard cigarette lighter hot in her hands.

More Angelenos: Look, it's a girl having fun sticking out her impossibly long tongue. There's why-you-taking-my-damn-picture scowly woman, with a, yes, impossibly long Salem 100 between her nicotine-stained fingers. And a sleepy kid, no, two of them, one up front, the other in the backseat, both sucking on their thumbs. One can only imagine the orthodontia bills!

And just to counter the I'm-gonna-kill-you guy and the bird-flipper, here's some cheer: a smiling dark-haired girl flashing the peace sign, and pages along, Santa himself. No doubt sweating on his way to his gig at the long-gone Galleria mall at Ventura and Sepulveda (where I once mock–bowed down before a signed copy of Moon Unit's "Valley Girls" in a Licorice Pizza record store).

So I like this book because it's my old home, but what about you? Well, the range of expressions, emotions, composition, and downright humanity in Mandel's car photos should enchant anyone. *People in Cars* is a fine example of the one-subject book: How many great photos can you come up with around one thing? Mandel isn't alone in going with automobiles. I just pulled Lee Friedlander's *America by Car* off my shelves. The main difference: Friedlander is shooting the country *from* his car, most often the driver's seat (all those rear-view mirrors!) as he roamed about. (Snapping endless photos as you putt along ... as dangerous as texting? Let's write a *Times* op-ed.)

Friedlander, as with Robert Frank before him, uses his car to cruise through America as he digs deep, deep, deep into it.

Mandel is first of all looking *into* cars; he's also far more interested in people and their endless ways of acting out while inside an auto. His is a more interior book, no pun intended, but I'd argue still quite rich in its examination of America. Again, just think about the variety of what people are up to while they tool along the Valley streets.

And just to make the book better, there's a playful touch from the photographer who created the iconic *Photographer Baseball Cards* (in 1975, Mandel spent a lot of time in rattly gas-guzzlers driving around the nation grabbing shots of photographers such as Ed Ruscha and Imogen Cunningham, then working them, pre-InDesign, into mocked-up trading cards): In *People in Cars* he's included a bumper sticker in the back of the book. If it were still the 1970s, I'm sure I'd slap the sticker on the rear bumper of my car; I also probably would have chewed up the gum in the baseball card packs, too, if I'd been lucky enough to buy a set (no doubt diminishing its collectible value by half). As it is, I'll just admire a sheaf of fine photos replete with Mandel's characteristic light touch and joy in the simple act of making pictures—and always his subtle, telling jokes.

Not so playful is Larry Sultan, in the new version of his autobiographical *Pictures from Home*.

Sultan, a pal of Mandel's and a fellow Valley-ite, and Mandel's co-author on the essential catalogue of found corporate photos, *Evidence* (recently rereleased by D.A.P.), sets his own books in the San Fernando Valley. As mentioned above, there's *The Valley*, his study of the houses used as sets for the porn industry, pornography perhaps being the Valley's only unique business once the dairies turned into tract homes and aerospace and the Chevy plant shut down. Not my favorite book; personally, I'd rather just watch *Boogie Nights* again.

But in *Pictures from Home*, Sultan goes deep, deep, deep into his and his parents' lives, and the book is, and always has been, a keeper. (The edition I'm reviewing here is Mack's reissue/revision from earlier this year.)

In a recent article, *The Guardian* called *Pictures from Home* a "visual memoir that is also an exploration of the all-American family." That it is, but what struck me, growing up at exactly the same time—and as Google maps just showed me, less than a mile away from each other—is how far Sultan's folks are from my own family. My dad *was* in aerospace (till it went the way of coal mining); Sultan's dad is far closer to the flim-flam salesman world (he sold razor blades for Schick all his life). Look at his silver hair, his perfect suit, all the pictures in a bedroom that could in later years be reborn as a porn set. I read *Pictures from Home* as I would read any autobiography: to discover a life, a history, and to plunge as far into all of it as one can.

And also to hugely admire Sultan's nerve. I mean, lots of people *write* autobiographies, about their parents, home life, difficult upbringing. But that's done probably miles and miles away in front of a computer screen.

Larry Sultan instead went home and took pictures of his parents doing everything they did. Here's how that went: "I wake up in the middle of the night, stunned and anguished. These are my parents."

The photos are truly telling. There's his dad in shorts practicing his golf swing on a shag carpet in front of a picture window, a perfect Valley day outside. There's his mom in a lime-green dressing gown in the doorway of her lime-green room with the lime-green shag carpet (or is it avocado; I'm not as up on my grotesque suburban color schemes as I could be). There's a shot of the parents in their living room, furniture-less, getting ready, as the text tells us, to abandon their former lives and move out to the desert to retire.

Then there are the dozens of historic photos, snapshots of Sultan's folks when they were younger, as social as can be, dressed up or out mowing the lawn, loving golf, in swimming pools (ah, the Valley, a swimming pool in every backyard; ours was kidney shaped, and my friends and I spent all summer in it), even a shot of Irving Sultan's Dale Carnegie self-improvement course's full class, lined up in the style of a grammar-school-class photo.

This is the whole story of his family, narrated by Sultan in clear, matter-of-fact prose. He looked at his world, his life, his upbringing, his parents ... and did it unflinchingly.

And with far more order and wildness than the last autobiographical photobook with words I already wrote about, Jim Goldberg's *The Last Son*. In *Pictures from Home* the personal story is typeset, not hand-scrawled. Unlike with Goldberg, we don't learn that much about Larry Sultan (at least not advertently; the book's true focus is more ambiguous), but it is easy to infer that Sultan was far less rebellious.

But no less an artist. And no less a writer.

Pictures from Home is a good read. Yet it's more than that, too: an exemplary model of how to turn what in some ways is a family scrapbook, potentially barely interesting even to the family in it, into a compelling work of art, meaningful to anyone. Sultan pulls you into his family history, and you can't put the book down. He also masterfully blends his own anxieties about the project he's undertaken with his father's own story, along with comments by his mother (both in italics in the book), and the plethora of historic family snapshots with the beautifully composed shots Sultan made for his difficult project.

As with all biographies, auto- or not, there's a bit of invention involved. As *The New York Times* reported in Sultan's obituary (he died in 2009, at 63), after telling his father how to appear in a picture taken of him on his bed, Sultan says that his father told him, "Any time you show that picture, you tell people that that's not me sitting on the bed looking all dressed up and nowhere to go, depressed. That's you sitting on the bed, and I am happy to help you with the project, but let's get things straight here."

Hmnn, maybe it is more Sultan's story than his father's. But the story is also so vivid and well told (through both the writing and the photos) that it could be anyone's; it's that identifiable, and the themes are timeless: How did our parents come to have us? What choices led to their establishing our homes? What happens when we leave those homes? Can we ever go back? And, ultimately, how do we hold on to our parents, as they age, move, sweep ever closer to death?

And that eternal question with any group of photographs: Even with an exact representation (photographic evidence, indeed), where does truth truly lie?

Again, Sultan's father seems to get it: "All I know is that when you photograph me I feel everything leave me. The blood drains from my face, my eyelids droop, my thoughts disappear." Mr. Sultan is worrying that Larry's shots don't capture his truth at all. "If anything," he says on the next page, "the picture shows how strained and artificial the situation was that you set up."

Larry responds: "Sure, it was a charade, but I'm talking about how the image is read rather than what literally was going on when it was made. There's a difference. Don't you think that a fiction can suggest the truth?"

And of course his dad has the perfect rejoinder: "Maybe, but whose truth is it? It's your picture but my image."

A timeless question: Where does ultimate truth lie in a photobook, with the subjects or with the photographer? And one explored so well here, in an enduring book that lifts beyond scrapbook to the power and sweep of a novel.

Daido's Tour Keeps on Never Ending: Daido Moriyama, *Pretty Woman*

September 2017

As I wrote above, the first time I met Daido Moriyama, I told him I thought of him as the Bob Dylan of photography. A small smile, an undisclosing nod. I can't say how he felt about my comment. Yet now more than ever, with new Daido books coming once, twice, thrice a year, it looks as if he's emulating the aging Dylan (Daido's 79, our current Nobel laureate 77), who's well-known for his never-ending tour. (I see Dylan every time he comes to town, and he just keeps getting better.) Nope, these guys won't stop ... and won't stop putting out great work.

Just as Dylan's changed course again in the last few years, recording Sinatra standards, intriguingly, Daido's throwing in some new twists to his oeuvre in his exceptional new book *Pretty Woman*. (Be warned, there will be numerous Dylan correlations throughout this piece, so I can't resist mentioning up front the great Roy Orbison song "Pretty Woman," possibly inspiration for the book's title; and of course Orbison was one-fifth of the Traveling Wilburys, along with Dylan, George Harrison, et al.)

Back to Daido, back to the book. *Pretty Woman* is a mix of rich, saturated color shots worked in with high-contrast black and white, nothing new for Daido in essence, though he doesn't usually mix color and b&w. It's a large book, nine by twelve inches, and as is customary with Daido, the photos are printed full-bleed. They're mostly street shots, Daido prowling the narrow streets of Tokyo, camera in hand, looking for that photograph only he can take. As we shall see, *Pretty Woman* is in many ways a compendium of classic Daido tropes, but it also breaks a lot of new ground in subjects and his approaches to them. What's truly astonishing is that the photos here are not only his best work in years, but some of his best photos ever.

Like Dylan, Daido seems to like to work fast. He appears in

the book's final shot framed in a street mirror, his small, presumably now digital camera up to his eye, his Beatle-esque moptop rising above his camera-clenching left hand—the image of the travel-light, shoot-what's-great street photographer. Daido's art, like Dylan's studio work, is a practice of in quick, out quicker. With Dylan we know it's all about instinct. I've been working my way through eighteen CDs of every extant take from his three best mid-'60s albums, and there are great songs that, just not clicking on tape, Dylan abandoned. I mean, truly great songs that stand with his finest, such as "She's Your Lover Now" and "I'll Keep It with Mine." It's all feel ... the quick flash of gesture, the word images and musical moment seized before they fly away.

So with Daido on the street. The shots in *Pretty Woman* were taken recently, over a one-year period, and mostly in Tokyo. The eternal beauty and power of Daido's work (as with Dylan's) is that it's simply one man with flaming intuition and world-divining vision out taking in everything that comes his way and wresting art out of it. As he courses the streets with his tiny camera, Daido shoots not so much what's there but grabs what only he can see. It's a flood of rich details, a woman's earring, the fluff of a legless mannequin's costume, the tarot-card-esque Madonna before a blue-tiled wall ... and that's him just getting started.

In *Pretty Woman*, amazing image piles atop amazing image, just as in Dylan's best songs. Allow me a small conceit. Let's think of Dylan as a kind of photobook maker. Take his epic "Desolation Row," with its flow of vivid pictures: postcards of hangings, brown passports, beauty parlors swelling with sailors, a circus new in town ... and that's just the first four lines of the eleven-minute song. Followed soon by this alltime great street shot: Cinderella with her hands in her back pockets, Bette Davis–style. Talk about a pretty woman revealed in a new way.

That's the Dylan effect at his best: a cascade of images making no clear literal sense but always sweeping us into a visionary world ... somewhere within his own Gates of Eden. So bear with me as I pick shots at random from *Pretty Woman*. A scarlet shopping bag next to a discarded cigarette pack. A moon-eyed woman on a light-splattered street. A vivid red tulip arcing over

The Mysteries of Light 131

a blue cityscape. A pouting owl snuggled against a man's chest. A midnight-blue ribbed hose snaking over a mottled floor. A back Shinjuku alley, lone bar chair on the street. Black sunglasses (classic Dylan-style) on a corrugated-cardboard mannequin. A red-tutued woman, white mask on her face, parading down a wide avenue. Blue earbuds slipping down the side of a pretty woman's face. A silhouetted miniskirted woman smoking in a backlit doorway, no doubt whispering of escapades out on the Marunouchi Line.

The above paragraph is composed of images I got from randomly flipping through the book. Meaning, I could go on and on. Put a crack band behind these shots and *Pretty Woman* would rock!

I said earlier that the book captures some of Daido's best work in years. I'm addicted to his photobooks and pretty much pick up each one he puts out. I'm always happy to see what he's up to, where he's gone—Marrakech!—but some books feel a lot like some guy just walking around with his camera shooting crowds on streets; they don't possess a full draft of Daido magic. But his best work has always come out of Tokyo, his own mythical version of the city, perhaps, and so *Pretty Woman* feels inspired by familiarity even as it rings new changes on not wholly unfamiliar Daido imagery.

There's a flood of little toy frogs, not unlike the pictures of Daido's from decades back of towering soup cans. (A pause here while I say that both Daido and Dylan have borrowed from numerous places, and Daido's '60s wall of soup cans references Warhol at just the time Dylan was dipping his toe into the Factory and writing "Like a Rolling Stone" for Edie Sedgwick.) Looking for red lips? There's a stick-on set on a ghostly white mannequin. Even better is a flame of lips on the beautiful dead-eyed face of a woman under cellophane wrap, presumably a mannequin? But best of all is a quick red-kiss paint dab atop a pair of sexy black stockings, just below the crook of a knee.

The latter is an alltime classic Daido shot, as if after all these years he finally found a way to reduce his obsessions to one image. (This photo is reproduced over and over in miniature on the book's inner cover.) A late career epiphany, not unlike Dylan discovering his own genius all over again, this time by making those Sinatra covers sound like Dylan songs, as he's done on his last five discs. It's the power of a compelling artist swaying all he comes across into his own way of things. Deep inside the Gates of Eden indeed.

In *Pretty Woman*, as mentioned, there are wholly new kinds of Daido images, too. Particularly striking is a red mouth with teeth and braces just there on a white background. A looming lattice of suspended stairs ominous before a gray sky. Sun–glowing wheat-colored strands of hair flying across a woman's ear.

And more. How about a spookily revealing street photographer shot: Daido snapping a man before a public urinal, half of him and his camera caught in the rest room mirror. Another voyeuristic shot, this time through a car window, short skirt rising up the female driver's left leg. A three-girl pop group, mikes in hand, just a tease of petticoat under one girl's skirt. And most unexpected, a small, touching street moment: a groom adjusting his bride's bodice as a pant-suited woman friend cools them both with a yellow fan. A shot almost sentimental yet lovely just the same.

(Small personal note: In my own work I hesitate taking photos on the street of people on their cellphones. Daido doesn't have many, but inevitably a number of phone shots appear in the book. Why won't I shoot them? Because people on their phones have abandoned their attention, indeed, forsaken their souls, to the devices; and so a shot of someone gazing screenward captures little but blankness, nothingness. I can't say Daido has avoided this problem. The phone-gazers might be endemic today in any cityscape, but the little magic screens have still wiped out anything human or interesting from photographs of people immured in them.)

Still, not many smartphone shots, and just think of the abundance, the grandness, indeed, the overwhelming delight of turning the pages of *Pretty Woman* not knowing what mind-blowing photo you'll find next. Oh, my, how'd I miss the black-and-white spread of checkerboard tiles, a woman's crossed ankles above them. Or the gold-toned mannequin with the presence of a Roman statue. Or one of my favorite shots, the watch-capped

The Mysteries of Light 133

tough behind a graffitied blue plastic pane, pen scrawls scattered over his stare-you-down face, most telling a small pair of red lips floating over his own.

O.K., I fear I'm having too much fun turning Daido's always striking photos into words, but what the hell ... it's that kind of book. Indeed, I can't stress enough that *Pretty Woman*, while replete with these amazing photographs, is at heart simply a great *book*. Just as we can single out towering Dylan songs, especially from his early masterpieces like *Highway 61 Revisited*, no one song—or anything else—compares with the effect of that album as a whole.

That's what a great photobook must be: Not simply a collection of photos but choices and orderings that make the book so much more than that. That's the toughest trick, whether it's a record album, a collection of short stories, or a photobook: to make the whole vastly richer than the pieces.

Daido's done it. Again. *Pretty Woman* is a book that stands alongside his previous masterworks *Japan a Photo Theater* and *Bye Bye Photography*.

Consider that a main reason we collect great photobooks is to not simply own a few prints by a photographer we like but to own a whole museum, not to mention the book as a work of art in its own right.

Pretty Woman is your best museum visit in years, reading it an experience that will knock you out loaded. The book is a strange fever dream, a walk through a city that surprises at every turn, a clash of vivid, stirring images that whisper manifold mysterious things to each other even as they shout out the boundless magic of street life itself.

This year the Nobel Prize committee in Sweden saw fit (finally) to give its literature prize to a musician and songwriter, arguably the Shakespeare of our time. Does it have the vision and guts to expand literature even further and award the prize to a photobook maker? If so, it can only be Daido Moriyama.

Weird, Weird, Weird: Feng Li, *White Night*

October 2017

IN MY FICTION WRITING class, after a piece has been read out loud, the first question we ask is: What's the story? I like to have the students kick around what they think the story they've just heard is, how it sets out, where it takes us, how it turns, twists, resolves. That question gets to the center of the writing, and from that the rest of the piece opens up.

With a photobook my first question is often: Is there a story? By *story* I don't mean a plot or even any clear sequence of events; photobooks move differently from other art forms. What I am asking, though, is: Is there a shape behind the array of shots? A sense of correspondence, of pace, of theme, of direction? Simply, what holds all the images together—images that might not reveal any literal sense but should be composed, and ordered, as in a private poem. The late John Ashbery, a fave of mine, did this exceptionally well in his poetry books: Lift us, take us on a journey of images (and language), and always keep us a bit lost as we try to make sense of what we're reading.

With Feng Li's powerful *White Night*, I'm sensing just that intention ... a strong story he has to tell, but one which I don't have much of a clue about. It seems a natural tale of his wholly unnatural world of Chengdu, China ... a photobook that's part surreal, part hallucination, all street work, and the product of a powerful artistic intent.

Come, let's jump in.

The cover of the book intrigues. It's a thick, black, almost solid sheet of plastic, just translucent enough to let the outlines of the photo underneath through: The back of a shapeless woman, in a huge fur coat, her knock-off tan designer bag at her side. She's alone on a gray street, a brooding image countered immediately by the first shot in the book itself, branches of what look like cherry blossoms before a turquoise sky, a common enough Chinese image that leads to ... a moody shot of a man carrying what looks like a fake tree of cherry blossoms down a murky street.

Immediately we know the photos *are* talking to each other, and observations undercut by visions of artifice is a theme in play. That's all the more true in the next photo, a plaid-jacketed soul spinning a giant fireworks sparkler, followed immediately by a similar band of colors in a rainbow stretching above a ledge topped by broken shards of glass.

Private images, private poems. And pairings across spreads that are so far from accidental they seem almost uncanny. A few pages in we find a young Chinese woman gazing mysteriously heavenward across from a line of black-leather-clad women, each wearing over-the-knee leather boots and brandishing a long cat-of-nine-tail whip.

Ohhhh-kayyyyy. Chengdu, where Feng Li lives, is evidently a pretty curious place, at least through his eyes. From a fascinating walk-around-town interview with him that appears in *American Suburb X*, I learned that Chengdu is the historic capital of Sichuan province, and through Feng Li's work, a place with more than a hint of surrealism rising up from its ancient streets. Feng Li is evidently one of the most successful professional photographers in this artistic city, but the photos in *White Night* are the private work of a decade. As Leo de Boisgisson, the lucky writer strolling around town with Li, puts it, "[Li] is not into 'the decisive moment,' or aesthetic settings. For him, the decisive moment is now, and he would never settle somewhere to wait for it. Every snapshot is an unexpected and sometimes inconvenient encounter with fate."

Is that what underlies the deep story of *White Night* ... fate? It seems as good a theme as any. The world of Chengdu is being modernized, changing rapidly, and Li captures the gaps between the old and the new ... the way fate plays out inside the everyday. A stunned-looking woman on an escalator across the page from a goofy-looking guy with old-school bad teeth. A one-legged man in an unzipped bunny costume followed a few photos on by an ingénue in a much more formal bunny-cotillion costume (shades of Hugh Hefner, late between draft one of this piece and now), this photo paired against one of a guy in a tiger T-shirt so realistic the beast's snout extends at least as far from his stomach as a pregnant woman.

What? Where the hell are we? I take a lot of my shots in New York's Times Square, looking for that concatenation of hordes of different people, layers of reflected images, strangeness, astonishment ... and I've never seen a guy wearing a tiger shirt that looks like it would be happy to rip out your throat. Spooky stuff.

And lots of it. *White Night* is 184 pages long, the product of at least a decade of *flâneur*ing around town, very much the private work of a very busy professional photographer. (According to the *American Suburb X* piece one can find Li's professional shots on huge digital screens around Chengdu.)

But not in his book. Who's going to put up on a billboard the photo of a woman held high aloft on a white pole, enwrapped inside some kind of cloth bulb like a bright-red Hershey's kiss. To sell what? The absolute surrealism of daily life here? Where's the money in that?

Somewhere, evidently, because people sure are acting out in Chengdu. The next spread contrasts a string of nippled breast balloons with a bald man's head almost squeezed in a window frame, and that's followed by a man surrounded by flame-red lamps presumably in some kind of quack medical treatment, that shot paired with a fur-wearing woman shot from the back (like the cover shot), but this time with just the same red-yellow-orange fiery glare erupting from the scalp below her thinning hair.

Weird, weird, weird ... and on and on. I'm just getting going with *White Night*, and already I've seen shots I've never seen before, and could never have imagined. Brilliant. Disturbing. Breathtaking.

There's a bit of Bruce Gilden here, though the subjects are not at all uniformly grotesque. There are traces of the intense colors of the late Ren Hang, though not many actual portraits and no apparent undertow of sexuality. Really, Feng Li is his own photographer, his own man. As Li puts it, "My wife often tells me my pictures are weird, and I tell her it's not my fault if so many weird things happen right in front of me!"

Besides the weirdness, one thing that's consistent is wit, especially in the way the photos line up. Here's another spread: Four women on their backs doing exercises, white panties vivid, paired with a man carrying two plastic-wrapped costumed dummies down another of those murky Chengdu walkways. And another: A child with its hands up and pressing against a pane of glass paired with a kid in a folkloric fox costume, also with its hands up. That last pairing is about as obvious as Li ever gets; most pairings are far more ineffably appropriate than clever, more mysterious than just a visual pun.

But as I said above, all the photos talk to each other, the pairings particularly engaging, similar themes and imagery fluttering, darting through the whole book ... until the images end with another tree of budding flowers, though here the buds are all glowing white lights, the life and beauty of the cherry blossoms buzzing now with manmade electricity.

So what is Feng Li's story in *White Night*? That everything connects; and that life is amazing, absurd, and just when you think you've seen it all, you ain't seen nothing.

Which is, perhaps, the best, most timeless story of all.

Inventing the New Photographic Language: Christer Strömholm, *Poste Restante*

October 2017

There's a very helpful quote on the back of the reissue (finally!) of Christer Strömholm's masterpiece, *Poste Restante*, from a contemporary review in the Swedish evening tabloid *Expressen*. "As far as I know," the review goes, "this is the first time a book publisher (Norstedts) has dropped all demands that a photobook must have a subject in the ordinary sense—or at least that it must work on a social, documentary, or generally decorative level. *Poste Restante* is as exclusive and private in its conception as a modern lyrical poetry collection and in its expression, almost as closed and inaccessible....

"*Poste Restante* shows that Christer Strömholm is probably the person in photographic history who has been most effective in using photography as a symbolic or formal language for private experiences, for a subjective sensibility of life."

I don't usually quote other reviews, but I do so here to raise a historical question: Did Strömholm invent the poetic photobook?

That's not exactly *Expressen*'s point, but still an interesting question, leading us to consider such forebears as Man Ray; Germaine Krull and her ode to metal; Moi Ver and his surreal superimpositions; Robert Frank's breathtaking song of the American highway (Walt Whitman in photos a century later, now singing the radiant jukebox); and even William Klein with his "I also contain multitudes" epic bebop prose poem of New York (and of Rome, Moscow and Tokyo). But *Expressen* does have a point: In *Poste Restante*, Strömholm works with a far more private language of secret images and not-quite-explicable meanings than photographers before him. That in its way *is* a first.

I've written in these pages many times about how I look for story in photobooks, *story* as shorthand for a way of shaping a book, giving it direction, pulse, a rise and fall of emotion; but in essence my deep argument is that the best photobooks constitute a new form of literature. So why not the photobook as a form of poetry book?

What then has Strömholm written for us? What is this "modern lyrical poetry collection?"

Well, first off, that stark, disturbing cover photo of a dead, rotting dog on harshly pebbled ground. Not the only image in the book of death, of course: there's the lurid wall drawing of a tiger biting into a terrified man's shoulder; what looks like an Indian woman in her burial shroud; and a casting of a shrieking head in a box that's easily the photographic equivalent of Munch's famous bridge-screamer—perhaps not death itself, but surely an image bearing down hard at us on the Hades Expressway.

Poetry thrives on running motifs. For Strömholm, death is a powerful theme; the magic in found images is another.

Indeed, Strömholm loves found images, the crocodile snapping at a she-lizard; a cast-off painting of a mustached burgher, a chip of canvas torn from his forehead; and a lurid drawing of a spotted carnival woman flanked by two bemused apes, this photo flanked by the actual carny woman in her two-piece swimsuit, the spots liberally strewn over her mostly naked flesh.

Strömholm also loves carnies, it's clear; further, he harbors a deep fascination with outré life-styles, too. *Poste Restante* has eight photos from the series that would make up his other great photo book, *Les Amies de Place Blanche*, his shots of transsexuals along the Boulevard Clichy in Paris back in the 1950s (unexpectedly quiet photos, pace Henry Miller), but almost every shot in *Poste Restante* is curious if not downright strange and unsettling. What's that child doing hanging at least a dozen feet up hoisted on a bamboo stick? Where did the photographer find all those oozy snakes? How about the wicker basket of broken-up doll parts? That demented looking blind child that might have given even Diane Arbus the willies?

In a way, *Poste Restante* resembles Ed van der Elsken's *Sweet Life*, as it roams the world seeking out the strange and curious, but when put side-by-side, Elsken's book is more travelogue; Strömholm's truly is "modern lyrical poetry." How else as imagistic poetry do we explain why he chose to shoot a Pere Lachaise grave statue of two thick arms reaching out, two huge stone hands clasping? Or a white-cloth-covered motorcycle before an ivy wall? A couple splots of vomit on a brick road? A board full of hanging pocket watches? Two plastic bags carrying goldfish home?

The only explanation: All these images spoke to Strömholm. They contained a poetic magic that caught his eye, that only his camera could capture, and that this great photobook—each photo speaking to the next, in discord and harmony, in mystery and heightened consciousness—could bring to life.

That's the essence of the poetic photobook: Images powerful and personal, correspondences between shots inexplicable yet telling, the power of a strong, vivid internal vision finding its correlatives in images somehow snapped by one's camera. That's the true secret: internal mysteries only the artist understands (or intuits) made manifest in photos, not words. In a phrase, *This speaks to me, and my poetic soul is so certain and present that what I photograph will speak to you, too.*

Poets make poetry, meaning that those souls privileged (or damned) enough to see/feel what no one else does can render those transcendent glimpses into words. Poetic photographers, those who see/feel what we can't, make poetic photobooks. Perhaps as simple as that.

I'm fortunate to own an original copy of *Poste Restante*, and after comparing it with the reissue, it's safe to say that every photo in the new edition is crisper and richer than the 1967 version. Also different is that the interview with Strömholm that opens each book on gray paper (O.K., the gray paper in the original version is textured, thus more interesting, but so what?) is now in English rather than the original Swedish. Which means I can read it. And it's worth going through. Strömholm was an intriguing cat. There are numerous tales of fighting Nazis in WWII, then wandering the world, especially the world's brothels. Here's a telling quote: "Personally I can't cope with the same woman day in and day out. I want new bodies under me, want new confessions and new stories."

New confessions, new stories ... add to that new photos, new placings of images, new mysteries, new passions, new visions ... and you get *Poste Restante*.

By the way, the title translates as "general delivery," and as with any great poet, Strömholm's work can see into the future. Those world-sweeping images of desirous geishas and pornographic wall scratchings, of snake ladies and Parisian transsexuals, are no longer so forbidden, so outré. Indeed, you can probably have all of it turn up in the post with a few clicks on Amazon. General delivery, indeed.

Strömholm: poet, visionary, inspiration for photographers from Arbus to Elsken, from Frederick Sommer to Daido Moriyama, and all-around mysterian, to our great benefit back again in this reissue of his classic work by the Christer Strömholm estate. Simply essential ... and ready to inspire other poetic photographers well into time.

Joy, Mischief, Life:
Saul Leiter, *It Don't Mean a Thing*

November 2017

Here's the one time I met Saul Leiter. It was a couple years before his death, he was signing a new book at his gallery on East 57th St. There was this jolly, smiling, army-and-navy-surplus-store-dressed old guy, rings of silver hair circling his face, sitting at a table with a pen and an array of rubber stamps and ink pads. (My first decade in NYC I had a place around the corner from where Leiter lived for fifty-plus years; on my old block on East 11th Street there is still a custom rubber stamp store, Casey, run by another silver-haired East Village gent, most likely where Leiter got his own stamps.)

I put Leiter's new book in front of him, told him how much his work meant to me. The book was Kehrer's *Saul Leiter Retrospektive*, and when he first signed it, he did so on the page that already had a printed signature, so it simply looked as if his signature had been printed twice. I asked him if he could sign the title page, and he obliged, with gusto. I got the second signature, then with a gleeful grin he started stamping like crazy with his little rubber stamps. Along with a huge red heart, there are two bold blue "HELP!"s, a red "IT'S NOT MY FAULT," and a red circle and a black circle, both with SL inside it.

I shook his hand. He beamed.

So there was Saul Leiter, eighty-nine years old, full of joy, mischief, and life. A year later he was dead.

I go on at such length about this meeting because it's expressive of an essential joy, mischief, and life that comes through in virtually every one of Leiter's photographs, which makes each new shot from his archives that turns up in print such a notable occasion. Which makes the latest release from the Gould Collection such an important book.

It Don't Mean a Thing gives us dozens of heretofore unseen Leiter images, many as good as the indelible classics we all

The Mysteries of Light 143

know, combined with a short story by the eminent New York City author Paul Auster. (This is the Gould Collection's second book. Their mission is to combine the photobook with short fiction, and they're accomplishing that far better than I ever thought it could be done.) One simple aspect that makes these books work is that the photographs are printed on full sheets of white luster paper, while the short fiction is on a gray textured stock that ends an inch and an eighth (less than three centimeters) short of the larger paper. So *It Don't Mean a Thing* is primarily a photobook; that is, the printed words at the least don't get in the way, as they do in so many mixed-media projects.

As more and more Leiter shots see public light, we learn ever more things about him: his strong black-and-white work; his deep interest in nudes; his continuing magic with color. All these qualities (except nudes) are resplendent in *It Don't Mean a Thing*. Personally, I like his color work best, and there are photos here not unfamiliar in style to those in Steidl's transformative *Early Color*. There are snow shots, mirror shots, window-reflection shots, even one of those wonderful Toulouse Lautrec–like faded-café shots. The astonishment? These are not B photos compared with those in *Early Color*. Most are at least as good; some better.

And what a great color photographer Leiter is. Among other things, he reinvented Impressionism for the mid–20th century, finding a way to uncrisp lines, blur figures, float wonderful clouds of color all in service of truths and emotions far greater than the realistic representations a lens usually captures. And he was doing much of his best work in the 1950s, when color photography could barely be imagined as actual art. (To Leiter's credit, he turned down an invitation to Steichen's dreary "Family of Man" 1955 MoMA show and book.)

The pairing up with Auster in *It Don't Mean a Thing* is inspired, not only because some consider Auster an important New York City novelist, but also because his story in the book is somewhat Impressionistic, a not uncharming (if very slight) tale of coincidence comprised of a Matisse scholar, an indigent poet, first readings of *Le Petit Prince*, a wildly enthusiastic recital of the Ellington classic "It Don't Mean a Thing (If It Ain't Got That

Swing)" by the narrator's daughter (lending the book its title), and a building on Central Park South. Written by Auster in 2000, the story complements Leiter's pictures, as an aura of decades-ago New York City rises from the words and subtly backlights the photos.

Now back to the photos.

There are some somewhat conventional black-and-white street shots that Walker Evans or Louis Faurer did better, and one shot taken near ground level on a NYC street, a man's suit legs taking up the foreground, a woman looking into her purse the main subject, a flock of other women blurring past with a distinct William Klein vibe—though since it's dated only "1950s," there's no telling who came up with that type of shot first. (My money's on a tie, since both Leiter and Klein always seem to beat to their own drums.)

Even the shots in *It Don't Mean a Thing* that can only be Leiter's—a spread on pages 32 and 33, for instance—push our ideas of his work further. Page 32 is a 1950s shot of Times Square, one of those Leiter complex mirror/window deals, though this one piles up the crowd thicker and more abstract than shots in *Early Color*. Likewise the next photo, another snowy street with a red and green traffic light (the colors more muted than usual in Leiter), but this shot is nearly half blacked-out by a blurry man in a hat walking by, simply a dark shadow over the already blue and melancholy winter street. This photo is also not as crisp as the well-known winter ones in *Early Color*, where the snow is more fun as it falls on postmen, or more simply a backdrop as it is in "Red Umbrella," the white back-dropping the umbrella's frame-leaving pop of color.

There are shots in the book new for Leiter's work, at least to me. Curiously, I see a photo or two here much like ones I've taken walking around NYC, shots that made sense for me to take ... and now I see that Leiter was thinking similarly sixty years earlier. For instance, there's a photo of the reflection of tall city buildings off the trunk of a shiny automobile. I took a couple like that just a few months back.

Likewise new to me in Leiter's work are black-and-white weather shots (the weather ones I know are in *Early Color*) and some very emotional black-and-white street shots. On the cover of *It Don't Mean a Thing* is a photo of his longtime companion Soames Bantry, but it's clearly not a studied portrait as so many in *Early Black and White* are. Here we have a woman sitting on a street-side bench, mouth pressed up into a raised fist, looking at best contemplative, at worse concerned or deeply troubled. It's a powerful picture of anyone, even if not a loved one; but that she's Leiter's mate makes the photo even more intriguing.

Leiter has always drawn powerful emotion from his shots of friends and lovers, just as he can wring stirring emotions out of casual street scenes. More than most photographers other than William Eggleston, the power of Leiter's work is in his use of color, like Matisse or Rothko or even Mondrian, whom Leiter imitates in a shot or two. As with the artists above, Leiter's work is all about feeling, and in *It Don't Mean a Thing* every picture new to us (a small percentage are from earlier books) takes us on a new artistic journey.

Which is not to say that *It Don't Mean a Thing* makes us reevaluate Leiter in any major way, just that it makes clear that the depths of his singular vision and photographic art have not yet been fully known or enjoyed. And for that, the new book is essential and a true delight ... and we hope a taste of further joy, mischief, and life to come.

I Gotta Make a Photobook: Stephen Gill, *Night Procession*

January 2018

FIRST COMES THE HUNGER. An actual physical urgency to make pictures. I feel it all the time, especially if I haven't been out shooting for a couple days. I'm in New York City. I hit the streets, take the subway to different parts of town, camera ready, more important, my *mind* ready, seeing everything. It's the seeing *everything*, the way my eyes sweep the streets, wanting to catch every subtle detail—any movement, gesture, even color fluctuation—that might make a picture. Or a person whose expression is redolent of emotion. Or a store window replete with an intriguing arrangement of objects. Or ... something I don't know will make a good picture till I lift my camera and try to grab it.

Daido Moriyama works this way. He called his third book, from 1972, *A Hunter*, and explains in a reissue that "I hunt images." Daido, inspired as he says by Kerouac's *On the Road*, heads out to "feel actuality and chaotic pulses of splinters of external world littered on, and of crossing narrations and lyricisms."

That sums up a type of photobook I'm often most drawn to: books created by an inner urgency simply to take photos, to discover pulses of meaning, then cross narrations and lyricism to make a photobook from them. This is usually not a book to fulfill an external assignment, or follow a planned theme. It's inner compulsion. Private beats. Spontaneity. Working with what's around you. Discovering in that world a poetry of images that speak to what's within us all....

Which is why I'm so impressed by Stephen Gill's new book, *Night Procession*. As Gill explains, he left England in 2014 for south Sweden, the town of Österlen, where his partner, Lena, was from, to raise his family. No more East London, he was in the wilds now, yet still with that need to make photos, to hunt images.

As Gill explained in the *Financial Times*, he was ready for the new challenge, "looking forward to making work that would not feel restricted and suffocated by modern photographic technology, nor would project an inaccurate impression of the natural landscape we had become part of." Gill has always experimented wildly in his photobooks, and now he saw a new opportunity: to take shots of nature teeming through the forests at night.

From an essay included with the book by the esteemed Norwegian author Karl Ove Knausgård, a neighbor of Gill's in Österlen, we learn that Gill was out every day, afraid of boar, for sure, but also hiking and kayaking through his new land. And hunting pictures.

Knausgård also reveals that Gill has a singular condition in which he's "unable to separate information," meaning that to Gill in any given scene all information has the same value, the same relevance even if one element is truly important and everything else not. Gill tells Knausgård that he believes photography is his way of controlling this recently diagnosed condition, which makes total sense since at essence photography is the art of choosing significance out of a rush of information—choosing this shot, not that one; this edit, not that one. As I've often put it to myself, I hope *to see* everything, but always know (to photograph) only that which is most telling and meaningful.

But to overcome an actual psychological condition? Safe to say that for Gill his hunt for pictures sounds truly urgent and necessary.

So here he is in this new land, new terrain, doing what he does: making photographs. Yet also cut off from the totality of the forest until a new idea comes to him. As Gill tells us, he found himself particularly curious about the "idea of stepping back as the author of images, to give space for chance, and to encourage the subject to step forward." So it wasn't enough to stomp around the intense forest, he needed to step away from it, let the forest be itself. To do that, he did his best to imagine where a deer would drink from, an owl perch, and set up cameras with motion detectors, "so that the subjects would orchestrate and perform and take on the role of author while I was likely to be sleeping. This was nature's time to speak and let itself be felt and known."

As coincidence would have it, I was recently in a cloud forest in Costa Rica, where I took a night walk looking for any kind of wildlife. We didn't see much, though I did turn up on a leaf an inch-long national-symbol tree frog! At the end of the walk we saw a short video made using a motion-capture system similar to what Gill employed. Nice shots of monkeys and ocelots ... but nothing remotely artistic. So what is it about a photographer who can create his singular art while dozing far from where his camera is set up? Does his dreams somehow cast forceful spells into the forest? Move the birds and animals into compelling, revealing position? Let their true spirits come forth?

I can't answer that, of course, but the photos in *Night Procession* are uniformly vivid, spectral, haunted—the work of a true artist.

In Gill's book there's plenty of fauna: startled deer, glaring boars, water-sniffing fox, death-eyed elk, wing-flapping owls; and plenty of flora, too: stark tree branches, heavily patterned leaves, snow-catching reeds. It's nature! Many shots lean heavily toward abstraction. Gill is happy to show us water swirls, woodsy streaks, ripply boar skin, a deer's hind legs, snow flows, shell whirls, even photos with nothing distinguishable in it except that purest of photographic truth: patterns of light and dark rendering their own meanings. (There are also a few shots of humans, a couple presumably of his children, another of a pair of hands picking berries.)

As he's done with many of his books, Gill doesn't simply print the photos he's taken (though his publishing house, Nobody Books, has done a beautiful job rendering the shots onto the thick matte paper), he often physically fools with them. Some shots are close to a simple black-and-white print, others are tinted (most often a yellowish green, though there's one photo that's reddish-brown with splashes of ice blue), and a number are messed with more extensively, a quality of Gill's work we've seen many times before. In *Night Procession*, he tells us in the *Financial Times* piece, he used "plant pigments ... from the surrounding areas to make the final master prints." The simple change in how each photo has been prepared keeps the book always surprising, and full of near physical delight.

And a true book it is. Broad in its range of shots, but all of a piece. A book with an intention, true: capture the forest (Gill's homestead) at night. But as with any work by a great photographic hunter, what results takes into account happenstance, luck, dismay and surprise, then is edited down into a book that feels inevitable. The hunt is all, whether on the streets of Tokyo or New York City or in the wintry forests of southern Sweden. And the reward? A book full of these magical shots no one would otherwise see, nocturnal forest rituals far from human eyes.

Footnote: The enclosed Karl Ove Knausgård piece is one of the least cantish, most revealing essays accompanying a photobook since Kerouac's be-bop intro to *The Americans*. Knausgård says insightful, brilliant things about *Night Procession*, photography, and the nature of reality—especially how reality, in photography, is both actual and unreal, always a secret world of transmogrifying detail and compelling abstraction. As Knausgård understands, what Gill has done here is to leave behind the personal that usually defines meaning in a photograph (by selection and editing) and let it float into the nonpersonal, the forest doing its nighttime thing. Gill "has moved towards the zone in which the local content of the motive and the universal content of the image have scraped and grated against each other."

Yes, somehow Gill is *in* the forest even as he sleeps miles away, even as he's in each photo even though in truth the image is just a deer gazing dolefully at a hidden camera. Because it's his book. And his secret place (now ours, too) so wondrously captured in *Night Procession*.

Can You Make Too Many Photobooks?: Nobuyoshi Araki, *Blue Period/Last Summer*

March 2018

Nobuyoshi Araki doesn't need me to write about him. He probably doesn't need *anybody* to write about him at this point, five hundred or so books in (or is it five thousand?), and a long, serpentine, impressive career behind him (with, one hopes, much more to come). I mean, what is there to say anyway? That he did breakthrough work back in the early '70s, discovering along with Daido Moriyama just how exhilarating a bunch of blurry photos reproduced on a crappy Xerox machine could be. That in the '80s he became a rapscallion celebrity photographer, especially in the pages of the girlie-rag/serious photo magazine *Shashin Jidai (Photography Age)*, that would feature Araki sex shots and Daido Moriyama serious-photo spreads (or vice versa). That Araki went on to a series of strong street photographs; perhaps the most powerful (and far from appetite-arousing) photobook dedicated to food, *The Banquet*; and, yes, way too many bondage shots. Every time you flip a page of even one of his more anodyne-appearing books, there's a good chance you'll hit yet another bondage picture. (Like, what's up with that squid in *The Banquet*?) Alas, I'm not a connoisseur of pics of women trussed up with black leather and chains (tend to turn my eyes away from them, actually), but my sense is that Araki takes a pretty damn good one. Seems to put all of his heart (and other body parts) into the bondage snaps. It's just that there are so damn many of them ... not to mention all kinds of #metoo issues.

Which means I approach *Blue Period/Last Summer*, a new book by him, though of older work, with some trepidation—or at least a sense of *Why bother?*

Well, I am bothering because the book is beautiful, and beautiful in a way that it turns out only Nobuyoshi Araki can be.

The Mysteries of Light 151

Published by Session Press/Dashwood Books, *Blue Period/Last Summer* is two books in one, published that way at Araki's request. Both works derive from a series of slide-show and music performances he gave starting in the '80s. (There have been over 30 films made to project these happenings through the world.) *Blue Period* and *Last Summer* are comprised of photos from the '80s, many first published in *Shashin Jidai*, then shown separately back then, and put together for a 2005 flick.

So how do all these photos made for many different occasions and performances work as a book? Amazingly well ... so much so that I'd call *Blue Period/Last Summer* one of the most beautiful, thoughtful, stirring Araki books ever.

One reason the book (and photos) work so well is that Araki threw external processing at the original photos. He tells us that *Blue Period* is about the past, and captures that quality by having dunked each slide into a chemical bath to tint the shot blue in unique ways. There are many shots of nude women—and yes, one with a long red cord bound around her ankles and chest—but they're 1) artful and inventive (as well as dubiously erotic) in the way Araki almost always is when shooting nudes; and 2) with the liquid splotches, blurs, and etching into the film, each shot gains a cool beauty. The past indeed ... as if each shot is seen through a bluish dream haze of memory.

Last Summer, Araki specifies, is about the future, and in that half of the book he's dabbed or thrown paint at each color slide, mostly primary colors, reds, greens, oranges, blues—colors haphazardly half-concealing, blobbing, scraping, even hovering ominously over the various shots. There are still plenty of nudes but far more street shots here than in *Blue Period*. Perhaps the future for Araki meant not just looking at naked ladies but getting out of the studio. Or maybe it means something wholly other.

No matter what the intention, the painted-over photos (printed perfectly in the Session Press/Dashwood book) are uniformly fascinating, beautiful, disturbing, exciting, mysterious, and truly one of a kind. My take: Except for his most personal and moving books, the two *Sentimental Journeys* (about his late wife, Yoko), and maybe a few intensely focused works such as *Tokyo Lucky Hole* and *Banquet*, Araki's photos seem always to benefit from being treated by outside media, chemical wash or paint or whatever.

They sure do here.

It was also interesting to learn more about *Shashin Jidai*, the Japanese art-girlie-hookup mag from the early '80s. From what I can tell, *Shashin Jidai* looks like a combo of *Aperture* and Al Goldstein's *Screw*, with spreads of great Daido Moriyama photos intermixed with a slick-mustached Araki disporting with all manner of ladies in-between ads for such ladies (pre-internet) replete with phone numbers and personal qualities.

Have to say, though, that if most of the photos in *Blue Period/ Last Summer* came from *Shashin Jidai*, then that "alternative journal" was on to something. The breathtakingly sexualized photos in Araki's book are all creative, unexpected, and lovely in surprising ways. Just as a coincidence I recently got a copy of Richard Prince's *Bettie Kline*, the fanciful thesis examination of the nudie photos of Bettie Page and their "inspirational effect" on the painter Franz Kline. So I've been looking lately at more conventional last-century sexual subculture photography than, well, ever. As good-looking and creative as Ms. Page was, it's a stretch to call the whips-and-chains shots of her art. Which makes Araki's achievement all the more extraordinary. His nude model shots are almost always about color, composition, emotion, wit, humor, pathos; and they always push the erotic imagination. And that's before the added blue wash or dabs and swirls of colored paint.

And of course, the erotic work is only a portion of what he's up to.

At bottom, that's the astonishment of the Araki photographic achievement. Works of impassioned, moving autobiography and a lot of breathtakingly inspired street shots (and, alas, legions that are more banal than not). Inspired color work of flowers and food and trussed-up women, all glorious and imaginative and beautiful, and a whole lot more good ol' bondage shots that even Irving Klaw (the impresario of Page's gallimaufry of porn) might've gotten tired of. And, yes, there are those photos smeared and streaked with paint, and coruscated with who knows what chemicals, all as timeless as any photo anyone's ever shot. (I have an intuition that Atget is behind them all but dare not push the notion.)

Nonetheless, when it's finally time to weed out the whole five hundred (or five thousand) Araki photobooks, the ones that will remain, including *Blue Period/Last Summer*, as well as the ones mentioned above, will stand as tall on the shelf of photobooks as any work by anyone.

Love Stories and the Photobook: John Sypal, *Zuisha*

April 2018

How important is an actual story to a photobook? By *actual story* I mean an almost literal narrative, with characters and situations: a mini-movie or a play in photos. Clearly the best photobooks carry aspects of story such as theme, structure, motion, even narrative drive—as in, you can't wait to turn to the next picture. But an actual story? That doesn't happen that often in important photobooks. I can think of Ed van der Elsken's *Love on the Left Bank* and ... not a whole lot else. Photobooks are not *fotonovelas* or film storyboards (and *Left Bank* is pretty close to a photo novel, in truth).

So just as a photobook can have no story shape at all (and lose much of the force that holds a great book together), a photobook can also have too much story and veer toward comic books.

But there is a sweet spot of actual narrative in a photobook that still remains purely a photobook. That place is where the pictures do delve into character and dramatic situation and actual narrative yet don't succumb to it; they stay books of pictures that move us by the force and power of the photos themselves. And that brings us to John Sypal's new book *Zuisha*, which mostly hits that story-laden sweet spot. There are characters, well, at least one visible one, apparently Sypal's girlfriend (photos of a woman who in the afterword he explains were first exhibited under the title *An Endless Attraction*, so I believe I'm drawing a reasonable inference; more on this to come), and also an only-twice-shown character, the fellow taking the photos of her, John Sypal.

What is Sypal's story? Ah, that's where the magic of photography and the photobook comes into play. The photographer explains in his afterword that the book's title, *Zuisha*, comes from a piece by the eminent scholar Donald Ritchie on a

The Mysteries of Light

Japanese literary genre called *zuihitsu*, "an informal essay created through an approach where it is not 'the assumptions of the writer's controlling mind that are followed but, as the Japanese phrase it, the brush itself.'"

That is, the story in *Zuisha* isn't what Sypal has in his mind, or what he wants to tell us, it's the story written by his camera alone; and that's presumably the story of the intriguing and mysterious woman we first encounter half concealed behind a street pole as a motorcyclist blurs by.

And that's what intrigues most about this subtle new photobook: How "an endless attraction" begins to reveal its own tale, with its own rules and mysteries; and how Sypal's camera was there to capture it all.

Of course not all the photos are of the young woman; and that's what also makes the book mostly work. We're not seeing a forced narrative, we're simply rolling through time with the photographer and his fascination.

(Notably, before the actual book *Zuisha* came a series of thirteen shows, also called Zuisha, at a gallery in Tokyo. Sypal, a Nebraska native who lives and works as a middle school teacher in a Tokyo suburb, would put up a series of twenty shots at the gallery when they were ready; the book presumably is a distillation of them.)

So, what is the story Sypal's "pen-like" camera is writing for us? First of all, simply a series of black-and-white photos that feel right together. Most are street shots, those moments when you're walking along and see something worth chronicling: a couple taking a stroll by a lake, the woman gazing up at tree blossoms; a man dozing on a hard-surface park path, a scatter of petals over and around him; a couple dining outside, the woman lifting cigarette smoke into the air.

But then the narrative heats up. Sypal catches a couple cats in a window, follows that photo with a coy look from his girlfriend (an old-fashioned pendulum clock behind her) and another of a shot of her right eye reflected in an oval mirror, and then—jackpot—those two cats captured copulating in the very same window.

I can't explain the meaning here, but I sense it. Just as in the next pairing of shots: an intensely gazing girlfriend followed by two birds in flight outside what looks like a barn. Or even stronger, a few pages on, another cat, this time perched upon a stand-alone coat closet next to a shot of the woman supine on a bed, her doe eyes gazing up in tender expectation.

This is the way literal story works best in a photobook: enough shots of a recognizably significant character paired with shots that inchoately expand the narrative—and never give away anything too overt or obvious.

The plot, such as it is, ticks on, thickening. There is what appears to be a blurry selfie of the photographer and his inamorata, next to a Robert Adams–looking backside of a building, and then a few pages later another mirror photo, this time the photographer standing almost hidden behind the woman, whose left eye is concealed by a rectangular spot of white, possibly another reflection, with this photo matched with the first stirrings of buildings under construction.

The pairing of shots of the woman and chance buildings or landscapes builds. Finally we get an almost Tomatsu-like blurry photo of a soccer field, followed by the photographer shooting into a blurry aquarium, and in the final shot the woman in full frame, garbed in a loose flowery robe and high-thick-heeled shoes walking down what looks like a suburban sidewalk, and smiling widely.

What holds *Zuisha* together is the implied sense of endless attraction, and the unknowable way all passionate relationships unfurl. Is there a plot? Possibly one known to Sypal if not to us, though that final smiling-girl photo does suggest a happy ending.

I'm reminded some in *Zuisha* of Araki's early book about his honeymoon, *Sentimental Journey*, which while mostly photos of his newlywed, Yoko, also mixes in shots of landscapes, buildings, what have you. Since it's Araki, *Sentimental Journey* doesn't stint on what was back then called the wifely arts (fellatio, mouth gaping throes of passion), and thus there's nothing coy about it, with no doubt what the book's about and what its story is. I mean, there's Nobuyoshi and Yoko's wedding-dress photo on the cover (at least of the original) to clue us in.

Which is appreciated. The more we understand the basic story—their honeymoon, their love—the more moving the photobook is. Indeed, *Sentimental Journey* is one of the few photobooks that rise to the status of enduring literature. And not the least for Araki's boldness in his range of what he shows us.

And that's a problem with *Zuisha*. It's not even close to as clear a work as Araki's, or Masuhita Fukase's equally lovestruck book for his wife, *Yohko*. That is, I feel I'm working a little too hard to find a story here, and worrying that perhaps I'm getting things wrong. The woman on the cover of *Zuisha*, the woman most often shot in the book, I assume is the woman of "an endless attraction," Sypal's girlfriend. But I'd feel more comfortable knowing that for sure, and also drawn deeper into the book without the uncertainty of who she is. The love story, if that's truly what *Zuisha* is about, would lend the book a far more compelling mystery if we know for sure that's what we're looking at. (And by nailing down the certainty, Sypal might then feel free to let his camera-brush sweep into wider ranges of material.)

See what I mean? I want to read the book as more than simply a collection of photos taken over a few years, I want to draw out the story. So a thought for Sypal, for anybody intending their photobooks to reveal narrative: make sure we know the set-up, the grounds of the tale about to be told. Build that foundation strong, then go as far as courage, will, and heedless abandon will take you.

Only then can you let the camera, as free and unaware as a brush, paint what happens as it happens, with not only our eyeballs but our story-loving souls rapt.

Bring on the Literature:
Mary Frey, *Reading Raymond Carver*

June 2018

IN MY LAST PIECE for *Photobookstore Magazine* I looked into how story works in photobooks. By story I meant something less than an out-and-out narrative, but also something with a shape reminiscent of a story: a beginning, an end, and at least the feel of a narrative arc as we move through the book. In effect I was talking about the photobook as a form of literature.

For the last couple years I've been teaching a university course in making photobooks, and when I have to explain what I'm doing to layfolk, I tell them that I consider the best photobooks analogues to literature: you know, up there with volumes of poetry, a short story collection, even a form of novel. (How far away in truth is Dorothea Lange's *An American Exodus* from Steinbeck's *Grapes of Wrath*, William Klein's *Life Is Good and Good for You in New York* and his Paris fashion shots from Capote's *Breakfast at Tiffany's*?)

Well, here we have a photobook in which the literary nature is explicit: Mary Frey's *Reading Raymond Carver*. As Frey says in her intro to the book, she wasn't setting out to mimic Carver's short fiction, just that she remembers "that I was reading Raymond Carver." Which is at it should be. I can't quite imagine a photobook that would set out to mimic or directly be influenced by a work of literature: I mean, what, make a photobook of *The Great Gatsby*? *Crime and Punishment*? Plath's *Ariel*? (Even most films made from true literature suck.)

But there are photobooks that if not exactly inspired by literary, historical, or film works, are at least coincident with them. Think of Christian Patterson's *Redheaded Peckerwood*, inspired by the same 1950s Midwest James Dean–wannabe and blond teenage moll crime spree that captivated the nation, and led to that great 1973 Terence Malick flick, *Badlands*, not to mention Bruce Springsteen's "Nebraska." The power of a photobook can come from the literary or cultural overtones it captures.

As a novelist (as well as a photographer), I may be biased, but, indeed, I think all serious photographers would benefit from spending less time worrying about f stops and more getting turned on by Walt Whitman or Dante or Aristophanes or *King Lear*. (My own photos often have their own great writers lurking in my consciousness—or unconsciousness—as I'm out snapping shots for my books.)

In *Reading Raymond Carver* we have a book that doesn't shy away from the literary connections. So what does it tell us about the relationship between strong writing and powerful photobooks? And how does that brilliant and doomed American short story writer make Frey's book stronger, better?

Again, and key, is that Frey's making of her photobook was coincident with *reading* Carver short stories; she never set out deliberately to capture his work in pictures. Carver's world of small towns, complex domestic arrangements, lives unambitious but nonetheless profound, also appears to be Frey's world.

Hence, we have a lot of shots of children: playing shoot-'em-up, riding a trike on a broken-brick sidewalk, hanging upside-down on a jungle gym, in their jammies getting ready for bed. We have a housewife proudly holding mouth-high a huge fresh-baked pie, singed oven mittens protecting her hands. There are heaps of teenagers, too, keeping busy in teenager ways: playing Monopoly, applying mascara on a friend, twirling a basketball, holding up a print of a Hopper lighthouse, at a picnic scarfing down sandwiches made with Wonder Bread.

That is, American suburban life, conventional life, day-to-day life ... pictures of lives that couldn't look more normal. And yet, just as with every Carver story, each picture is resonant. Frey's gift is to give us photos that look like anybody's shots of their family, and yet to make them interesting, compelling. That was Carver's art—the boundless depths of "normal" life; and that's Frey's, too.

How does she do it? How come her book resonates and moves us far more than our own neighbors' endless Instagram feeds?

The ultimate explanation is probably right up there with the usual mysteries of art, but I have a few ideas. Each photo is quite telling. We immediately get what's going on—the kid on a couch sucking his candy, the girl in the next shot guzzling some beverage out of a bottle in a doorway—and somehow each shot rouses, at least in me, my own memories of the deep, meaningful banalities of my own former suburban life.

That word *meaningful* is key. Here's how Frey explains her project: Stuck at home, pregnant, "Out of necessity I photographed my family and neighbors, seeking out the most banal situations and challenging myself to find or construct meaning in the everyday. For me, a simple gesture, the quotidian moment, or a descriptive element could hold significance beyond its purpose."

Frey captures the whole point of her art in those couple sentences: to find meaning in the everyday. This, of course, was Carver's gift, too ... and that "finding or constructing meaning" should be the primary challenge of all photographers, all writers, all artists.

Certainly, Frey succeeds, and the effect is cumulative. The impact of her work probably wouldn't come across in a single photo on a wall; it's seeing all the shots together that moves us. And that's the power of a great photobook: These photos tell a singular story. They add up, as do the best short story collections, to far more than any single piece. Simply, these photos belong together.

Carver's stories are mostly set in the 1970s, as are Frey's photos, but both have a 1950s feel, which Frey acknowledges. All this gives the book an interesting *Happy Days* twist—the hit (and unwatchable) TV show from the 1970s that took off on an *American Graffiti*–like vision of the American '50s. So the cover, instead of a 1950s-era picture of, say, *me*, leaning over, transistor radio pressed tight to my ear, listening to Vin Scully broadcast an L.A. Dodgers game with Duke Snider, Maury Wills, and Don Drysdale, we have a teenage girl leaning over, portable eight-track player pressed tight to her ear, a cartridge of Led Zeppelin's final album poking out of the slot.

It's homey stuff—purposefully homey stuff, as that '70s Watergate decade yearned for the fantasy stability of two decades earlier (not that far from the U.S.'s 1950s-stuck current leader)—and the book rouses intriguing memories. Except that nothing's sugarcoated ... nobody's going to make a nostalgic sitcom out of *Reading Raymond Carver*.

Just as they won't out of Carver's stories themselves. Which raises the question of how close this book comes to the richness and complexity of actual literature.

One primary way Frey's book succeeds is that each photograph projects not simply what we see on the page, but streams of action leading up to the moment, and after. At random I flipped to a shot of swimsuited teenagers, three boys playing a video game, a boy and girl making out. The scene is rich enough that we can imagine the kids out on an endless-summer, *whatta ya wanna do?* lark; and that the lucky guy and girl just found each other ... and there they are going at it. Something in the shot suggests they won't be a couple after this night ... or maybe I'm totally wrong.

But the implications—the constructed meanings—are there for us to make as much of as we can. Take the next shot, also the one on the cover. The cool intensity with which the girl presses the eight track of Plant, Page, and Bonham to her ear, fully rapt to the music ... easy to hear Zep's thunder pulsing and squeaking out of the little speaker. The disco LP behind her, what do we make of that? She also has a Bob Seger eight track ... O.K. And a wood LISA sign on her door. So we have Lisa, her urgent need to hear Led Zeppelin, ear pressed tight to the speaker, yet also the flat, unreadable emotion on her near blank face....

The more time I spend with *Reading Raymond Carver*'s photos, the deeper I fall into their world; and the more intrigued I am by the idea of making my own short stories out of the book.

Richness of art in all its forms. Two-way streets. We can take these photos and find inspiration in ordering them into a collection as if from Raymond Carver; then it turns out that each photo is so rich somebody else could come along a write their own story from it ... and it all goes round and round.

Which is at bottom what literature, what art is: Creations that stay alive, always inspire, always move us, continue to intrigue, explain, enrich, and inspire.

And that ... that's the answer to how close this book comes to literature right there.

Back on the Road:
Vanessa Winship, *She Dances on Jackson*

June 2018

THE DREAM SPRINGS ETERNAL. Hit the highway (preferably along fabled Route 66) and discover America. Jack Kerouac did it, so did Robert Frank. So what that was over sixty years ago ... the soul of America has to be out there somewhere, right? (We hope our 2018 soul isn't best expressed by racist demonstrations in Charlottesville, Virginia, school massacres in Parkland, Florida, or as I write, just this week toddlers ripped from their parents in Texas.) Trouble is, you head out the actual Route 66, it's a too-full-of-its-own-myth tourist byway. You course the other main roads through the nation, they're mostly get-out-of-the-way-of-the-Walmart-truck superhighways barely holding up all those years after they were built in the nation's last great infrastructure push—sixty years ago.

Still, that's an enduring portion of the American dream, that somehow even now one can light out for the country (pace Huck Finn) and discover the damn place, then bring it back in prose or photos.

And damn if British photographer Vanessa Winship didn't pull just that off, turning up America's soul (and the way, as with its highways, the nation is crumbling) by poking mostly along the country's back roads for her 2013 Mack photobook, *She Dances on Jackson*, reprinted now to go along with her first major solo exhibition, at the Barbican Art Gallery in London. The book is the product of Winship's being the first woman awarded the Henri Cartier-Bresson Award, which allowed her the time to travel to and dig deep into America. (Just guessing here, but Frank got a Guggenheim grant for his travels; when you're out on your pilgrimage faced with endless asphalt and long, dying afternoons in no-count small towns, it might cheer you up to think, Hey, I've been given prestigious money to be out here bored and stupefied while trying to take enduring photos—and make sense—of America.)

Of course, grants or no grants, on any given day countless people are out roaming America looking for something, most probably going from one tourist spot or national park to the next, but many (having Kerouac or Frank or Peter Fonda and that excellent photographer in his own right Dennis Hopper in *Easy Rider* lurking in their minds somewhere) are no doubt hoping to discover that deep American soul ... and instead filling up their phones with pictures of diner breakfasts ... which, sorry Instagramers, as his recent huge MoMA show reminded us, Stephen Shore was doing definitively forty years back, and still is. (By the way, I proudly wear a Uniqlo T-shirt imprinted with Shore's knife, spoon, orange peels, and daisy-adorned juice glass ... a garment someone a few weeks back told me was the strangest T-shirt they'd ever seen.)

So as usual, it's not the notable award that creates the impressive work, but the impressive artist who takes advantage of the financial assistance to follow her vision and ability to do the best work she can—to in Winship's case certainly bring back the goods.

So what does Winship discover in America?

First of all, as with almost all Mack books, beautifully printed black-and-white photos, about a 50–50 blend of landscapes (mostly rural) and staged portraits of people she met along the way. The first photo after the title page is of a twisted, spiky tree on a literal bend in the road; parked below it is a long 1970s gas-guzzler. It's an empty landscape, a bit forlorn (that endless afternoon America does so well), subtly adorned with a speck of a no-pedestrian sign. That shot's followed by a portrait, a large, shirtless, tattooed man shot from the side. All he has on is a baggy pair of gym shorts, his perfectly curved too-many-cheeseburgers belly swelling over them. The expression on his shaved head? Determined, wistful, almost blank ... indeed, there's an intriguing blankness to many of Winship's portraits, a challenge to us to try to figure out what the subjects are thinking; or perhaps even more, where they see themselves fitting into this new-century America. Answers ... you know, they don't come easy.

The next photo, more spiky trees, but also a thick flock

of flying-away birds. (This is the shot printed in chiaroscuro on the blood-orange cloth cover.) As one whose near favorite photobook is Fukase's *Ravens*, I can't not see an allusion here, and yet there's little other acknowledgment of Fukase's book, though the image two further along in Winship's book is of a statue of an elk atop a tomb, a shot that would be at home in Lee Friedlander's recently re-released *American Monument*. (Turns out it's a tomb in New Orleans's Greenwood Cemetery.)

The allusions in *She Dances on Jackson* float lightly, and don't get in the way of the author's own vision. Indeed, every shot is Winship's, in a style of her own. And yet to even begin to capture America, it can't hurt to reach back to past works that also set out to nail down the nation in photography and literature.

And nail it down Winship does. All the photos are strong, but the portraits reveal (even as they conceal) the most. After that first profile portrait mentioned above, all the other subjects face the camera ... no, actually stare it down. Some are world-class shots: One of an African-American young woman, gazing resolutely into the lens from the passenger seat of a car, is crisp, powerful, and ambiguous. There's definitely something unflinching in all of Winship's subjects, which (we hope) speaks to an indomitable American spirit. But, again, there's also something unreadable. They don't seem happy or sad; indeed, any emotion is unclear, even from the two Sunday-best young men, one playfully tweaking the other's ear, or the young couple, the girl holding her boyfriend's left hand and pinching his T-shirt, wholly ignoring the fox head and fur wrapped around the boy's right arm.

What? Fox head and fur wrapped around his arm? You almost don't notice it. Indeed, these strong and unrevealing portraits are in a way just there, and they anchor the book. Apart from the kid's fox hand, it's really in the nonportraits that the true American weirdness turns up.

The large heart shape on a stick in an empty field (with hints of Frank's shot of crosses on the scene of a highway accident in *The Americans*). The storage lot for presumably Mardi Gras floats, a blackface mime head fronting the most immediate one. The scatter of mushrooms on a bed of fall leaves. A highway snaking through badlands. Rows of ripped and torn cloth seats in a presumably abandoned movie theater. A tall tree stump festooned with dozens of forsaken pairs of shoes.

Winship doesn't push weird America too hard. Really, she doesn't seem to push anything very hard. The photos are there—just there—as is the country itself. And for all of that quiet and dispassion, the book is exceptionally strong ... and pure. And kind of empty, too. And yet full of that still indomitable spirit.

It's hard to pin down exactly what Winship found out about America at the end of her long road, though just as *She Dances on Jackson* leaves the countryside and hits city streets comes my favorite photo, and one that expresses the book best.

It's a portrait of a teenage girl, loose, shoulder-length red or blonde hair hitting her shoulders, a big white chrysanthemum pinned on the left. Her lips are pronounced, perfectly-bowed Daido Moriyama lips (red as can be, I'm sure, even though all we see is black and white), with two studs piercing the lower lip a half-inch in from the fetching corners. She has on a cheap metal necklace (it's actually a long beaded key chain), a Boston Red Sox medal hanging from it. She's looking at the camera the way all these other souls in Winship's book do: with a blank face, eyes in an unrattled focus on the camera, her strong spirit vivid and untrammeled.

Then there's the script tattoo sweeping in a perfect curve below and in harmony with her neck line: "young heart, old soul."

This is the fourth-from-last photo in the book, yet if any photo sums it up, this is it. (The book leaves us with a nearly empty one-way city street, the Stars and Stripes hanging forlornly from the Old Colony Building—another Stephen Shore–like shot in its perfect composition, only in black and white.)

Still it's that tattooed girl I come back to. If in a way an artist's vision comprises the choices she makes, unyielding and expressive (even in their inexpressiveness), then Winship has come up with her own strong vision of America. It's a book of the Trump era, even as it was photographed a few years before he came to power.

Which means there's little uplifting at the end of Winship's long road, and yet one hopes that her dark truths about the nation may simply be truths of a certain time. That her (our) America that feels so lost and sad, gone profoundly astray, is also unyielding and unconquerable ... a world of millennials willing to spike ink into their flesh visibly and forever with phrases such as Young Heart, Old Soul.

As in ... kids, all of us, let's get out there and vote.

These Books Are Made for Walking: Morton Andersen, *Fast Cities*

August 2018

Here's one way to make sense of the world now, the unsettling of the old order, the historical tipping point we all seem to be on. The Nigerian novelist Chimamanda Ngozi Adichie is having her main character in *Americanah* reflect on wealthy Nigerians' predilection for shiny new things, while affluent Westerners are wholly into farm-to-table restaurants and restored historic homes: "But of course it makes sense because we are Third Worlders and Third Worlders are forward-looking, we like things to be new, because our best is still ahead, while in the West their best is already past and so they have to make a fetish of that past. Remember this is our newly middle-class world. We haven't completed the first cycle of prosperity, before going back to the beginning again, to drink milk from the cow's udder."

In a phrase, if a society has never known McDonald's, McDonald's is truly the Golden Arches ... till you realize it's just overpriced thin patties of meat and gobs of sticky sauce.

What Adichie still calls the Third World is racing with all their energy (and universal cellphones and Chinese infrastructure investment) toward the golden dream. And they're going fast.

Which is why *Fast Cities* is the perfect title for the Norwegian photographer Morten Andersen's new book. His first photobook, from 1999, was *Fast City*, zippy, punky shots taken around Oslo, almost all black and white with a few in color. All of Andersen's work is high-energy, he's known as a rock 'n' roll fan and shooter, and *Fast City* has some Provoke-like blur, a bit of a Stephen Shore whatever's-in-front-of-me vibe, yet the book is all Andersen.

Here's how Andersen explains what he's up to in *Fast Cities*:

"With curiosity, camera and boots made for walking I set out to explore the streets of Mexico City, Cairo, Mumbai, Kolkata, Dhaka, Shanghai, Sao Paulo, Djakarta and Lagos" ... all cities experiencing huge population growth, heaps of new money, wide swaths of intractable poverty ... and out there somewhere boundless dreams of golden arches.

So what does he find? Here's my best summation: There are a whole lot of people out there, all different. A lot of life. A lot that's new, a lot that looks just as tangled and impossibly poor and messy as when I backpacked around the world forty years back. A lot of streets. A whole lot of what the media calls tribalism, venerable ways of dressing, conducting daily affairs. A lot of the way the past insistently presses into the present.

To that end, we have (in the book's second photo) a teenage boy micturating against a streetside wall. We have hideous snakes of electric cable trying to hold a city's power together. We have an actual cobra proudly lifted out of an ancient wooden box. We have Indians sharing banquets atop rolling railroad cars. We have Nigerian women forgoing purses or bags and elegantly carrying their goods in large metal pails atop their heads. We have a middle-aged Chinese woman in red miniskirt and boots, right after a shot of a scatter of dogs in the middle of a highway, followed a few photos on by a mysterious board game played with red and white stones on a chalk-drawn scribble on the sidewalk.

We have a world of cities that, if they are rushing fast to the future, sure are deep-dyed in the past. A couple hundred pages into *Fast Cities*, and I haven't seen a McDonald's yet; which, much as I like my trope above, may mostly mean that Andersen (anyone?) doesn't think a picture of somebody eating a Big Mac is that interesting, which of course doesn't mean that right outside his frames people aren't dreaming of Big Macs, as well as gobbling them down them by the millions.

It's just that these fast cities are also pretty damn slow. Andersen's world still hasn't completed that "first cycle of prosperity," the people in it are still drinking milk from the cow's udder ... or at least, as one photo shows us, a boy carrying a raw-meat carcass from an animal (cow? horse? something I can't recognize?) with its tail attached. (Even McDonald's probably won't put horse-tail burgers on the menu.)

But of course what we see is the choice of the photographer, and that leads to an interesting thought on how anybody takes the photos they shoot.

First off, *Fast Cities* is a book of journeys, eyes alight, not any kind of treatise. It reflects a choice: Take in the world but don't impress your expectations on it. Which thins out my conceit above. Sure there's a shot of a lovely hijab-wrapped girl with an iPad in hand, a dog happily riding a skateboard, a middle-aged Chinese woman in a red miniskirt, but Andersen clearly isn't out to show us only the way modern Western accoutrements have invaded the Third World; no, he's really just a photographer after the best photograph.

And damn if he doesn't get them. There's not a weak shot in the book, but, interestingly, there aren't any that will win Andersen the Pulitzer Prize. The news (and the book is full of news, subtle and almost incidental) is not explicitly *newsworthy*. And the photos by themselves don't ring out as Once-in-a-Lifetime shots.

No, what Andersen's photos in *Fast Cities* do is add up to a book. This is what he's always done, make photobooks; and it's the purposeful making of photos-that-will-endure-in-a-book that demonstrates so well the strength of a photobook over just any ol' group of shots.

Lately I've been going out shooting around NYC with a more traditional photographer friend, and it's clear we see things differently. She's looking for a more Pulitzer-like photo, or at least one she can sell to a newspaper or website. I can think of another photographer who told me he thinks of every shot he takes as an 11 x 14–inch print hanging framed on a wall.

Not me. Essentially, I shoot to make photobooks, not to take stand-alone pictures. Photos that will speak to the ones around them, harmonize or be discordant, yet always reveal complex meanings bound in with other photos, creating a whole greater than their parts.

Here's another way to think of this, going back to Robert Frank's *The Americans*. Sure, budget willing, it would be cool to hang one of Frank's *Americans* photos on your wall, and there are shots of his I love more than others, but would you trade any of the individual pictures for the complete book experience? And when you do see one of Frank's shots in a gallery or auction, don't you immediately think of how and where it sits in his timeless book?

Simply put, a photobook becomes great when all the shots in it add up.

This feels like what Andersen is up to, too. He's in these foreign lands with his camera, walking around, grabbing every shot he can—he's only in each place for a week, so, sick or well, he's there busy-busying about with his camera every day—and then back home putting the best of them together into *Fast Cities*.

One curiosity of Andersen's new book is portended by the final page of his first. The back of *Fast City* is a street shot of a building through aqua-colored netting, a direct link to the twenty-years-later *Fast Cities*, with the new book's overall blue tint, the layering of images with reflections and scrims and fences, the concatenation of portraits and street shots and advertisements and all kinds of crazy activity all over the world.

But after hundreds of pages of *Fast Cities*, I was asking, Why the overall blue-aqua tint to almost every photo? Does Andersen see that as a signature?

Personally, I'd prefer a wider range of colors and tones, one that doesn't tend to make each locale look such a counterpart of the others. The blue tint, as well as the quick, Daido *Record*–like recording of what's around him, are certainly Andersen trademarks. His work is also similar to the New York City photographer Ari Marcopoulos, another fast-on-the-shutter rock 'n' roll street photographer. With both, their style is their work is their style ... it all goes round and round, personal style at times expansive and illuminating, but often closed-in and circular.

Which is not to take away from what's grand and important about *Fast Cities*. I can think of books that go deeper and richer into distant cultures, but none with quite the breadth and ambition (over 300 pages of full-bleed photos!) of Andersen's new book. *Fast Cities* adds up to a wide portrait of our crazy, mixed-up world, ever changing, ever resilient.

Andersen's boots made for walking? Indeed ... and not only Nancy Sinatra should be proud of the latest photobook he's given us.

Feed the Feed
Social Media and the Photobook:
Nick Sethi, *Kichari*

September 2018

IN MY LAST PIECE for *Photobookstore Magazine*, I wrote of Morten Andersen's roughly 8 by 12–inch, 300-plus-page, full-bleed-color photobook on his travels to the so-called Third World. Here I'm writing about Nick Sethi's roughly 8 by 12–inch, 400-plus-page, full-bleed-color photo book simply of India. Andersen spends a week in Kolkata for *Fast Cities*. Sethi, an Indian living in New York, spent a decade working on *Kichari*, his bright and shiny opus of all things Subcontinent.

I was in India once, way back in 1978, and in the parlance of the day, it totally blew my mind. I liked to avoid actual hotels so found lodging in a grim, cheap concrete hostel on the Main Bazaar Road, not far from the central train station. I checked in, then hit the street. Here's how I explained to people back then the sheer overwhelmingness I found: Imagine women in flowing saris, one more brilliantly colored than the next; men wrapped in what looked like white sheets; urchins darting and dashing along; slow-ambling cows; legless men pushing themselves on platforms on wheels; elephants; beggars chanting for relief, one hand out, another holding a baby they'd press into your face; souls with skin diseases erupting over all their bodies, and on and on … and imagine this all passing by you in less than one minute.

As in, I was *overwhelmed*. Forty years on, I'm sure India has changed vastly (back then, for example, you couldn't buy Coca-Cola, only locally produced, and pretty much undrinkable, soft drinks; Indira Gandhi's own Make India Great Again program), but from the evidence of *Kichari*, Sethi's lovingly produced photobook from Dashwood Press, the nation is as overwhelming as ever, as is his eye-popping photobook.

Here's a street-side minute of *Kichari*, photos flipped to at random.

The Mysteries of Light 173

A Hindu holy man, scraggly black hair and beard, white powder drenching his fully naked body; a woman shopping, her own brilliant red blouse, green skirt, and purple scarf offset by muted yellow, blue, and pink plastic bags; a plaid-shirted smoking young man hanging on the window of his friend's white Mercedes; a tatted-up muscly dude, his Indian guru painted on a red sheet hanging next to him, gold emanations radiating off the guru's head; a mysterious catlike animal (head cropped off) doing a wild dance; a visual cacophony of stringed lights; more muscly guys carrying a Ganesha elephant god float; a teenage couple making out on a burlap blanket on rocky ground; three shots of another white-powdered man, a bamboo shoot skewering his testicles; a sky-tall float of a Hindu god made up of flowers, eight half-naked men woven into it; pages of smiling men in tee shirts proclaiming phrases such as "Every Man Dies Not Every Man Really Lives" and "Help You I Well"; more pages of smiling kids cutting up for the camera, and ... and ... and....

That is, I'm barely scratching the surface of *Kichari*—pots and pots of colors and images and smiling folk are cooking away in Sethi's kitchen. (The word *kichari* means a mung beans and rice porridge used as an Ayurvedic purification cleanse.) I'm not sure the book *Kichari* will cleanse you; certainly it will fill you up, if not quite blow out your senses.

That's the thing with the book: There's a lot going on, but it becomes repetitive. There really are an awful lot of smiling kids! There are stunning photos, pages and pages of simply strong ones, and yet they're vitiated by piling on more and more banal ones or everyday ones or even more kids-grinning-for-the-camera ones.

Which raises a very 2018 question. If *Kichari* is a book that feels like a boundless Instagram feed, and the aesthetics of Instagram are now going to inform serious photobooks, will there still be a place for a tightly edited work? A photobook that doesn't put in just any ol' shot but the ones that matter. Books that speak subtly from photo to photo instead of just bellow at each other. Books that say more than that there's a whole lot of stuff going on out there, and look at all the pals I have and what they're up to. Books that understand that the right photos in the right order, the strongest photos leading to even stronger ones, will have a greater impact than just what one's iPhone captures, and what the bottomless maw of Instagram will devour.

It's a little like when records segued into CDs, and all of a sudden an album was twice as long because the CD could hold a lot more minutes of music. Quickly turned out that twice as many songs didn't make for better albums, though, just longer ones. (When was the last time you pushed through all 62-plus minutes of the Stones' *Bridges to Babylon*? *Out of Our Heads*, with "Satisfaction" and "Play with Fire," is just 33 minutes long.)

So now there are no limits to how many photos you can put out there for those interested in your work, but does that mean you should?

A question worth raising ... and one that Sethi's book engenders. But of course he also has all of India to work with. I'll put it this way: India is an abundance of colors and imagery, *Kichari* is also an abundance of colors and imagery ... but does that make it the best book it can be?

Yes and no. There are certainly a great book's worth of strong, moving photos—children dancing amid a deluge of white confetti; a discarded elephant god statue, face broken up; a pair of braceleted hands painted with henna circles—and there are pages with multiple photos all collaged to capture a Hindu parade or the breadth of daily life. But there are an awful lot of pages that read like Facebook posts, as in, here's a friend smiling for the camera, here's somebody showing off their tee shirt, here's who we were hanging out with last night.

Which makes this a new kind of book ... and raises questions of whether it should be a book at all. A photobook fixes a body of work. Simply by a photobook being a physical book it's implied that what's in it is a product of a choice of photos, arranging them in a specific way, then expending the effort, and the money, to turn them into the physical book.

Safe to say that the physical *Kichari* is a beautiful piece of work. Thick as a mid-sized city's phone book, printed in India, hand-bound in India with signatures held together by red and silver string and a powerful invisible glue, a brilliantly colorful cover with images laid on top of each other suggesting it could

The Mysteries of Light

use 3D glasses (not supplied) to see it clear ... there's no question that *Kichari* is impressive. The only question is how important it is.

The publisher's page on the book refers to how Sethi's "intimate and complex images push the boundaries of where art, photography, and daily life intersect." Sounds good, eh? But to me that vaunted boundary in *Kichari* is just another way of saying, *Hey, I'm an artist, and here's my daily photo feed.* Nothing wrong with that, of course, but the all-inclusiveness of *Kichari* is both the book's undeniable power and that which diminishes it over the long haul. Could Sethi's experience of India be more concise? Could we not start turning the pages faster because, oh, look, more pages of kids cutting up for no apparent reason?

That seems to be the issue with Instagram, or any social media service, and serious photography. Are the photos posted ones that have been mulled over and uploaded because there's richness and meaning in them that will be of deep interest to you and me and anyone? Or are the shots we're looking at just something that happened the other day, banal as breakfast, silly as friends out drinking, and posted with intentions of self-aggrandizement and that pernicious we're-having-a-better-life-than-you social media one-upmanship?

And what does all that have to do with photo *books*?

Times change, media change, the delivery of media changes profoundly. CDs of course have virtually disappeared, replaced by the endless streams of Spotify and the like. And yet records, actual vinyl discs, have for years been coming back strong, because people need fixed and finite works: an album, a record, a book.

The best photobooks hew tight to a clear, intense idea, and they always will. Each page is a revelation, and each journey through the book brings something new.

By the end of *Kichari* you've seen it all a dozen times. (All those kids eager to beam at the camera, those pals happy to pose with arms linked!) You're thinking, O.K., India is a big, wild country, always was, always will be, and there's sure a lot going on, so maybe there's no other way to capture it in the twenty-teens than with this near-endless banquet of a book. An argument I could easily make, and leave it at that.

But it's just that by book's end I feel as though I've been there, sure, and that I've seen an awful lot, yet a lot of it seems pretty superficial. In a way I learned more about foreign lands from Morten Andersen's *Fast Cities* mentioned above ... the book of a seasoned photographer who knows how to get what matters, even if he's only in a place for a week. (Quick line from my review: "There's not a weak shot in the book." Certainly not the case with *Kichari*.)

Sethi is not even thirty. I'm sure he'll keep shooting, wildly, ambitiously, and will no doubt keep on making books. I'm glad I own *Kichari*, and I'm still discovering more of its abundant mysteries, in particular a number of all-orange pages with ghost faces on them (oh, wait, two thirds of the way through the book we find the page with five of these "faces" painted on a stone wall—typical of the book, a full flush of photos from just one wall ... mystery solved).

Still, if you're going to throw everything you have into a book, the ultimate Instagram-feed work, where better than India?

I'm definitely looking forward to his ten-years-on opus of India, when what I'm reading isn't just *all* the shots that poured out of the kitchen—or streamed across social media—but *a book* ... weighted with greater experience (life highs, life lows), knowledge, understanding, and a further-developed artistic vision.

Indeed, *Kichari* here is impressive enough that for this more developed work I'll be first in line (unless I've seen it all already on my iPhone).

Time and Street Photography: Janet Delaney, *Public Matters*

October 2018

H ERE'S THE THING WITH street photography, it's too easy to just take pictures of people walking down the street. And pictures simply of people walking down the street, or bunched up on it, or even a solo soul taking in the sun, are just about as interesting as walking down the street yourself. (You know, thinking about important stuff: What do I want for dinner tonight? Anything good on TV? What outrage will the president perpetrate next?) Indeed, that's the fundamental challenge of serious street photography: how to make a photo of people walking around the streets more than just a photo of people out walking around the streets.

Historically, there are a few approaches. The most well-known, of course, is Cartier-Bresson's fabled "decisive moment." He could nail down moments we still can't understand how he captured (like that opening chord to "A Hard Day's Night"), such as the shot of the man leaping off a floating ladder over a pool of water, his movement perfectly reflected in the water, mimicking a leaping woman in a circus poster behind him, the geometric ladder harmonizing with the spiked iron fence and another fence near a clock tower, and, oh, there are those (what look like) barrel hoops in the water also picking up the arc of the man's leaping body. Decisive moment indeed: one millisecond later, and the photo is just some guy splashing into a flooded yard.

I go on about this well-known shot because it embodies the true magic of perfect street photography. What makes it great is the way every part of the photo picks up on every other part, layer upon layer of harmonizing images, the mystery of infinite reflections … ultimately, the sense of something akin to divine presence arranging everything in so ideal a moment.

Cartier-Bresson got more than his share of moments like this

... but he also put in his books shots that are just, well, people out on the street. Other masters, of course, are Robert Frank and William Klein and Garry Winogrand, each of whom made pictures so perfectly composed or captured or even intriguingly lit that they are timeless; we can never puzzle out all their mysteries. And then there's the poetic flow of the best books by Japanese Provoke masters such as Daido Moriyama and Takuma Nakahira, photographers far less interested in showing us what takes place on the street than what percolates in their own artistic consciousnesses, erupting in furious blurs of street life.

So that's the trick to any street photography: Either turn the street into theater, replete with telling moments of drama and human insight, and/or find a way to compress the quotidian into poetic moments (vivid or obscure) that resonate and never bore us. Not that easy to do. Simply capturing a witty gesture, a person grinning or sighing, or a couple kids cutting up rarely resonates, unless, say, you're Helen Levitt with an inexplicable gift of making any old person (or kid) on the street always interesting.

Again, street photography's a tough challenge, especially since the practice in ways reached its pinnacle decades ago with the artists, and their peers, mentioned above.

Still, there is one further way a book of street photography can work for us today: If it captures a historical moment both true to its time and important for ours, those "some people on the street" rendered engaging because of the passage of time itself—layers of history, changing fashion, and unexpected relevance rising up from a book's pages.

And that brings us to Mack's new release *Public Matters* by Janet Delaney.

In the 1980s, Delaney lived in San Francisco's Mission district, a mostly Latino part of town known for its then-cheap rents. (A decade earlier I lived in the Mission, paying $30 a month for a small room in a shared flat; and yes, that's *thirty* dollars, *not* a typo. Today the same flat, swarmed by Googlers, would probably fetch 200 times that.) Back in the day, Delaney went out with her color film and captured public events, parades, street festivals, political marches ... people out living their lives. There aren't really any Cartier-Bresson–rich shots in the book, though as a rule they're all pretty interesting, though that may in large part be a product of the book as history. People marching for civil rights, against AIDS, for gay identities, for Hispanic acceptance, and in one striking photo, three people (it's not clear if they're women, or men in dresses) in Girl Scout uniforms, one sporting a sign that reads "Cookies Not Contras."

That's one of the best shots in the book, since it both captures its time and contains a plenitude of mysteries ... not to mention the photo's emotional energy, with the lead "scout" shouting out.

There are other strong photos in their own right: a kid with a Transformer model atop his curly-haired head; a large-hatted man checking out his dominoes as if they were a poker hand, a sixer of Buds on the table before him; a pink-clad girl gobbling down pink cotton candy; a Mexican couple tangoing atop a street-side stage, a near Cartier-Bresson–esque arc to their bodies; another woman waving a Mexican flag in a photo nearly as well composed as Frank's cover shot of the New Orleans streetcar for *The Americans*.

Then there are lots of not all that distinguished shots that capture our attention because of historical signifiers, as in, Wow, look how big those '80s boom boxes were! Remember how AIDS was ravaging the community. And that people still used payphones.

There are also political parade shots that, except for puffy '80s hair-dos, wouldn't be that out of place today, protesting against discrimination and for greater human rights. Then there are some shots that are just people on the street doing not-that-interesting stuff: two guys getting on a bus; two schoolgirls standing by a boarded-up doorway; three construction bros sporting tool belts shot from below; a woman holding a baby; and four or five photos of regular people just looking at the camera lens.

As noted, all of the shots in *Public Matters* are in color, and a vibrant, conscious playing around with color, coupled with a vivid sense of composition (see Alex Webb or Jeff Mermelstein), can also enliven a book of street photos—play rarely present in Delaney's shots, which, except for the pink-dressed girl and her cotton candy, don't seem to care much about how colors interact or flood the frame. (Ditto composition: she seems mostly interested in simply photographing what people are up to, not how they sit in or fill the frame itself.)

Still, *Public Matters* is a photo *book*, so it should be judged (as I always do) as more than just a collection of photos but instead a narrative with its own purpose and power.

In that regard it mostly succeeds. The picture of a long-ago time, the passions of its street energy, the subtle ways politics inform almost every shot in the book (Delaney herself says the book is here to document a time redolent of our own), the way even the not particularly distinguished photos don't sink the book itself ... all this makes *Public Matters* a work that matters.

"The Presence and the Living Energy" Three Weeks in a Foreign Town: Anders Petersen, *Okinawa*

January 2019

I'VE COME TO NOT like the term *street photography*. I feel in a way it's time is over; it's what Robert Frank and William Klein and Garry Winogrand and Joel Meyerowitz did so well fifty or sixty years back (put nicely in historical perspective by the book *Bystander: A History of Street Photography*, by Meyerowitz and Colin Westerbrook). So much of what calls itself street photography today (just Google the term, see what comes up) seems to be just people out walking along the street, doing whatever, without the mystical moments when everyone in the shot is arranged just perfectly (Winogrand's bench full of folk at the 1964 World's Fair), or caught at just the right angle (Frank's elevator operator), or with just the perfect crazed expression (Klein's alltime untoppable kid-with-a-toy-gun shot). Don't get me wrong, there's no reason street photography can't still be vital, alarming, magical. It's just that if it's not those things, instead just photos taken on the street, then what's the point?

Which leads to Anders Petersen, still busy out there around the world and still taking shots only he can. His latest book, *Okinawa*, is actually comprised of photos from 2000, when he was in that Japanese city for a three-week residence. It's a slightly different photobook than his other recent city books such as *Roma*, *frenchkiss*, and *Soho*, not to mention Steidl's three-part *City Diary*. The classic Petersen book, of course, is his *Café Lehmitz*, where he dives deep into Hamburg's red-light district and comes out, well, not the Beatles, but with one of the classic works of lowlife excess. *Café Lehmitz* is all interior shots; the later city books blend interior and exterior shots. They're also uniformly printed in intense high-contrast blacks and whites. (Too bad Petersen missed the gravure age; his books cry out for those meaty slabs of poisonous ink.)

What makes *Okinawa* a little different is that it's all exterior shots, a number taken on a beach (I haven't found a grain of sand in Petersen's other work), and that the printing is more muted, with a brown-gray tone rather than stark blacks and whites. It's also a slightly quieter book, with less of the in-your-face personalities resplendent throughout his other work. If the crazy drunk antics of the *Café Lehmitz* set a tone of behavior often captured by Petersen in his other books (women smoking cigarettes with their toes, men with six-inch scars on their cheeks, couples copulating in cramped rooms, oysters acting up), well, *Okinawa* is downright tame. The wildest we get is a schoolgirl inexplicably flashing her nipple while two friends look away indifferently.

Otherwise, we find in the book basically what a brilliant photographer comes up with during three weeks spent walking around with his camera in a place halfway around the world, i.e., what turns up in front of him, and which he's fast or, when speaking with a stranger, charming enough to catch. So we get a lot more almost conventional street shots than are in books such as *Roma* and *Frenchkiss*. Petersen, known for tight focus, getting right in his subjects' faces, here in *Okinawa* stands back, puts people in their environment: a hatted man with flowers on a park bench; a family settling into their beach chairs on the sand; six people in a sidewalk shot, one a boy in his father's arms, dozing on his shoulder. Want strange in *Okinawa*? Well, there is a guy walking by with a ten-foot-long stuffed dolphin on his shoulders, which is….

Well, not very kinky, but still all Anders Petersen. And resplendent with the gift a great photobook maker has. Each photograph on its own might not be amazing, but they all add up to a strong book. As Paul McCartney said to criticism of the Beatles White Album (fifty years old now!), "Hey, it's the bloody Beatles White Album." Sure, it might have a "Why Don't We Do It in the Road" or a "Honey Pie," but as a complete album it's timeless.

I'm not sure *Okinawa* is quite a timeless book, but it's a worthy addition to Petersen's body of work, and also an example of an intriguing photographic challenge: How do you make a book in three weeks halfway around the world in a place you can

(I'm drawing on my own experience here) barely understand.

If you read my recent three-part Japan Journal for *Photobookstore Magazine* (reprinted at the end of this book), you know I recently faced the same challenge: How to make a photobook of a city (Tokyo) in which I spent most of my time trying not to get lost on the streets and subway. Well, I did what I always do, wherever I am. I put my head into the place where I see everything around me as intensely as possible, constantly looking for photos, then take my camera and do my best to capture them. (My two Japan photobooks, *Shibuya Time* and *Lost in Tokyo*, are out now.)

In an afterword, Petersen talks about how he tackled Okinawa (city and book): "My timetable was short. I made a choice and dived into the diversities of the streets, the presence and the living energy, no matter what it was. It's about the desire to be surprised by the unpredictable, and the magic of innocence. And it has always been the wish to get closer to other people and learning something, that's what counts."

The presence and the living energy. I couldn't put it better. That's what we want in, well, if not what's tiresomely still called street photography, how about in photographs taken out on "the diversities of the streets." It's capturing human force and weakness, disparate and rich personalities, inexplicable happenstance, and the essential magic lurking within daily life that's always made photographs on the street worth celebrating.

And we can still do it, as long as a photographer with true vision and originality is behind the lens. As Petersen also writes, "The authenticity of documentary photography is punctured since long ago. It refers only to the author."

Yes, yes, yes. That's exactly what we want: the *author* present in every shot taken, every choice of photo for the book, the order of the photos, the way the book reads to us. (And if there's any doubt that the author *is* present, in the second photo we get one of Petersen's trademark stark-eyed, feral cats, though in *Okinawa* it's only a small part of a photo of an outdoor cigarette machine.) There is nothing dead about street photography when it's written by a true author, a true artist.

So check out what Petersen could do in three weeks far, far

from home. Pick up *Okinawa*. Then after enjoying his presence-rich street photographs, do as I've been doing for the last few days: try to make sense of some of the koans he drops into his afterword:

"I am primitive and need to be touching distance to know I exist."

"When shooting I want to know, but I'm unsure if I always want to understand."

"Looking at the colorful life in front of me, exposed to the exposed ones."

"Photography has never been innocent."

"I learned that photography is not about photography. And being strong is not going to help you much. But being weak opens up the presence."

Think about that last sentence in particular. That's what anyone heading out on the streets to take photos has to keep in mind. You're there for one simple reason: to open up the presence.

And, boy, does Anders Petersen do it in every book he puts out.

The Defamiliarization of Ephemeral Reality: Issei Suda, *The Mechanical Retina on My Fingertips*

March 2019

IT'S PRETTY OLD-SCHOOL. Just bang out photos, taken on the street, and let them amass, then put them out in an inch-thick book of four hundred and thirty shots, and have virtually every one of them be interesting and telling, placed next to another photo that makes them together even more interesting and telling ... and have the whole book simply blow you away.

Who did this? Well, the book is from Zen Foto, the innovative publisher in Tokyo, and the photographer is the great Issei Suda.

The photos in *The Mechanical Retina on My Fingertips*, we learn, come from shots Suda took from 1991 to '92 with his Minox "spy camera," snapping away on the streets of Tokyo and getting photos with a Moriyama-esque profound casualness. Indeed, the book reminds me a bit of Daido's *Bye-Bye Photography*. Not as radical, not a total dismissal of all photographic conventions, but still a wild hodge-podge of quick shots, glimpse shots, even a fair number of missed shots ... that all work.

And a book that works better than any of the many other Issei Suda works I own.

Recent Suda books treat him with great respect (well-deserved, of course), but that means beautiful, luscious black-and-white prints in elaborate hardcover books such as the *Complete Fushi Kaden, Tokyokei*, and *Work of a Lifetime*. But with *The Mechanical Retina on My Fingertips* it turns out that Suda's mostly street photographs are best presented piled on, one atop the other, in a five-by-seven-inch paperbound book of 480 pages priced around fifty bucks. (The Suda book closest to it is Super Labo's recent *Sein*. Those pictures are far fewer and all in color, though equally diverse and rich.)

Some of the photos in *The Mechanical Retina*, we're told, were in exhibitions of Suda's work in the 1990s, but most of them—

photos from a camera of which no other one "ever accompanied my activities so closely"—were kept in what he calls a "Box of Lingering." (I like the appellation; next time my wife bugs me about all my own photos stuck away in her flat-storage drawers, I'll tell her that they're all just out there "lingering." I'll let you know if that mollifies her.) But now the book is out, and, again, it's for me the one indispensable Suda book.

Unlike his more formal portrait shots in the fancier books, almost every photo in *The Mechanical Retina* is different, and interesting. You never know what you'll find. Here's a run of photos from my randomly opening the book about one-third in: a toy barge powering down a concrete canal; a man (alive? dead?) chained to a rack, a glimmering liquid being poured through a funnel into his mouth; a naked female's fleshy torso, forward and back (in a mirror); a votive-appearing candle burning bright in front of a low-resolution woman's face; a flock of cranes; a businessman looking away on a subway; two women in the door of another subway car, patient and stoic through the doorway windows; two geisha-dressed women looking surprised in a phone booth, a WHIRLA WHIP sign behind them; a bike-helmeted man staring at the camera next to a case displaying life-sized models of Japanese desserts; a gardener on a walkway in a park; a non-Japanese woman taking a bite of a sandwich on the far right of the frame; and a pompous male politician about to speak into a microphone, police and bodyguards looking on.

Again, the above are simply twelve photos in a row, picked totally by chance from the book, and at least half of them as good as anything Suda's ever taken.

The casualness of the shots, that magic that can happen when you're not worried about anything with your camera other than squeezing off the shutter; the askew angles, totally uncentered composition; glimpses of people unnoticed or maybe wondering who this dude with the spy camera taking my picture is, surprise lighting up their faces ... *The Mechanical Retina* is a rich banquet of happenstance and street-side mystery; in no way a well-planned and produced feast, but a little this, a little that ... and the best photographic meal you've eaten in memory.

The Mysteries of Light

I don't know if Suda was thinking Daido as he was taking these shots. My guess is he was more enrapt with his little spy camera and the way it liberated him to just go banging down the street grabbing whatever caught his eye. Kind of like Daido does it. Kind of like legions of other street photographers try to do it. The key line: what caught *his* eye. As in: Issei Suda is one of those rare photographers who can make almost every shot he takes interesting. Think about it: How many others can fill up well over four hundred pages like this?

And the title, how beautiful is that. *The Mechanical Retina on My Fingertips*. Yes, seeing through your fingers, through your whole body. That's how you do it. A great photographer's "eye" implies everything about him or her: their actual eyes; their skin and their bodies; the feelings bubbling away inside them; the thoughts they woke up with and those they fell asleep to; the books they've read, paintings they've studied, other photographers they've envied or despised (or both); a wide swath of all the people they've met; the power of their empathy; the emotions—the joy, the despair, the accomplishment, the frustration—they've celebrated and cursed; and, well, every previous photo they've taken and all the ones they simply know they'll take in the future. That's what a great photographer's "eye" is, all of the above, and everything else.

On a page well into the book Suda writes about how much his little Minox meant to him. "The camera fit into my pocket, with a shutter release as light as the blink of an eye.... Scenes from yesterday were quickly swept away into the past. The ephemeral reality that we call the 'present moment' is defamiliarized. The Minox effortlessly handles the manipulation of time that I was always struggling to achieve. I was very satisfied by its capacity to reveal new aspects when I looked again at images of those scenes that I had once viewed."

"New aspects" of scenes once viewed. What more can we hope for from any of our photographic efforts? And reality? The common notion is that photography freezes reality so we can look at it over and over, and understand it. But here, for Suda, this "ephemeral reality ... is defamiliarized." We're not talking about Instagram shots that show everybody what you've been up to. We're not talking anything actual at all. We're talking, I guess, moments that pass before us ephemerally, as all moments do, but that in these photographs, the more we look at them, the more they *lose* their familiarity. Is that it? Do Suda's shots become something *other*? Something strange or inexplicable? Or become almost nothing at all?

Here the allusion up top to Daido's *Bye-Bye Photography* gains new resonance. In *The Mechanical Retina*, Suda is moving in a way beyond photography, or at least he's taking it to whole new places. The cacophony of small, blurry images. The way we leap from a jiggle of city lights to the photographer grabbing his own image in a car's rear view mirror to a rusted umbrella sign to an old air-conditioner amidst a jumble of angles of tin roofs to people on motorbikes to a woman at the left edge of the shot petting her cat on an asphalt parking lot while her dog wonders who's taking our picture … O.K., I'm doing it again, just running through random photos and marveling at how each shows us something that is there; and perhaps, by Suda's lights, in the photo's grainy, smudgy depiction, not quite there. Defamiliarized. Mysterious and startling as the best photography always is.

I mentioned above the glimpse of Suda and his spy camera in the car mirror. There are other shots of him in *The Mechanical Retina*. Eleven photos in, we get a side shot of Suda snapped fast, "in a blink of an eye" in a mirror as he walks past, his mouth at the top of the frame, an arm at the bottom, and in-between that cherished ("Minox … which held me in thrall from 1991 to 1992") spy camera.

Simple, casual, yet also furiously and profoundly powerful, upending and defamiliarizing reality over and over again in four hundred and thirty photos.

The Master at Work.

✳ ✳ ✳ ✳ ✳

AND, ALAS, A master no longer to work at all. Word came as I was writing this piece that Issei Suda passed away, at age 78 on March 7, 2019, a saddening loss. He was working as hard as he could till the end. All his work will live on long and just as profoundly powerful as in this magnificent book.

Yep, The Dream Does Spring Eternal: Mark Power, *Good Morning, America*

April 2019

THE DREAM SPRINGS ETERNAL. *Hit the highway (preferably along fabled Route 66) and discover America. Jack Kerouac did it, so did Robert Frank....*

Wait, I already opened a review with those three sentences, writing about *She Dances on Jackson* by Vanessa Winship, and not that long ago.

Well, evidently the dream does spring eternal, for here we go again. This time it's a book by Magnum photographer Mark Power called *Good Morning, America, Volume 1*, from Gost Books, in which he courses the highways and byways of the U.S., circa 2012 to early 2018. That is: America today.

Or at least one version. That's the thing with calling a book *Good Morning, America*; you're pretty much announcing that you're setting out to take in the whole broad country in your fifty-seven photos. Inevitably you find certain aspects of America, which you depict instead of the vast number of other possible takes. And more, you set yourself a nearly (post–Robert Frank) impossible burden: Oh, wait, this book says it's about *all* of the United States. O.K., so what does this photographer think our country is? What's he trying to say?

With Frank's *Americans*, it's not clear he's trying to say anything other than: I spent two years driving the country with my wife and children on a Guggenheim grant, there are all kinds of people in America (most of them, black, poor, gay, never seen back then in conventional media), and here are eighty-three amazing photographs of them.

With Power (and Winship, and other chroniclers), it's not always clear what the photographer is trying to say, but the underlying feeling is that Power is trying to say something.

One photo to consider for this is ... well, side note first: The book is big, each page 9.5 by 12.5 inches. Photos are often stretched across both pages, and a number of them fold open with a leaf to be approximately 12 by 20 inches. These are nearly gallery-sized photos.

The shot I'm going to first is a two-pager, a suburban road in Memphis. Looming large in its center is a worn, rusted sign for METRO SHOPPING PLAZA. The neon that once lit up the letters is gone. Lower down on the same sign is a straightforward THINK GOD! To the sign's left is a brand-new-looking ACE LOANS/CHECKS CASHED/DEBIT CARDS/PAY BILLS sign. That's basically what this photo seems intent on showing us; its raison d'être. America is falling apart, religion-addled, and near bankrupt. But is that all there is? Well, down the road is a thriving Checkers fast food joint and other suburban establishments, and right across the street is a new-looking elementary school. With its stripes of red brick and stone, it actually looks like a school you might be happy your kids go to.

But in Power's composition of the photograph, Larose Elementary School looks like something that just happens to be in the picture. It's hard not to focus on the bankrupt shopping plaza, the Bible Belt sentiment, and the quick loans for people drowning in debt ... ah, America.

How bad are things in Power's vision of the nation? Well, how about the dead cat in a plastic Western Family grocery bag left to rot in a clearly polluted stream. How about prickly bramble bushes rushing up to and nearly swallowing a yellow house most notable for the fact every window in it is busted out. How about a water-warped hymnal cast out in fall leaves, open to the song "Holy, Holy, Holy." How about a vinyl Stars and Stripes flag twisting above a shadowy green background.

All these photos are in *Good Morning, America*. And they all contribute to its tone of quiet despair. But there are certainly many other types of shots. Power seems intrigued by the range of flora throughout the States, and in truth it's difficult to ascribe intention to photos simply of trees and bushes. So maybe the photographer just likes his out-and-out country shots. Weeping willows in Louisiana. A scatter of rotting oranges inside an orange barn. A scraggly, barren tree in Oklahoma. And, more interesting, an actual pine tree in front of a wall-sized mural depicting a forest of pines and other trees.

In its play of actual and depicted, that last picture implies a quiet wit apparent in some of the shots. There's another of a prominent sign proclaiming SI LOS AMAS DEJA DE FUMAR (Quit Smoking for the Ones You Love!). Guess what: It only takes a few moments to find, out of the four people waiting for a bus, the one stocky guy drawing on a cigarette. And one of my favorites: a Loan Max store high atop a maze of climbing white stairways so intimidating as to make you consider getting evicted from your no-doubt-a-hovel rather than try to get CASH LOANS ON CAR TITLES, as the sign atop the building offers.

Then there's the opening photo, which looms symbolically over the book: a picture of train tracks in another thick forest, the tracks forking left and right, directly before us. Is Power suggesting that America itself is at a critical historical fork, having to choose one direction or another? Well, just read the news every day and answer that one for yourself.

Which means that politics as practiced in the Trump years is not absent from *Good Morning, America*. There's a photo of a sign attached to a trailer that reads "One Bad Ass Mistake America … Repeal Obama Care." Two photos down we have an office building door under a window professionally painted with the words "Liberalism Is a Mental Disorder"—as in, what the hell kind of business is this? Perhaps one run by whoever lives in the one-story foundationless home in the middle of nowhere with the Confederate flag covering a window. Nope, no shots of Alexandria Ocasio-Cortez in this version of *Good Morning, America*.

Which raises a question of the book's title. Is the British Power being ironic? Are we expected to see actual hope rising amidst the sweep of despair in his book (like the silver-embossed sun wedge on the cover)? Or is he for some curious reason simply alluding to the ABC network morning show, also called *Good Morning, America*?…

There are strong photos in the book, no question, but I'm not sure how many will stick with me. Here's what I mean. I've probably looked at Stephen Shore's famous Chevron station in L.A. at Beverly and La Brea a hundred times, in books, at the MoMA show last spring ... and I've never gotten tired of it, nor felt I'd even half-begun to understand what makes the photograph so powerful and endlessly intriguing. So I'm looking right now at a Power's photo of a nondescript street corner in Milwaukee. It's an overcast day, rain on the ground. A prominent street light is green; the red number of seconds left to walk across the street is at thirteen. There's a man waiting at the corner to cross the street, another walking toward us fifty feet back, and a gray car parked behind a bus stand to our right. That's about it. This is certainly a photo that rewards a long look, but I'm not sure how often I'll want to come back to it. Further, what makes the Shore photo eternal is that everything in it feels exactly right, as in: How did Shore capture this banal street corner at the exact moment when every part of the picture belongs? (I was able to ask him about this once. Shore said he spent all morning moving his boxy camera around, inch by inch, till he found the perfect angle.) The Power's street corner doesn't carry any of that timeless sense of perfection. Indeed, I just put my finger over the guy standing at the corner, and arguably it's a better photo without him. Likewise removing the parked car.

There are photos I like better, though. One has another thick forest, a tall telephone pole dead center, and stuck onto it are seven stuffed animals. Right there in the middle of nowhere. Some odd back-country rite? Something to scare away actual animals? Or??? The photo intrigues, though the white plastic shopping bag to our left ... again, just stuck my finger over it, and I think the shot is stronger without that distracting splash of white.

Another nice one, with some historical reference: a shot of the flat front of a shut-down shop, newspapers taped to the window, and next to it a wide-open barber shop, a man shadowed in the doorway checking his phone. At the exact juncture of the two shops is an American flag; to the right, on the other side of the door, is a red-white-and-blue barber pole. And in front of the closed-up shop are four modernist plastic chairs atop bird's feet, incongruous furniture in shades of strawberry, orange, lemon, and lime. This picture has a Walker Evans Depression-era storefront purity, as well as the Robert Frank Stars and Stripes (nicely harmonized by the barber pole). A classic shot subtly redolent of earlier journeys in search of America, yet true to our time.

Then there's the final photo in the book: a white ranch-style home billowing a thick gray smoke that has already erased its roof. A house on fire? A vision of destruction? The final end of the journey that one (or both) of the two train tracks in the book's first photo has brought us to?

All possible, and certainly more evidence that we should take *Good Morning America* as a book that does tell a story about the nation, though to its credit not a literal or too obvious one. A photobook like this is all about its cumulative power; the larger vision (*this* America) that rises almost inchoately from it. The more time I spend with Power's book, the stronger it feels. As I read it, I feel I'm sinking into something hard and true about our country in the twenty-tens. I'm not sure what all these harsh truths are about—just as I'm not sure how hopelessly lost as a democratic enterprise the U.S. is, both as depicted in Power's book and as reported daily in the news—and I'm not sure Power knows, either.

Which is a good thing about his book. It engenders deep thoughts, profound questions. I'm glad it's here, though I also don't love it enough to say I'll purchase Volumes Two through Whatever when they come out. But I'll certainly give them a look, in the same spirit in which every day I devour *The New York Times* and watch the news: I'm eager, desperate, to know what our odd, crazed, unhinged time truly means—and where we're all headed.

Will and the World in Photography: Alec Soth, *I Know How Furiously Your Heart Is Beating*, Part 1

April 2019

IN THE PROMO MATERIALS for Alec Soth's long-awaited, and quite wonderful, new photobook, *I Know How Furiously Your Heart Is Beating*, Soth says, "I went through a long period of rethinking my creative process. For over a year I stopped traveling and photographing people. I barely took any pictures at all." As a photographer who finds himself compulsively taking his camera out every time I wander the city (all the time), and if I don't have my camera with me always seeing potential photographs loom up before me, and kicking myself that I don't have the one tool to at least try to grab them, I found this a curious thought: In effect, Soth says he's been having photographer's block, the equivalent for writers of sitting there before a blank screen with nothing coming out.

For novelists, being blocked is often a sense that the task at hand—creating a full world wholly out of one's imagination, a heavy lift in the best of times—is just too much. So you sit there and feel terrible. In case anybody's curious, my best advice as a longtime novelist for being stuck is simply to sit there, even if you don't write. You can't get up, can't fiddle with Facebook, can't do anything but stare at your screen. If you do this long and disciplined enough, you'll start writing. Anything is better than just sitting there doing nothing. *Anything* ... even writing.

So I'm curious about what this photographer's block is like, what gets in the way of doing what seems so natural, and also how Soth in particular broke through it in such spectacular fashion.

Fortunately for my understanding, Soth has been giving numerous interviews about his new book, including a long one in the back of *I Know How Furiously Your Heart Is Beating* itself.

I think it helps us know the book better by seeing how he came to make it. So in Part 1 of my article on Soth, I'll look into the process of how he got going, before tackling the actual book in Part 2.

The key to Soth's hiatus seems to be not at all that he didn't feel he could do photography; indeed, the problem appears to be that he knew he could do it too well. That is, if at bottom any photograph comes from some degree of distance between the photographer and the world outside him- or herself—a gulf, a chasm, if you will—and if both sides of this space are defined by degrees of power and intention, then Soth seems to have fallen into the pit. In effect, he lost a true understanding of where the balance line between photographer and subject should be drawn.

An intriguing predicament! What seems to have gotten to Soth is that what he wanted from a photo (and a person sitting as subject) was coming too easily. Here's how he puts it, in an interview with the *Guardian*. "When I started out I had so little power," but with his editorial work and increasing fame—arguably, he's the best-known of his generation of photographers—he got far more power, and found he could "push things in order to get a better picture."

That is, Soth was able to manipulate scenes, mostly for his editorial work, and get the shots he wanted ... and yet for Soth there appears to have become less of the true world in them, less of the fluxes of air and light that move beyond our own will and concentration. In the book interview he speaks about how predatory his earlier way of taking portraits was; how he would be out "driving around, snagging people, talking them into stuff they don't want to do." Too much power, too much ego, too much being wrapped up in himself.

Then Soth had a "full-on mystical experience" in Helsinki that made him see the oneness of the universe and everything in it. And he stopped taking photos.

Writers have jokingly likened his experience to an acid trip, but think of it this way: Over fifty years ago the Beatles did drop LSD, and came up with *Sgt. Pepper*. George Harrison contributed "Within You Without You" to the timeless album, and that's as good a way as I can think of to describe the photographer's eternal search for the correct balance between what they want and what the world itself wants them to put into images. Every photo you take should be equally within you and outside you. In the song, Harrison talks about how if you see beyond yourself, peace of mind can come. You see that we're all one, "and life flows on within you and without you."

If Soth's own power was blinding him, of course he couldn't take the photos he needed to; in effect he realized he needed to step back, let the world and the people in it reassert themselves. For Soth, a notably good guy, it might be a stretch to invoke Harrison's words about the people who gain the world and lose their souls, but I'm guessing that was in a way the dynamic at play.

So for a year he did nothing, cheerily. "I was just so happy sitting around looking at the light," Soth tells us in the book interview. He finally again felt the need to take photos, but in a new way. He purposefully searched out people with identities and power to match, or at least balance with, his own. He has said he wrote to people he knew in different cities asking for names of people with singular presences, powerful personas who fill up their home spaces, then arranged to meet and photograph them. In his words, "to have an encounter that is visually strong."

He also wanted to photograph people he didn't know at all. In the book interview he intriguingly says, "The more I know you, the less likely I am to take your picture." When asked why, he says, "I don't understand it. I honestly don't understand it. It just doesn't work. I have to get on the therapist's couch."

Well, I'm no therapist, but I think his inability to shoot people he knows too well has a literary explanation. Henry James speaks about the *donnée*, the small given that informs a writer's imagination. I've always thought of it as seeking out glimpses of actual intriguing scenes, the way you can get a tiny peek through an open door into somebody's personal world, and then imagine full lives around that glimpse. If you see or know too much, everything you've taken in can shut down what my literary mentor Bernard Malamud called "necessary invention."

Soth seems to understand just this. Earlier in the book interview he talks about how "when I was in high school, I used to deliver Chinese food. I loved that moment when the customer opened the door and I could peek into their interior world. It always felt magical and mysterious."

That's exactly it. Gain too much power and control in the world and you lose not only your soul but also the world of magic and mystery.

Maybe that's what photographer's block comes down to. Losing the balance in the universe. Letting your ego subsume the sublime. And the cure? Being honest and clear enough with yourself to know that good photography—good anything—isn't a pure expression of personal will and power, but the focus and force you bring to a situation in which what's around you is equally forceful and focused. In that balance comes a loss of self, which leads to a greater expression of self; your art is not confined by your own boundaries but extends into the world, reaches an understanding with the world; and both your art and the world are richer for it.

And, oh, yes, you have to be always looking for, and respectful of, those quick glimpses through the door ... into the inexplicable, the mysterious, the unknowable, the sublime.

A hard lesson well-learned by Alec Soth. A year's personal sabbatical that brought a wealth of new photos, and a very special book, which I'll write about in detail in Part 2 of this piece.

And all the while the world flows on within and....

Artistic Faith and the Photobook: Alec Soth, *I Know How Furiously Your Heart Is Beating*, Part 2

May 2019

IN PART 1 OF my piece on Alec Soth's new book, *I Know How Furiously Your Heart Is Beating*, I wrote about how Soth, to get the book going, set out looking for subjects with singular presences, "to have an encounter that is visually strong." He says he wanted to shoot people who filled up the spaces in their own homes. And more than that, he wanted to bring less of his own will and intention to the photos; didn't want to manipulate anyone but let each shine in their singular way—a difference from his more produced photos, including those in his masterpiece, *Sleeping by the Mississippi*.

So how did he do?

First off, these are clearly Alec Soth photos. The richness yet subtlety of color. The intention (and success) of invoking deep character in each shot, even if no actual person is in the photo, it's just their cluttered den or a faded pink makeshift doorway curtain, hanging between stove and drier. The quiet and unexplained oddness, here a furious stuffed hawk above a few laundered men's shirts hanging off the TV cable snaking its way along the top of the room; and in the photo right before it, nothing but a white plant holder set dead-center atop a round table. The gentle perfection of light. And at bottom, the way the human subjects seem to be embodying their essences no matter what they're up to.

I Know How Furiously Your Heart Is Beating is not a radically different book from *Sleeping by the Mississippi*; in a way it's like an extension, yet also its own work. It also feels to me more mature, though I can't explain exactly why. Soth is many years older than the man who put together *Mississippi*, and it's to his credit as an artist that what greater understanding of the world he's picked up infuses each shot in the new book in subtle but clear ways.

He's shooting *Heart* the same way he shot *Mississippi*, with his big glass plate camera, but this time he's mostly indoors. As he puts it in the *Guardian* article, it's a camera that was "built for Ansel Adams to photograph the American deserts and prairies and I'm using it in confined interior spaces." He disappears under an old-fashioned scrim to keep out the light, and spends his time focusing on people's eyes as he shifts the plane of focus. What does he get from using such an old-fashioned camera, and hiding under cloth? For one, quiet, and a kind of non-presence in the room, which, he hopes, relaxes his subjects. As for the image, probably the same thing a vinyl lover like myself gets when I play a record: something "almost sensual in the way it caresses surfaces," as Soth puts it; or as I would, a richness, a fullness, the gentle bloom of palpable color and light.

Yet the camera also makes him most definitely *there*. No escaping the man under that blanket focusing that big lens right on you … or, interestingly (and different from *Mississippi*, in which each shot was perfectly clear), at times *not* focusing the lens. To the latter point, one of my favorite Soth works is *Looking for Love*, his 1996 book of photos in black and white. I just pulled it down from my shelves, thinking I'd find the photos had a Provoke-like blur, but I'd misremembered; each shot is clear and in focus. Which makes a shot in the new book of writer Vince Aletti that blurs out the lower right quadrant of his portrait all the more surprising. The focus in the photo is on Aletti's desk, stacks of photographs, two magnifying glasses, flowers, and a large print of a man's nude buttocks on the wall, not of the silver-mustached writer on photography. Though Aletti is at best a human streak before his desk objects, it's hard to argue against this shot being the truest of portraits.

Likewise the final photograph in the main part of the book, one of "Simone" at a blonde wooden table, arranging stones before her. One rock at the apogee of the circle is in focus, but Simone's hands and top and, most of all, her silver hair are as out of focus as if they'd been shot from a moving car.

Which is impressive. Every photo in *Heart*, whether it's the two just mentioned above; or the stark portraits of people such as that of a middle-aged man in his white cotton briefs, fluffs of what look like wigs scattered on the floor next to some exercise-looking device; and the dead-eyed stare into the camera of "Hanya" as she lies in her pajamas on a banana-colored pillow; or then on to the portraits without people, instead just the way they live, for instance the two-page spread of a mauve day bed on a worn parquet floor with an old-school telephone on the ground across from a photo of half a large dog on that same-looking parquet ... all the shots in *Heart* capture a mysterious center of personality. You can never sum up or reduce or dismiss a Soth portrait.

Or forget it.

Or not know it's a work by Soth. As I said, I pulled *Looking for Love* from my shelves, and I'm looking through it now. Black-and-white shots most likely developed by Soth himself when, at 26, he worked in "a large, commercial photo lab." Just photos from walking around his Midwest town. Yet each photo from back then captures a telling moment, some loudly speaking without people in them; yet when people are present, we can read exactly what's going on ... and yet not come close to fully knowing or understanding what the deal is with these characters at all.

Which is Soth's great gift. His camera, beginner's 35mm or Ansel Adams–approved 8 by 10, always sees more than we do. And his "writing" capabilities mean he always gives us mostly a rich glimpse of a character in his photos, leaving our imaginations to fill in the rest. In my writing course I always talk about the Hemingway iceberg theory of fiction: how Hemingway shows us only the tip of what's going on, and through the power of his art we infer or imagine the whole mass. Same with Soth. He's really strong at portraits that capture our fascination, then lead to our own story-making around the glimpses of character we observe. And as I said above, even his people-less rooms evoke rich insights.

Until we get two thirds of the way through the book, to a full spread of nothing but books on shelves, behind a flood of tattered and forsaken-looking volumes pouring onto the floor. It's called "Irineu's Library, Giurgiu, Romania," and try as I can, I only see chaos and disrespect. It reminds me of when a writer friend of mine years ago bought a used bookstore going out of business on Fourth Avenue in Manhattan and invited everyone he knew to pillage it. Even in my office, where photobooks pile up, I know (almost) where every volume is, and they're all reachable. Not here in Girugiu. Soth, who always paints with such lightness and grace (even when depicting extremes of human possibility), drops two photos here that just sit like sodden clumps of refuse.

No doubt he has his reasons, and I respect them, but I'm also happy to move along, especially to the two photos mixed in with the final pages of text: a light, floaty spread of pages from the book *Birds of America* somehow nearly the size of a glowing floor lamp before wispy pink curtains (a dollhouse?), and the final shot, "Sabine's View, New Orleans," which is an empty wire birdcage before a waxed- or frosted-up window.

No doubt these final photos have meaning, for Soth—and as we enter into the book, for us, even if we can't explain everything. Each photo implies significance, they carry us beyond ourselves … that is, they do what the purest art always does.

And do we really need to fully understand? If, for instance, we're looking at a vintage electric organ with sheet music to "Little Red Corvette" spread open atop it, how important is it to tell ourselves a story of how the sheet music came to be there? Likewise, the man in dress shirt, underwear, and socks curled up in a sheetless bed, clutching a stalk of dried seed buds. (O.K., I just asked my wife to help me describe what's in the man's hand, and unprompted she said the picture is about desiccation; fair enough.) But even if I choose not to explicate Soth's photos, just appreciate them and feel them, I do always believe they're there for a reason. That's simply how a great photobook artist works: you trust them; you don't go, What, sheet music of a great Prince song on an organ, so what?; no, you intuitively feel the book is richer for the mystery of the photo.

At bottom, this is the trust we extend to any true artist who has earned our faith: we are willing to take our time to come to "why these photos, in this book"; and more, believe that knowing this will enrich us. Of course even this simple faith can be tested with any artist's new work (that flood of books in Romania!); and the artist can lose us if the work isn't good enough. Fortunately, *I Know How Furiously Your Heart Is Beating* redeems all our faith. It is that good.

Trusting Nature: Stephen Gill, *The Pillar*

May 2019

Time to head back to Stephen Gill's farm. Earlier I wrote about *Night Procession*, Gill's first book from his new life in south Sweden, where he studied the wide range of fauna on his land far from the city work of earlier books such as *Hackney Wick* and *Hackney Flowers* (though in many earlier volumes Gill was interested in local flora as well as, shall we say, human fauna). We saw all kinds of animals and birds living their mysterious nocturnal lives in *Night Procession*, but now in *The Pillar*, it's just birds, out in an empty field before mostly cloudy skies, and the work is all the stronger for it. Indeed, *The Pillar* already feels to be a work of enduring literature

Here's what Gill did, in his own words: "In January 2015, with the inkling of an idea that their activity might be more prevalent than I first thought, I decided to try to pull the birds from the sky. On the edge of a field next to a stream I set up a 6-cm-diameter stage in the form of a wooden pillar about one and half metres high. Opposite it I placed another, the same size, on which I mounted a motion-sensor camera. When I visited the camera a few days later, to my surprise, it had worked. The pillar had funneled the birds from the sky, offering them a place to rest, feed, nurse their young, and look around. I was captivated."

Well, I'm captivated, too. It's not just a hidden life of so many different birds of such different species, it's the photos themselves. An owl staring the camera straight down. The wing of a buzzard sweeping across the empty plain, the bird itself soaring out of the right side of the frame. Another buzzard, beak wide, screaming at us. A swarm of fowl streaking across the field, the dark pillar mute before them. In one of the occasional color photos, a kestrel cheerily munching on its rodent lunch. And further along, another buzzard looming before the reader like their worst nightmare.

O.K., I've gone this long before bringing up Masahisa Fukase's alltime classic work *Ravens*, but that's the quality of book we're talking about with *The Pillar*. These are pictures of birds doing all kinds of things, sure, but they're also shots that go straight to the world of dreams, nightmares, and personal artistic vision ... and, again, all without human agency.

Which brings up once again the intriguing question of where Gill was in the making of this brilliant book.

Well, it was his idea, for one. His farm, his landscape. His choice of where to set up his two pillars, certainly. His love and long experience with birds, unquestionably. And of course his most important personal and artistic contribution, the making of the book itself: editing the photos down, sequencing them, making sure they were printed well ... all the stuff any serious photobook maker does.

I can't help but think of Doug Rickard's celebrated *A New American Picture*, comprised of photos he pulled off early iterations of Google Street View. That was a startling new vision of street photography that came about simply because 1) Rickard had the great idea of combing Google for telling shots; and 2) working them up into a book. Nobody argues the art behind these found shots; and nobody should argue against the same power in *The Pillar*.

The book is even richer because not every shot is of a bird. Just as in *Ravens* Fukase startles us with non-bird shots (that half-asleep, corpulent nude woman!), in *The Pillar* Gill drops in the occasional birdless shot: mist over the field, stretches of snow, a coyote strolling by. These non-fowl photos help pace the book, as do the muted-color shots. There's not an unnecessary picture in the book, and the cumulative power rivals that of Fukase's masterpiece.

As with *Night Processions*, the celebrated author Karl Ove Knausgård (Gill's friend) contributes a wholly worth reading essay, printed in a separate enclosed booklet.

Knausgård riffs for a bit on memories he's held on to of birds in his past, all in the service of his main point: "How each of these birds opens up a unique moment in time." He goes on about *The Pillar*, writing, "I was shaken, as a person so often is when confronted with an extraordinary work of art. I'd never seen birds in this way before, as if on their own terms, as independent creatures with independent lives. Ancient, forever improvising, endlessly embroiled with the forces of nature, and yet indulging too. And so infinitely alien to us."

True, all true. Then Knausgård goes wide, invoking Heidegger and Kierkegaard, and ends up writing, "Above it all is the sky. The bird's eyes are round as marbles ... and their light is nevertheless recognizable to us, for it is life itself, and the soul that lives it."

That's the reason no doubt Gill's book immediately resonates so powerfully with us. The birds' lives reflect our own lives, the glimpses of soul "still a soul, which is to say a being filled by the world, and sentient in relation to it."

Can any of us ask more than to be just that, beings filled by the world and sentient along with it?

Yet there's one further question that keeps nagging me, from the young Bob Dylan, who in "Ballad in Plain D" asks, "Are birds free from the chains of the skyway?"

A question *The Pillar* answers for the birds we witness in the book somewhat affirmatively, those "independent creatures with independent lives" apparently free to come and go (though their eye-souls remain haunted by who knows what).

And also a question that, for us humans, has long haunted me. One that I've never been able to answer with anything close to, *Sure, of course you and I are free from the chains of the skyway. Why would you ever ask that at all?*

Literary Ambition and the Photobook: Jason Eskenazi, *Black Garden Trilogy*

July 2019

How ambitious can a photobook be? In a handout to accompany the publication of Jason Eskenazi's two new books, *Black Garden* and *Departure Lounge*—the completion of a trilogy launched by *Wonderland* in 2008 (to be reprinted in 2020)—Eskenazi tells us: "I've always seen bookmaking as cinematic and in musical terms. The images though authentic are taken out of their original context in order to make another, more personal and universal visual narrative. All the books have three chapters each adding up to nine, for the nine muses. And the sequence of all the books are numbered consecutively from 1-314, as in Pi."

That is, his three books are as far from just some collection of photos he took as you can get. Indeed, here's a hint of the books' ambitions: They absorb music, myth, literature, history, and the profound transformations of the collapsing Soviet Union, the eastern Mediterranean world, and, finally, our planet itself, "once a garden in the universe, but now on the edge of annihilation by the hand of man."

And more, the books work like music and literature, with recurrent motifs, clusters of notes harmonizing and clashing with each other, abstruse numerological references, and established characters who change (or don't change), be they of people or of emanations of history, and relationships that grow ever more resonant and reflective. Scholars are still delving deep into such complex works of literature as Homer's *Odyssey* (a touchstone for Eskenazi) and James Joyce's *Ulysses* (inspired by Homer), debating symbol, allusion, and overall meaning; and it's not hard to imagine scholars years from now digging into similar depths in the three books the photographer calls his *Black Garden Trilogy*. Yes, they're that rich.

But this isn't an essay written years from now, this is in effect a review upon publication. So let's get to it.

All of Eskenazi's photos are in black and white, and each of the books is handsomely produced. The shots are printed in rich tri-tone, and the books are all bound in thick natural cardboard with a fulsome color cloth spine. In *Wonderland* the photos have a slight white border; in *Black Garden* each photo has what looks like a hand-drawn black frame inside a white-paper border; in *Departure Lounge* the photos have a black-paper frame—not huge differences, but careful and telling. As Eskenazi explained above, the books are also broken into numbered chapters, clearly noted (hand-drawn Arabic numerals in the first book, Roman numerals in the second, printed Arabic numerals in the third), three per book, nine total.

As much as any photobook I can think of, these are works not to be flipped through but actually to be read, and read deeply. Try it: You can curl up with *Black Garden* and go from boys tending horses in an animal market in Turkey to mummer-like figures holding up toy bomber planes on Fifth Avenue to a mesh-shrouded bird's-eye view of Ground Zero to a shop window back on Fifth Avenue with curiously Greek goddess–looking models amid a reflection of what looks like Doric columns, then back to the real Old World with a shot of workers putting up a cloth roof over chairs set up before the pyramids in Giza, Egypt. Each picture expands on Eskenazi's story as it loops back to photos you've read before. It's an immediately satisfying experience, even as all the complexities of the book tantalize and inspire further readings.

Oh, and the photos themselves are really good. Once you've seen the array of shirtless male bodies hanging off of bars doing sit-ups at a military camp in Kazakhstan in *Wonderland* you won't forget it. The shot has the complex composition of the best of Alex Webb's shots (sans the vibrant colors). Indeed, Eskenazi is great at bodies in motion, whether it's yamaka'd boys at a Passover festival in Jerusalem or the next photo of a host of kids clambering over a fence in Istanbul. He's a master of the telling moment, too, with the understated power of a Cartier-Bresson, and nearly as wide a geographical range. You also won't forget the shot in *Black Garden* of a man in Istanbul standing on his right leg, his left leg and torso fully perpendicular to the ground, a Molotov cocktail about to be launched. Oh, and to enrich the photo, in the foreground is a fully shrouded figure with an unlit cocktail bottle atop their head.

This is a newsy photo, for sure, a shot taken with all the implied danger of being smack dab in a battle zone; but it's not a mere news shot because it's so strong and timeless, and the story it bears isn't the disposable kind that graces newspapers but instead a photo that links tightly, through form, subject, and implication, with all the other photos in the trilogy. Furthering the pairings and resonances of the book, the above isn't the only Molotov cocktail shot. A few pages earlier we see two homemade bombs launched into the smoky air by a hooded man before a dumpster fire. Those two bombs soaring during a street fight in Cairo are on the right side of the page. On the left? A Veteran's Day parade on Fifth Avenue, men in minuteman costume tootling pennywhistles marching along beneath four helicopters in the sky in the near exact positions as the flaming bottles in the adjacent shot.

Yes, *that* degree of duality and complexity. Some college school student will someday write a paper on just this one page spread ... if not a graduate thesis on the whole three books.

A small hint to that future thesis writer: The first photo in the trilogy, a lovely nude-torsoed woman looking out a hotel room window in Moscow is from the same contact sheet as the final photo in the trilogy, the same woman now putting on a dress and lit up by a curtain before the room's large hotel window.

Does that mean the whole trilogy takes place in the few seconds between the photos? Are all the shots in all three books simply that woman's dream? Or is she the trilogy's heroine, who, escaping mere temporality, has adventures on many continents over many years and many political and social upheavals finally to arrive back just where she began? I'll leave it to my hypothetical scholars to work it all out as best they can.

As for me, can I pick a favorite volume of the three linked books? Nope, they're each full of powerful, amazing photographs, and they each radiate Eskenazi's deep intent in how his story is coming together. I do have photos I like better than

The Mysteries of Light

others, but even thinking like that in such a complex work seems to be missing the point, like deciding that the scene with Miss Havisham burning up in Dickens's *Great Expectations* is the only chapter in the novel you like, the rest of it, Meh. No, in the *Black Garden* trilogy every photo has a reason to be there, and as much as in any photobook I can think of, the sum is far larger than the very impressive parts.

This last thought is most manifest dead center in the middle book.

Before I describe the array of photos in that center spot, I should tell you that Eskenazi worked for a while as a security guard at the Met Museum (great first job, you wannabe photographers and artists), and he spent a lot of time with the Italian altar pieces. He says he fell for their three-part nature, the large middle panel, and the two flanking it—and that the whole trilogy is in a way based on that construction.

So what does the very middle of a book based on Odysseus's travels, a trilogy inspired in part by our current ecological crises, do? It opens up beautifully.

First you hit a photo that's spread the length of the quite wide book. It's dozens of bathers in a sun-drenched sea, in a broad circle, all holding hands. But that's hardly all. The initial spread folds back, revealing four photos, on the right boaters walking ashore, next to it a lump of an island in the sea, then three black-shrouded women gazing outward, and finally a handheld snapshot of the World Trade Center hovering inches from a camera trained on Lower Manhattan post-9/11. But then—breathless hopefulness—those two end photos fold back and we get one whole spread of events before a calm sea: a man lying on rocks, a woman looking out at a ship, that island, those shrouded women, then some sunbathers, and finally a woman using a primitive straw broom to sweep up trash before the wine-dark sea.

A still center in the chaos, a place the whole wild rest of the three books swirl around. True, world-saving hope? Not for me to say. (Turns out the man on the rocks is a dead refugee; and the book's next spread puts us right back in fire and Molotov-cocktail-throwing violence.) But that woman in that Moscow hotel dreaming this whole breathtaking photobook saga, I'm sure she—like us—takes her comfort these days where she can.

But comfort, of course, is not Eskenazi's job. Making strong, moving photos is. As well as creating a book that pushes the very boundaries of what a photobook can be.

That's the vastly ambitious job he took on ... and in the three astonishing volumes of *The Black Garden* trilogy, unequivocally pulled off.

Going Through the Drawers:
Philip Perkis, *Mexico*

June 2019

WHEN'S THE RIGHT TIME to put out a photobook? Is a book stronger when the photos are freshly taken, more or less of the moment, telling us a story of our time? Can a book work when the photos in it are decades old, pulled out of a drawer and shaped into a book? Or does the question even matter?

Thoughts raised by a new book by photography professor and essayist Philip Perkis, who has through the Korean publisher anmoc just put out a collection called *Mexico*. These are shots Perkis took while on a Guggenheim grant, in journeys through that country back in the 1990s, from what looks like back-road traveling, far from well-established gringo haunts, on juttering buses to small towns with wide plazas and a Mexico before big-box stores and machine-gun-toting *federales* took over.

It's a quiet world. Perkis's black-and-white photos are all printed in landscape mode with plenty of white border around them, and in many of them he prefers a solitary figure (or occasionally a dog or an object, a chair in an empty concrete garage space, a toilet and wastebasket on a dark-tiled floor). These photos are not rousing, not clearly about anything, but they do possess a simple dignity, a power that accumulates as you move through the book.

Also a deeply-felt loneliness. Many of the shots are steeped in emptiness; these solitary men and women looking lost or distracted even as they go about their business. In an interview by Blake Andrews from 2016, Perkis answers the question of how he would describe his childhood very simply: "I was lonely and frightened." Qualities expansively investigated in *Mexico*.

The book has a personal vibe to it, no question. These are Perkis photos. And the ongoing somber, quiet tone is effective. Indeed, maintaining a consistent emotion in any photobook is a true accomplishment.

Still, I find myself asking how far these are from tourist photos. They're not the obvious ones travelers take, of churches and markets and blatant local color, but I'm also not sure how penetrating they are, what the ultimate tale they tell is. Take for instance the shot of a woman in an open marketplace, peeling a potato into a white plastic bucket, a huge pig's head looming beside her. The photo is well-structured, the pig's head hanging close to the woman, a glowing bare light bulb dangling to its left, but the photo is also wholly contained in itself, it doesn't open up to anything else. It strikes me as somebody walking through the market going, Oh, look, an actual whole pig's head just hanging there ... they sure don't have that back home at the Kroger's.

And the shot of a bullfighter in the ring, sword drawn, ten feet from the bull? I'm surprised Perkis couldn't resist putting in a bullfighting photo in a book called *Mexico*. I also can't see how that tells us anything new about anything.

In the Andrews interview Perkis talks about the inevitable influence of Robert Frank, who along with Cartier-Bresson is probably the alltime great travel photographer. I can see Frank's influence in *Mexico*, but that's also why I'm talking about tourist photos. I don't find much close to the surprise and astonishment and radiant meanings of Frank's *Americans* photos. Most of Perkis's photos are not complex, they don't reveal great depths. There is resonance, but, again, it's a quiet and dignified significance, not one that's particularly revelatory.

Indeed, that's the prime qualm I have about the book, the lack of anything new and revealing. This isn't simply because we're looking at nearly thirty-year-old photos. It's that, as a self-described "unapologetic modernist," Perkis seems to be content with his take on the lessons of Frank and Levitt and Cartier-Bresson and Steiglitz (all of whom he mentions in the Andrews interview). As photographers, we all should learn from the past, and I'm sure Perkis and I are not the only ones who continually revisit classic works to find inspiration and sustenance. But when it comes time to put out a book, it's not enough to show how we've been influenced by "people in the canon."

Another qualm: mysterious chapter titles that don't seem to mean anything. The first is "What the bus driver saw." That's not very literal; there aren't any shots from a bus except for the final one in the chapter, which is shot over a bus driver's shoulder. Is it figurative? Are we supposed to ponder who "the bus driver" might be? Is he the soul who sees a man sitting alone at the end of a table in a room in an expensive hacienda? Far as I can tell, that's just a shot Perkis took, decently composed and redolent of that constant loneliness but not much more. Another chapter title is "The piano lesson." Needless to say there's no piano, no student. Instead we have a lot of shots of dogs on Mexican streets (and one with a *calle* full of wandering pigs). Perhaps it would have been better to drop the inscrutable chapter headings, as well as the rambling, oddly spaced nattering at the end of the book, some information helpful about the book in hand, but also a bunch of speculation on "the stuff that makes us 'tick.' "

I also wish I could describe to you one photo that hit me hard, pinned me to the wall. I can't. There are some I like better than others. A black-silhouetted dog gazing out from the top of the roof of a *carniceria* shop on a moody, rainy afternoon. A fountain of fireworks spiraling from the hand of a boy sitting on the shoulders of a man at a nighttime fiesta. A small parade of folk moving past an open doorway, a young man glancing at them, book in hand. And those pigs truffling down the middle of their empty street.

But we are talking photobook here, and *Mexico* definitely works as a book. Again, it has a deep and quiet dignity, a sense of a lost world, a cumulative evocation that any one (or group of) photos in it don't quite communicate.

Interestingly, Perkis himself has written "that if all the negatives that I've ever exposed were given to someone without any knowledge of me or of my prints or books—and they were asked to make 200 prints from the tens of thousands of negatives—I'm quite certain that it would have very little to do with the work I've done over my lifetime."

That is, somebody else would have chosen different photos, made a different book, in a different time and a different way.

Of course without access to all the negatives we have no idea what this other *Mexico* would be. My guess is I'd like my version better.

Photos to Books to Art Objects: Laura El-Tantawy, *A Star in the Sea*, Part 1

August 2019

Laura El-Tantawy's most recent work, *A Star in the Sea*, the latest in her string of highly artful self-published book productions, raises for me a most interesting question. One thing that makes serious photobooks unique is that we're looking at both photography and bookmaking, and where the line of emphasis between the two is can shift from book to book. My own preference is for more focus on great photographs (*The Americans*, Eggleston's *Guide*), less on the artistic expression in the book's actual construction, which of course is not to say I don't like a well-made, innovative book. It's just that as a rule, I want the quality of the images, and their flow and significance in the book, to be predominant.

The next-to-last work I looked at, Jason Eskenazi's *Black Sea Trilogy*, is a good example: books of strong, moving photographs, arranged with deep meaning, but also in a creative, unusual format (three books that all physically fit together, creative chapter making, the photos in each book surrounded by a different and meaningful frame) that suits both the photos themselves and the overall sweep of Eskenazi's artistic ambitions.

Pushing this mix of strong photos and innovative layout even further is El-Tantawy's magnificent first book, *In the Shadow of the Pyramids*—an almost perfect photobook. The photos are strong, from the family snapshots at the front of the book—it's hard to think of a more personal photobook maker than El-Tantawy; much more on this to come—to the perfect "build" that opens the photographer's own shots. "Build" ... I tell my fiction students to work on that all the time, draw us in, up the complicity and intensity, then deliver a payoff. So in *In the Shadow of the Pyramids*, El-Tantawy's first seven photos grow in size page by page until we hit her eighth, which is full bleed (the size of most of the rest of the shots in the book, interspersed by occasional photos from her family album, and finally a quiet diminuendo at the end, the photos tapering down in size to mimic the opening). And what a great, telling shot that first full-bleed one is: rich in vibrant and slightly off-kilter color, as many of El-Tantawy's photos are, this one swirls and sweeps with undergarments flapping in a breeze over a jaundiced-yellow Cairo skyline—a beautiful photo in its own right.

In the Shadow of the Pyramids was mostly shot during the Arab Spring uprising in Cairo. El-Tantawy was born in England to Egyptian parents, and has lived in Egypt, Saudi Arabia, and the U.S., but was hugely moved by the political movement nearly a decade ago. As she puts it in one of a few word essays in the book, "When people took to the streets on January 25, 2011, I had to be among them. It was a moment when my past, present and future came together as never before.... In Tahrir Square I found myself again."

The photos in the book, mostly from Tahrir Square, capture political force, and counterforce; excessive passions, rising hopes, outrage, and even one striking portrait of a woman with eyes uplifted, hands held together in prayer; powerful resolve and flowing tears; battles engaged and wounds dressed; and overall as powerful a photographic examination of a moment of dire political upheaval as I can think of, the rival of two other impressionistic protest books, Shomei Tomatsu's *Okinawa* and *What Is 10/21*, from a Japanese student collective in 1969, yet little else.

Much of the power for me of *In the Shadow of the Pyramids* comes from El-Tantawy's photographic style. Call it impressionistic, as I just did, or an exuberantly colorful updating of the Provoke era's *are-bure-boke*, (grainy/rough, blurry, out-of-focus), or the artist's own understanding that you don't need highly realistic documentary photos to best capture true moments. This is a book of rampant color, yellows, oranges, and most of all reds. I can barely find a shot in the book in which a person's normal skin tones prevail; most often they are furious eruptions of the colors noted above, the hues of passion and violence. (The 2011 rebellion successfully removed Hosni Mubarak from the presidency, but at least dozens of protesters were shot and

The Mysteries of Light 217

killed by police, and Arab Spring soon turned to Arab Winter.)

One advantage I've found from photographing into thick, emotionally engaged crowds is that you can easily get up very close to people, and El-Tantawy does that here. She catches faces from mere inches away, all pure expressions of palpable emotion. Chances are any citizen has only a single life opportunity, if that, to actually realize political change by protest, and El-Tantawy does a great job of expressing through these close-ups just what the moment means to the Egyptians involved. Simply, we're there with her.

And the shots that are mostly washes of color, near abstractions? Or the ones with bodies dark silhouettes before the stunning colors? The best photographs are not what you want to see but what the camera itself actually observes. So the blur, the abstraction, the shadows and shapes and bursts of unreal color ... they're all the truth of the moment, as captured by the camera, which of course is simply a tool of El-Tantawy's powerful vision.

The book itself is extremely well made, from its rough cloth cover with an image of two children on a camel (a family photo?), a dark, elongated shadow-man imposed upon it like an inkblot. The cloth cover makes the photo inevitably, and suitably, very grainy. Most of the pages in the book are folded-over sheets, perhaps to allow the colors to be richer on a page backed only by the white side of the paper. This unusual paper choice also gives the whole book a greater weight and thickness, which suits its importance. The folded paper also makes the book, looked at from its paper-side edge, an intriguing striation of colors, bounded by white sheets of the early and later pages, which are not full bleed. The overall effect of *In the Shadow of the Pyramids* is to embed interest and effect (and affect) in every aspect of the book, and in every moment of reading it.

I didn't set out here to review *In the Shadow of the Pyramids*, a book now four years old (and long out of print, alas), but it's a book well worth talking about, and one I'm sure will be discussed for years to come. So this here becomes Part 1 of my two-part piece on El-Tantawy's books. The next will be on her two major photobooks after *In the Shadow of the Pyramids, Beyond*

Here Is Nothing and the brand-new *A Star in the Sea*. Those books … well, that question I raised at the opening of where the line between photographs and book falls, and how it can be moved, that's the question I'll dive deep into in Part 2. As El-Tantawy puts it, "Trying not to repeat myself, every project deserves its own visual language. What that language will be and how I will consistently apply it across a body of work so it feels cohesive is always a challenge."

A challenge, indeed. For both the photobook maker and for us, her audience. El-Tantawy has not repeated herself, that's for sure (though in all her books, her palette remains somewhat the same). She's moved further and further in the direction of photobook as pure art object.

And as we'll see, she's done that most intriguingly.

Photos to Books to Art Objects: Laura El-Tantawy, *A Star in the Sea*, Part 2

August 2019

IN PART 1 OF my piece on Laura El-Tantawy's work, I quoted her as saying, "Trying not to repeat myself, every project deserves its own visual language. What that language will be and how I will consistently apply it across a body of work so it feels cohesive is always a challenge"—and I added, Not simply a challenge for her but for us.

Well, the first challenge I faced when I received her latest book, *A Star in the Sea*, was how to get into the book itself. Yes, actually how to physically get it open to read it. The first part was easy, slip a cloth pouch out of a plastic sack, then pull the small book out of the pouch. (The cloth pouch, a batik, was made by hand by El-Tantawy and her mother.) Then I faced a conundrum: The book was bound by many turns of a double-tied brown thread, but the five ties of thread were sealed by a lovely white glob of wax embossed with a five-pointed star. It wasn't clear how to get the threads out from the wax without cracking it. I consulted my art-director wife, and she said to carefully lift up the wax, which I did. I kept it intact! (As a photobook collector, well, I've never actually sold a book, but I like to tell myself many of them have value, and I of course understand that value can relate to completeness. I think here of Andy Warhol's *Index* book from the 1960s, full of little fun add-ons, a fold-up castle, a Velvet Underground flexi-disc, etc., and how often one sees copies for sale missing an essential part of the book ... I mean, what self-control for somebody in 1967 not to have ripped out the VU flexi and given it a spin. My copy of *Index*, I'm happy to say, is complete, including the time-melted balloon; and likewise, I'm planning to keep the circle of star-embossed wax close to *A Star in the Sea*.)

In any event, I got the book open, and....

Well, before I get to my review, in Part 1 I wrote extensively about El-Tantawy's first book, *In the Shadow of the Pyramids*, which though lovingly and creatively made, nonetheless is essentially a conventional photobook, read like a "normal" book, with one picture following the other in a linear page-turning fashion. O.K., El-Tantawy nailed that, so when it came time for her second book, *Beyond Here Is Nothing*, she decided to make it more of a challenge to both make and to read.

Beyond Here Is Nothing is definitely a production; indeed, its cover photo appears to be a window curtain cracked open just an inch, like a stage curtain about to sweep back. You open the book by folding back the cover board, then the board underneath it, then the board under that one (all rich with recognizably El-Tantawy photographs), and then you hit striking, mostly abstract photos on sheets of matte paper, of which the first set lifts up and back (in the direction of the final cover board). Another set of mostly abstract (and lovely) photos unfolds to the right, then the single word "Slow" in the center of a paper sheet appears. Beneath that is a diary entry, and another sheet of paper that reads, "I am lonely sounds like the most sinful confession to make."

The theme is set. A photographer's on-the-move style of life equals inevitable loneliness. (The photographs in the book were mostly shot with El-Tantawy's iPhone, and all around the globe.) Then you start turning pages haphazardly, some lifting up, some folding right, some folding left. There appears to be no correct way to "read" the book, and after you've turned pages, let me tell you, you'll never get them back in their initial order again. The photos are much less of a piece than in the Egypt book: natural moments, water, bugs, rocks, and humans mostly appearing only as shadow projections, through streaked glass or fog or just in imperfect distortion ... loneliness, indeed.

I could easily keep going about *Beyond Here Is Nothing*, but I'm really here to discuss the book that comes after it. So let me just say that with *Beyond* El-Tantawy fulfilled her challenge to move ahead, nailing a complex fold-out book, pictures not corresponding to each other linearly but more spatially ... so what next?

Well, *A Star in the Sea*. As mentioned above, I solved the first puzzle, how to simply open the book. Then I found out how El-Tantawy suggests we do it: "The wax seal on a *A Star in the Sea* should be broken. Basically pull the thread through and it will break part of it but some will stay intact. It's intended as a gesture of imperfection—I have a tendency to want to keep things in perfect form. The wax seal makes opening the book a careful decision. Once done, it cannot be reversed. I have to accept its altered state. It's a reference to what I'm trying to express with the book as a whole."

Which tells us that no detail associated with an El-Tantawy book is insignificant; and each moment spent with one of her books can reveal multiple meanings and possibilities.

So now I'm inside *A Star in the Sea*. What do I find?

In conventional terms, barely a photobook at all. Instead ... well, hold tight.

As I mentioned in Part 1, generally I prefer books with strong photos and sequencing; I'm less interested in books that let artful aspects of the physical book get in the way of the photography. Simply, I like a good picture, next to another good picture.

But I also know that when an artist goes all in, hand-dyeing and -sewing a pouch to put the book in, coming up with a decision rich in implication just to open the book, then insisting that we experience the whole physical way we handle the book as essential to the experience ... O.K., then I'm willing to consider going all in, too.

Which I am with El-Tantawy's new book. There are only a handful of actual photographs, mostly abstractions that appear to be sea life of some form (shells, coral, fish?). There is also a dreamlike tale that El-Tantawy explains as "three independent, personal life events: A love story; my first & only trip to my place of birth in the UK & a vision on a beach in Italy." In the story she goes to the house of an old, dear friend, sees the friend through a window, experiences a moment of visions, "a boat, a guiding light, a dream or a star in the sea," and then the friend disappears, the door changes color, silence prevails until a voice asks, "Did you see the star in the sea." No answer, but a kind of philosophical epiphany arises.

The book, El-Tantawy tells us, "is an overture for embracing the unexpected."

And the more time I spend with it, the deeper I fall into its magic. I'm not looking at pictures, I'm not reading a story ... I'm moving into a mild dream state myself, deep in my own personal memories, visions, and reflections. The book so difficult to know how to even open now for me keeps opening and opening, and expanding my consciousness with it.

This is a singular experience with a photobook. Even if El-Tantawy's final realization is a bit clichéd ("if it's meant to be, it will be"), and the promo video for the book too New Age–y, the work itself, in its gentle mix of images and tactile surfaces and pages folding and unfolding and folding back in curious ways, moves me. Its story draws me in. Somehow I've gone beyond simply photos and words and paper stock and cardboard to a place stirring and important.

El-Tantawy writes on her website, "The book is conceived as an artistic object demanding intimacy—something you want to protect & treat with care." Trust me, if I'd simply read that without knowing the book, I'd shrug and say something along the lines of "At least Marianne Williamson won't become U.S. president ... and good luck with Boris Johnson, eh?"

But, damn, I did experience a stirring intimacy, and I do want to protect and treat *A Star in the Sea* with care. I've finished looking at it, finished writing these words, and now I'm carefully—as carefully as I can—folding up the book, tying its five loops of thread around it, slipping it back in its batik pouch (careful not to harm the wax seal sitting at the bottom), and slipping all that into the plastic sleeve that lets me know I have number 38 of the edition of 150.

Oh, and now I'm worrying where I'll keep the book. Which books in my library should it sit next to? Will it befriend its companions, or perhaps annoy them? Reveal its magic, or just befuddle the likes of Josef Koudelka or William Eggleston?

At bottom, there is something nearly alive in this book.

And what other photobook can one say that about?

The Photobook as Pulp Fiction:
Tania Franco Klein, *Positive Disintegration*

September 2019

WHEN YOU THINK ABOUT IT, it's surprising there aren't more photobooks that simply set out to tell an actual story, with photos ordered to move the plot along, sort of like a comic book, or an old Mexican *fotonovela*. I can't think of too many serious ones that do, at least after Ed van der Elsken's *Love on the Left Bank*. There are probably more, but if a book is too story-book-like, well, that's what it is, too story-like ... burdened and shaped by its narrative, bled out of most of the art.

Still, there are important books that do focus on actual stories. Christian Patterson's *Redheaded Peckerwood* comes first to mind, with its investigation of the Charles Starkweather crime spree in the 1950s in Nebraska, which earlier inspired Terrence Malick's movie *Badlands*. What works in *Redheaded Peckerwood* is how far from a novel or movie it is—odd scraps of material that do anything but depict that literal crime drama, reproductions of diaries and maps, images out of the odd corners and dreams of the investigation, and always simple photos of quiet beauty.

In that same spirit comes *Positive Disintegration* by the 27-year-old Mexican artist Tania Franco Klein. I'm not sure if there's a single story, or even a crime at the book's center, though I'm also pretty sure it has a heavy dose of Mexican *fotonovela* lying at its roots. Those *fotonovelas* really were pulp fiction with actual photos rather than drawn art, filled with heavy doses of crime and romantic troubles, popular from the 1950s to the '80s. Needless to say, they were as heavy on plot as any soap opera ... which *Positive Disintegration* also seems to be, if you're willing to accept a plot that's so ungraspable as to sow only anxiety and confusion.

Franco Klein's book is lurid, inscrutable, ripe with alienation, fear, and mystery. (It's also beautifully colorful, in all senses of the word; more on this later.) Something seems to be going on in the book—something awful—but anything I can come up with to explain its story or meaning or simply its point feels like missing the point; that is, the book stands larger and more breathtaking than any simple tale, be it of crime, duplicity, or betrayal. Instead of an explicit story, what *Positive Disintegration* has in its mysteriousness is the heft and seriousness and simple beauty of a work of powerful art.

Last year Franco Klein had a show in Greece called "Our Life in the Shadows," and many of those photos are in her new book. At the series' center are shots of women (many are evidently of Franco Klein herself) in curly wigs, many of them black. There's a Cindy Sherman aspect to the book, photographer impersonating a character then photographing herself, but while for Sherman shots were static portraits (or film stills) one after the other, there's no escaping the implication of narrative in Franco Klein's book. (The title of the John Garfield adaptation of *Positive Disintegration*? How about, *The Woman in the Black Wig*?)

And that's what I love about Franco Klein's book: that something's going on, yet that I have no clear idea what it is.

Let me describe some shots, maybe you'll make more sense of them. A parked car on a lonely road, a plainly dressed woman facing starkly away from it. A blue telephone and a filled-to-overflowing ashtray atop a blue pillow. An orange telephone hanging off the hook next to a fruit-and-flower-patterned curtain in what looks like a forsaken motel room. A baby on its back in the rear seat of a car, the photo taken between the two front seats. A highly reflective toaster on a well-lit table, Franco Klein lying on the table, her own face reflected vividly (and exaggeratedly) in the toaster, a black-and-white photo of a boy next to her.

Now these are photos from early in the book, in order; let me skip toward the end, again describing each photo in sequence. A stunning photo of Franco Klein fully dressed in a blue-tiled shower, a plastic bag full of water held up before her face, blurring it, especially the carmine paint on her lips. The wig, now auburn, lying by itself on an equally rich carmine sofa. A woman (Franco Klein?) lying on her side on the floor, naked from the buttocks up, the whole shot steeped in spooky green tones. The bewigged Franco Klein sitting upright on the side of her bed, gazing through a bright morning-yellow curtained window.

Another woman (again, Franco Klein?) standing outside a small trailer-park home in a desert surrounded by tawny foothills. Another shot of the auburn wig, again not on anybody's head, this time lying on a ground of brambles and rocks. An old woman on the edge of another bed, almost facing the camera, in a turquoise robe and sporting what looks like a platinum wig.

I was going to stop describing the flow of photos here, but I can't. It's too much fun. So I'll show you the final run of shots, coming after a blank page. (If *Positive Disintegration* were simply an ultimately comprehensible film noir, I'd have to issue a standard warning here of plot points about to be revealed. No worries, though. If my descriptions give away too much of the story, I'll be astonished.)

So here goes, the final five photos. Back in that desert-y landscape, a long row of mailboxes along a road, at the end of which looks to be a kneeling woman, but that is actually pale pink high-heeled shoes, a gossamer white dress, with that auburn wig above it, as if atop the non-body a nonexistent face were looking away from us. A lime-green front porch with a sofa sitting on it. A woman (probably Franco Klein) in the same desert landscape, wearing bright-red slacks and a cream-colored bra, in what looks like the black wig again, gazing away from us. A deep-green seat on a train, and out the window through green curtains the desert scene with the pole of a power line faint under the blue sky. And the final shot in the book, picking up on a few of the early photos: a doll's hand, a semi-full crystal ashtray, an old-fashioned wireless telephone (antenna not extended), and an old-school portable cathode-ray TV, a tragic-looking woman on its black-and-white screen, the whole shot bathed in a light both orange and green.

Let me say here that Franco Klein's use of light throughout the book is brilliant. It's also overdone—little is shot in anything close to natural light—but the colors always feel appropriate for the film noir excesses of the book. I just know the use of color here holds great significance, though I won't begin to guess what each lurid orange or green or red or blue means.

And, again, neither can I tell you what's going on, or what the story means. Are you hooked, though? I am.

And while we're at it, here are a few more photos, from the middle of the book, just to let you see more about the scope of Franco Klein's full-blown pulp vision. A blue-and-white patterned sofa in flames. Yes, a sofa burning right there on the page. An ancient Electrolux vacuum cleaner next to pulled-out pieces of the black wig. A series of three shots of the woman, now in a blonde wig, face down on a green shag rug, her face atop a hand mirror, a scatter of liquor bottles next to a wooden bed. And one of the eeriest photos in the book, three bewigged women in nightclothes next to each other in bed, looking off as if at a TV set, their wigged heads shadowed deeply behind them. Oh, and one more: the loneliest of nighttime drives, a short yellow illumination of dirt road and an endless expanse of black night.

In a *Paris Review* piece by Anna Furman, she talks a bit about how the book came to be: "For this series, Franco Klein took most of the interior shots in Mexico City, her hometown, and saved exterior shots for trips to Long Beach, California, and small towns around Palm Springs. Because of ongoing violence in Mexico City—kidnappings, assaults, gun violence—Franco Klein is vigilant about her safety when working at home. 'In California, I feel so free to take these photos,' she says. 'I don't have the same paranoia.' "

That could be the best word to describe the book: *paranoia*. Even the most domestic of objects (beds, toasters, couches) are rife with anxiety and fear. And outside? In a way I'm surprised there aren't any guns in any of the photos, though I'm glad there aren't. That would be too obvious. What shakes and disturbs in *Positive Disintegration* are common objects right there in front of all of us.

As I mentioned, color is essential to the book, and it's safe to say Franco Klein is as good at a certain excessive luridness as good ol' William Eggleston. One photo of the photographer, in a red dress and the black wig, bent over in a deep blood-red painted room, immediately calls up the famous Eggleston shot of an equally blood-red room with the white light bulb. There's a green shower virtually the same green as the shower in *Guide*. Indeed, I just flipped through Eggleston's *Guide* to find the shower photo and felt as if I were reading a prequel to *Positive*

Disintegration. I mean that only as a complement to Franco Klein.

(Interestingly, there's a recent *New Yorker* magazine piece on the photographer Alex Prager, a possible photographic cousin to Franco Klein, who says that she went to see a show of William Eggleston's photos, and "I felt like I was struck blind by a vision and that was the path I was going to take for the rest of my life." Who said great photography isn't life-changing.)

Back to Franco Klein. What I can tell you for sure is that her book has strikingly composed, wonderfully colored, and mysteriously subjected shots, along with its inscrutable mysteries. Certainly there's probably more to be said, and one thing I find out about the title, again from Furman, is that "Franco Klein became interested in the Polish psychologist Kazimierz Dąbrowski's theory of positive disintegration (TPD), which posits that we are at our greatest potential for growth after periods of anxiety, depression, or trauma." Sounds good to me; indeed, basically sounds like a recipe for any old happy ending. (*Fotonovela* alert!) That is, bad stuff happens, as it appears to be happening all through *Positive Disintegration*, but good stuff—growth!—will come out of it. I'm all for that, but the final shot in the book, that mannequin hand, ashtray, phone, and portable TV, doesn't really suggest a huge potential for growth; it suggests more what you leave behind after a cocktail of vodka and strychnine.

Which is as it should be. Franco Klein evidently came out of making her book just dandy. But the book is all I know, and what I know is that *Positive Disintegration* is already haunting my imagination.

Soon I expect it to embed itself deep into my dreams, and my nightmares.

Color Film Changes Everything
Fun Times in the Soviet Union:
Boris Mikhailov, *Suzi et Cetera (Part 2)*

September 2019

FEW THINGS ARE AS interesting when it comes to artists than watching them discover their true work, what they're supposed to do, who they're supposed to be. When I first moved to New York City many moons ago I used to plop myself in front of Les Demoiselles d'Avignon at MoMA as often as I could, watching in one painting Picasso discover cubism. Likewise, the first Beatles LP I bought was *Beatles 65* (not their best, the U.S. bastardization of *Beatles for Sale)*, but notable because John Lennon had just heard Bob Dylan (and been turned on to pot by him on Sixth Avenue) and made a leap in his songwriting to the personal, and powerfully sad, "I'm a Loser" and "No Reply."

In the same spirit we now have Boris Mikhailov's *Suzi et Cetera (Part 2)*, early photos from the 1960s to the '70s, in which Mikhailov discovers not only the joys of color photography in general, but the stirrings of what he wants to do with it, his own style, his personal way of taking on the ridiculousness and horror of being a citizen of the Soviet Union. (Ridiculousness and horror, spread these days even to democratic nations, it seems.)

For Mikhailov the photos in *Suzi* are "like a capsule containing the embryo of all his following works and explorations," as a small booklet enclosed with the book tells us. (They remind me most of his later Red Series, casual shots of Soviet life with small curiosities captured; more on this later.) One of the fascinating aspects of the book is not only that Mikhailov is discovering his own artfulness, he and all of the Soviet Union are discovering color film, which became widely available there only in the mid-'60s. (Quick side note: On my one trip to Cuba I had the occasional joy of riding in Lada taxis, like cheap broken toasters juttering along on bald tires. Perfect evidence that Russia can't

The Mysteries of Light 229

produce anything other than vodka and political mayhem.) As the included essay, by Kateryna Filyuk, a curator in Kiev, tells us, "color photography was taken out of the pathetic-official, the collective, and came into the private, almost intimate sphere, at the same point in time when the consciousness of the Soviet person began to shift." I take that to mean that for a budding artist like Mikhailov, this new color film came at just the time people were discovering a true personal life outside the rigid Communist system. And what could be more exciting for him than to record this new freedom, in photos of private—and previously hidden and forbidden—experiences.

So what do we get? A lot of nudes, pretty girl nudes, plump girl nudes, dumpy guy nudes, and one crazy indoor shot of a dude wearing only his underpants with a bright orange pencil sticking out of his belly button, a woman in an equally orange bathing suit covering her face with her hands, but still sneaking a peek ... a curiously subversive photo.

Yeah, people were people, even back then in the U.S.S.R. Raw, up for anything, goofy, drunk, sometimes serious ... people. And photos that ... well, as a quote by a visitor to the show that inspires the book tells us, "You could only take [photos] like this in the U.S.S.R."

And what a range of shots there are. Along with the copious nudes (many of people cavorting out of doors), there are shots of all manner of regular folk. Here's one: two scarf-clad women in heavy blue overcoats dancing together on gray stone a great distance from an open-air band shell. Nothing to distinguish this picture at all. Indeed, it's one somebody might take of their own mother and her friend, then throw away because it's pretty boring.

Except it's not. For one, I'm assuming this isn't a photo of any of Mikhailov's relatives, not that it really matters. Since, for two, the photo has an intriguingly open sense of space, the women balanced in a dime-store version of a "decisive moment." There's another photo many pages on of another two women in heavy coats and scarves, this time nearly lost in the oppressive emptiness of a Soviet apartment complex. More common people dealing with Soviet life. Just to make sure we know where we are there's a subtly ugly/beautiful shot of a hammer and sickle sculpture above a car's rooftop with a smokestack in the background.

Sometimes Mikhailov goes for the purely commonplace in a close-up fashion that makes the photos anything but common. For instance, a brilliantly red purse before tall stalks of green grass, and a quite lovely/ominous photo of a purple cabbage sliced down the middle. Regular life glimpsed extraordinarily.

Then the photos get stranger. A woman fully clothed and lying on her side amidst a burning field, flames nearly surrounding her. Two close-up women sticking their tongues out at each other. A sculpted dummy hand, nails a ravishing red, sitting by itself on the arm of a broken wooden chair. That guy with the pencil protruding from his belly button.

And finally subversive: Mostly the outdoor nudes, a corpulent woman with a fur stole over her bare breasts and pudenda, supine on an Oriental carpet beside a river. A woman in a park, in a dress, but with her legs splayed open. Another naked woman indoors on a mat, posed like an Ingres nude. A woman urinating behind a storage shed. A curly-haired naked man squat with his legs apart, a female head covering his groin....

So here's the question: How much were regular Soviet citizens acting this way before they had color film to take pictures of themselves with? Sounds like a flip question but it's not. In the Instagram age we live in now we know all kinds of behavior has changed because of social media force, as in, I don't really want to go to the Himalayas and probably die climbing Mount Everest, but I really can't go on without spreading around a selfie of me summiting the top. Or, I don't really want to wait in line for an hour and twenty minutes just to get a kimchi taco (with edible flowers!), but how can I face myself if a photo of me smacking my lips into it isn't social-media'd around the world?

So here we have Soviet Ukraine in the '60s. Were people already throwing themselves around outside nude as can be? Eager to document perverse acts of the kind that presumably in Stalinist days would send them to a work camp because that was the way things went down? Or are all these crazy things people are doing the things they're doing because now there

The Mysteries of Light

are cameras out there, and their acts can be photographed and shared? Or is it Mikhailov enticing them to disport themselves in this way?

My bet's on the latter, since that's what artists do. They move the world around them at least as powerfully as a new iPhone app (and with far more depth and soul and meaning; I'm looking at you TikTok). That's why we love art.

And why we have to celebrate Boris Mikhailov's new book. Photo after photo expressing the freedom and thrill of a color camera finally in the populace's hands (perhaps a Smena or a Chaika or a Zenit, names all a marketer's dream), along with the Khrushchev thaw to help them make the most of it. And Mikhailov himself finding those casual, barely noticed moments—a man on a rainy street stooped over picking up something from the sidewalk, a brown-and-white cow by the side of a path, a woman casually picking her teeth, a boy's head popping up in the rear window of a bus in a snow-covered parking lot—those singular expressive photos that in the right hands will always conjure up a true world, perhaps lost to history, but fascinating for us forevermore.

We Are Family:
Masahisa Fukase, *Family*;
Guillaume Simoneau, *Murder*

October 2019

No question, Masahisa Fukase was one crazy cat. His photobooks range from the slight (photos of sidewalk cracks, yep, just sidewalk cracks ... except, well, some with paint on the prints, in *Hibi*) to his masterpiece, *Ravens*, the *Macbeth* and *King Lear* of photobooks, reviewed by me for *Photobookstore Magazine* a couple years back. Along the way Fukase has done books on the woman who would become his wife as she sweeps about abstractedly in a cape throughout a slaughterhouse *(Slaughter)*, and then that wife, Yoko, after they were married, in *Yokoh*, an amazing book I hope Mack can rerelease. *Yokoh* gives us the widest view of a marriage I've yet seen, from brilliant wedding photos, to Yoko cutting up here, there, and everywhere, to photos of her pulling faces suggesting she could have been one of the great actresses of her time. There's also a book on Fukase's father *(Memories of Father)*; assorted other books of photos abstract and mysterious (*Ravens* of course being the most powerful); and at least three books on his cats—yes, his cats—one of which, *The Strawhat Cat*, I just declined to purchase at the recent New York Art Book Fair because, well, I'm not a cat guy; and, really, it's just photos of his cat.

Fukase also did a book in 1991 called *Kazoku (Family)* that is most likely the oddest, most startling family album ever; a book now beautifully reprinted by Mack. A family album is ... well, just that, photos any of us might take of our family, then put together into a scrapbook or actual book. It's most likely done as a memory piece, who we were, where we were, how we've changed, and is thus autobiographical, though my guess is people using the local CVS drugstore to put together a collection of their iPhone photos, or simply posting them on Facebook, do not think that they're actually creating something as soundingly

The Mysteries of Light 233

serious as an autobiography. That is, I don't know if the book of shots of you and your folks at Disneyworld, and Uncle Jeff hitting another Bud, and Aunt Alice showing us her old Disco moves ... is that an autobiography? My life, contemplated, summed up?

Well, it is a life. And that's what Fukase has given us in *Family*, in spades. Of course most of us don't have a family-owned photography studio, as the Fukases did in Hokkaido in northern Japan until 1990, and most of us don't have family members willing to pose for formal group portraits time after time, especially when the first of them, and many others, have the photographer's wife topless.

Yes, in 1971, Fukase's first family portrait has most of his close family, all dressed in regular clothing except for his wife, Yoko, who stands there in a long white cotton waist-wrap, and nothing else. Her near waist-length hair covers her bare breasts, more or less, at least for the first few photos. In the sixth shot in the book, taken a year later, Yoko is replaced in the exact same position and dress by H, a dancer; and in the seventh shot, this prized position is taken by M, a singer, whose hair is far too short to cover her breasts, which are simply, and somewhat sur-really, present, along with the rest of Fukase's family in exactly the same position as in each of the previous photos.

Then things get even stranger. The eighth photo puts K, an actor, in the pole position, standing as straight and unengaged as can be; but then in the following shot, K is crouched down, standing on her left foot, her right leg crossed over her left knee, hands up and bent over with pinkies lifted, and her face going goofy, eyes pinched to the center, cheeks bulbous as if she's about to blow out a long stream of cartoon air. Everyone else, of course, is posing as usual for Masahisa's latest family gambit.

One fine thing about *Family* is that Mack includes two well-written, essential essays. (Essays worth reading? In my experience a rarity in photobooks.) One is Fukase himself writing about his life, the other is from Tomo Kosuga, the director of the Masahisa Fukase Archives, writing about how *Family* came to be.

The Fukase family photo studio in Bifuka, we learn, was very successful (it's pictured in the book's first shot, in its prime), and Masahisa was expected to take over the studio as the third generation. But after he went to Tokyo to study photography at the Nihon University College of Art, he shacked up with a woman and stayed on in the capital. His brother took over the family business, and Masahisa didn't return for ten years, when, in 1971, he headed home with Yoko.

Clearly the family was happy to have him back, posing willingly for the very proper family portrait, smiling and not batting an eye at the semi-naked woman to their right. As I described above, the family photos continued over this visit, and then the next, all the while Fukase trying out this and that. After the contorted-actress photo, the next is of just Fukase's parents, then Fukase and his father, Sukezo, in their underwear, then Sukezo and an actress both bare from the waist up, then Fukase and the actress also bare from the waist up, then both of them disporting wildly, one foot kicking high, arms thrust out, laughing joyously and/or demonically.

The whole book is this way, creative riffs on professional family portraits. You can just hear Fukase go, "Smile now—say, Cheese!" In one photo with Fukase in the far left position he's even holding his camera's shutter cable; in another with him in it, an assistant snaps the photo. There are photos of just Fukase and his father in traditional dress, then one of Fukase and Yoko also in traditional dress. (The essay tells us that the white cotton waist-wrap was traditionally worn underneath a kimono.) In one way, *Family* is an exuberant exploration of what a creative genius can do with the most limited of subjects and photographic approaches. What is also impressive is that Fukase never goes too far, never has his family, say, acting too outrageously or without dignity, never cheapens the solemnity of the family portraits. No, he just makes them like nothing you've ever seen before.

Then things change. Well, the time has changed ... the next set of photos is from 1985, ten years on. Sukezo has had a serious fall, and looks far more than ten years older, feeble and gaunt. One of Fukase's nieces, Miyako, has died, and a framed photo of her, lovingly held by her mother, is in the place Miyako stood in the earlier sets of photos.

The Mysteries of Light 235

The 1985 photos are really not that much different from the earlier sets, the family members grouped in the same places as before, the same "Say cheese" posing, similar expressions, ranging from somewhat forced smiles to more dour bemusement at the whole situation. Oh, and more nude women on everyone's far right.

This repetition also speaks to Fukase's genius, the way the *Family* photos suggest both an impromptu "Hey, let me take everybody's picture" and a simultaneous knowledge of what he's up to: I'll take these family shots every time I'm up here, everyone in the same positions, and the most minute yet profound changes will tease and move the viewer. My simple thirty-four photos will be a family saga to rival a literary family saga such as *The Sound and the Fury*.

Then Fukase's father, Sukezo, dies, and the story comes to its inevitable end. The family business is shuttered (the final photo in the book is of the empty building) and the family dispersed. In his essay, Kosuga hits this note hard, talking about how "the decay of the family setting ... brings to mind the way that a dead body gradually decomposes, leaving nothing but bleached bones." I don't know if I'd go that far. Time is inexorable, so is death. For me the greatness of *Family* is how all of that is captured so simply and quietly, and, again, almost inadvertently. Anyone taking photos of their family over twenty-eight years (the final shots have Sukezo memorialized in his own held-high picture frame) will show us time's ravages, as well as death. That's how it goes.

But in *Family*, Fukase does it as high art, trenchant, powerful, and true.

※ ※ ※ ※ ※

THERE are of course all kinds of families, if not of blood, then perhaps relations by artistic spirit. In my own photobooks, at my best, and most mysterious, I hope to share a small touch of Fukase's vision. There's another photographer who feels unusually close to Fukase, Guillaume Simoneau, whose book *Murder* has also just been published by Mack.

It turns out that around the same time Fukase was working

on *Ravens*, Simoneau's family in Canada adopted a nest of baby crows in a fallen tree. Simoneau's mother took numerous photos of the crows, many with her son, who in one photo looks cheery if bewildered to have crows perched on his head, shoulder, and right arm. Many of the mother's crow pictures are in the book. Then young Guillaume grew up to be a photographer himself, and in 2016 and '17 went to Kanazawa, Japan, the birthplace of *Ravens*.

In his book Simoneau has shot a bar whose red-and-yellow neon letters spell out RAVENS. He's also captured some nice sunsets, moody rocks, and crows whirling overhead in clear homage to *Ravens*. There are a lot of shots in the book that don't add up, but there are also touches of poetry, as well as a deep examination of how one photographer can influence another. He's followed Fukase's footsteps, captured some dramatic scenery, and caught a few local denizens of Japan's far north (though none with anything close to the startling appearance of the corpulent nude woman a third of the way into *Ravens*). A book mostly of straightforward photos, not the endless nightmarescape of Fukase's book.

And that's the thing here. At bottom, *Murder* is a book about homage, not invention. About crows, not ravens. Those black birds are the made-for-TV version of actual ravens, the unpleasant swarm you find picking around the garbage dump, not soaring ominously above misery trains hurtling through Japan's far north. And even though an enclosed booklet by Shino Kuraishi called "Crows as Messengers of Good News" tries to play up the metaphorical presence of those black birds, I don't see any photo in *Murder* with close to the ominous force of any single photo in Fukase's masterpiece.

Of course, whose photos do? Fukase, who in his own essay calls himself "a loser"—to me, invoking another troubled genius who could turn static popular forms into mysterious beauty, and who blatantly wrote the song "I'm a Loser," back in 1964—wasn't emulating anyone when he stuck his camera out a train window in northern Japan to capture circling ravens. No, his ravens were real, as were his demons, his wild imagination, and his enduring pain.

The Mysteries of Light

Which brings up those cats again. I was way too cavalier earlier. In his essay on his life Fukase tells us that during World War II "even my pet cat Tama was taken [from me] to provide the fur for a fur-lined collar for some soldier fighting in the north."

If *Family* is underlain with loss, so is all of life, everybody's, of course, though few have expressed it as simply and movingly (and strangely) as Masahisa Fukase. Will we see other books quite as metaphorically rich and sublime as *Family* and especially *Ravens*? My guess is, nevermore.

Opening Up:
Matthew Spiegelman, *Transmitter*

November 2019

So I'm at the New York Art Book Fair a few weeks back, head spinning from all the books and people, when I pick up a good-sized green-covered book, with nice orange type, called *Transmitter*. A quick flip through it, as one does at a book fair, and ... oh, it's nice color shots of people sitting on a shore before blue-gray water, a cityscape in the background. Not exactly what interests me most, so I put it back, but something's tugged at me and I pick it up again. Hmnn. I sense that something's going on in this book, it's kind of opening up right there in my hands, making me sense that there's a lot more happening in the book than just random shots of people by the water.

This is not a common experience for me, a book immediately demanding more attention, promising riches not at very first glance manifest. I'm intrigued. I end up with a copy of the book, *Transmitter*, by New York City–based photographer Matthew Spiegelman, and a chance to review it here for one simple reason: I want to explore this curious sensation of a photobook insisting that I look at it more deeply. How that works, what the book means.

As mentioned above, what *Transmitter* is comprised of are shots taken alongside water, in this case New York City's East River, from a small park at the end of Greenpoint Avenue in Brooklyn. It's called Transmitter Park because it was the site of WNYC's original AM transmitter, set up in 1935. The park was dedicated in 2012, and as I can attest, having stumbled on it once during a wander along the Greenpoint shorefront, it's a lovely, calm green space in the middle of the crazy metropolis. The park is a place of retreat, contemplation. A spot of quiet beauty, especially when the light is of a certain quality. A place to read, catch up with a friend, gaze out at the cityscape, smoke a pipe, work out a long-brewing domestic situation, or simply re-express one's love for one's partner. At bottom, as Spiegelman's book attests, Transmitter Park is a place to let one's essential humanity beam its essences, in all their grace and complexity, into the world.

Which is what I think I was picking up on when I first held the book *Transmitter*. Pictures that radiate—O.K., broadcast—a deep and true humanity.

Particularly strong in the book are the photos of pairs of people deep in conversation. There are couples both with pensive faces. A woman with her open palm on her chest, as if she's saying, "Really, it'll be all right." Two men at the end of a concrete jetty talking, then embracing deeply. A woman looking with love and joy at her male partner. Another man, brow creased, most likely saying, "Wait, what the hell are you telling me?" A figure in a brown hat before a golden sunset staring at the water; then in the next picture, bowing their head deeply over a metal railing.

That's Spiegelman's intent here, and his gift: to capture portraits that are in effect pantomimes, so easily readable as to their human meanings and emotions. And what a range of emotions we have: love, joy, calmness, consternation, yet most of all an expression of that deep solace we all can find next to water, nothing going on but the stillness growing and easing within us. Magical, rare moments.

What Spiegelman's so good at in *Transmitter* is to make everything so clear. We almost always know what's going on, we can write the dialogue ourselves. Take the shot of a young guy in a razored-short haircut pulling on a joint. Next picture he's holding the weed away from him, tilting his head back as his pal next to him looks to be firing up his own doobie. You don't have to be Raymond Carver to know he's saying, "Nice shit we scored, eh?"

And I invoke Raymond Carver purposefully, because in a way *Transmitter* is a book of short stories. I'm always beating the drum that great photobooks are a form of literature, and here we have as close to a collection of actual stories as I can think of, though in the way of all the best photobooks there's no literal narrative at all. The emotions and drama fall between and around the actual photos, and are all the more effective for that.

And sweet photographs they are. I mentioned a golden sunset before. Transmitter Park faces west, so you don't have to get up at dawn to get great light. I think one of the reasons for my first, quick *ehhh?* response to *Transmitter* was that I saw nothing but pretty pictures. Golden sunsets, orange sunsets, blue sunsets. Faces strikingly silhouetted before lit-up water. Manhattan hovering dark and abstractly beyond it all. Pretty pictures, which if that's all a photo is, leaves me ... O.K., I just spent a day at something called PhotoPlus Expo at the Javits Center, a photography trade show and a temple for the folk who pursue pretty pictures at all cost, and end up squandering the kids' college money on big, clunky lenses they don't need and cameras priced as much as a used car ... well, nuf sed.

But Spiegelman of course isn't at bottom after pretty pictures (though I'll admit their beauty doesn't hurt) but instead these deeply human stories. Though the photos were taken during 2015 and '16, they're not sequenced chronologically. Sequences appear to have something to do with the flow of time through the day, also color, and to some extent by the flow of visible emotions on the people captured by his camera. In any event, it works. The book is a pleasure to move through, and only gets richer the longer you spend with it.

And the title: perfect. If you go to the Google images page for Transmitter Park, you see clumps of people on greensward, the city and river distant in the background. Typically descriptive photos. (Not even PhotoPlus quality.) Look at them ... then take in what the book *Transmitter* has accomplished. It's not easy shooting parks, with people in them doing park things. Diane Arbus could find some curious souls in Central Park, and Garry Winogrand made a whole book out of taking his kids to the zoo there and in the Bronx, but for most people there's too much space, too much green, too much everyday whateverness.

But Transmitter Park is special. Spiegelman knows it, and, better, he captures it. It may not be a Navajo burying ground or a spot from which the earth radiates spiritual energy, but it is the home of New York City's first public radio station transmitter, a force that beamed voices and music over the great city and began to knit it together in a new way. Radio, like TV and the internet after it, was a new forum—and thus force—in history for the expression of human possibility, and complexity, and drama, and love.

Bravo to the city for sanctioning this special park and celebrating its place in our history. And bravo to Matthew Spiegelman for understanding how the ghost of those radio transmitters radiates its own special force, from which all the people in his powerful book express their own human complexity, possibility, drama, and love.

In Your Face: Street Photography and Jeff Mermelstein's *Hardened*

January 2020

WHAT DO YOU DO if you're into Instagram, but want to move beyond selfies and shots of food truck delicacies? How about becoming a street photographer? I mean, everybody carries a phone, which of course has a camera, and there the streets are, with people on them, sometimes doing something kind of interesting; so why not snap, snap, snap? Google around, there's a whole new world of street photographers, and Instagram to immediately publish your quick shots to that online world. As readers of my *Photobookstore Magazine* pieces know, I love photographs taken on the street, especially those of Japanese masters such as Issei Suda and Daido Moriyama, and that I practice the calling myself, always creating new books (all visible on my website, EcstaticLightPhoto.com). Yet I worry that these days it's too easy, the term *street photography* itself becoming too common, even banal.

As one website puts it, "Street photography is something anyone can learn," and while that's true, almost anyone can learn to play the piano, too. (And should! I can easily argue that being a musician, or at least loving music, is a key to becoming a better photographer.) But the deal is that calling oneself a street photographer is like saying "I'm a pianist," as opposed to the more-often truth of "I play the piano." Pianists are Arthur Rubinstein or Emanuel Ax or Professor Longhair, piano players are legion.

And the greatest of street photographers don't really seem to be street photographers at all. Sure their shots are taken out in the world, mostly while walking around cities, but in their work there's another dimension, a forcefulness of art, the power of personality, a strain of the visionary ... I'm talking about photographers not just shooting people having lunch on a bench (unless it's Garry Winogrand) or folk bunched up on a street corner. Robert Frank took pictures on the street, but nobody thinks of him as only a street photographer. There's too much going on in his work, every photo transcending its street (or elevator or barroom) subjects, every composition revealing, every shot imbued with mystery and personality and profundity.

The simple truth: Most street photographers shoot the street. The masters, the artists, make the street their own.

All of which is a long introduction to *Hardened*, the monumental new book by the masterful street photographer Jeff Mermelstein (who, I understand, is also ambivalent about the term *street photographer*). *Hardened* is a 330-page compendium of photographs Mermelstein took on the street, all with his iPhone (replacing his Leica) over the last few years. They seem mostly to be taken in New York City, where Mermelstein resides, though I'm sure he takes his iPhone everywhere he goes, and snaps what he finds along the way.

What makes for a signature Mermelstein shot? One aspect we see over and over in *Hardened* is the extreme close-up, whether it's a man hugging his roll of belly fat or a dog's front paw with brilliant red nails on a gray street. For me a classic Mermelstein shot comes three quarters of the way through the book: a close-up of a half-smoked cigar in a mustached man's lips. An eighth of the picture are the lips, most of the rest the brown cigar with almost an inch of crumbling ash, all with a sea of car windshields behind it. The shot is startling, personal yet abstract, telling yet wholly anonymous. It has some of the power of the cover of Mermelstein's earlier book *Sidewalk*, with the elderly woman chomping down on a ten dollar bill, though with perhaps not quite as much wit as the earlier shot.

Yet wit is another signature aspect of Mermelstein's work, and there's an abundance of humor and hard-bitten joy in *Hardened*. In one shot a woman gazes through a window at the back of a hula girl doll, her ratty straw skirt billowing. The next photo is of a puppet of an old straw-hatted man in ragged overalls hanging mysteriously above the sidewalk, and then, on the next spread, a cheery sight: a brightly laughing Robert Frank before a green wall.

Throughout the book the pairing of the full-bleed photos is almost always just right. (David Campany edited the book for the always thrilling publisher Aron Morel.) You can usually see or feel why two photos are joined in a spread, but it's never too obvious; or if you do get the reason (a harmony of shapes, a winking juxtaposition of people), there's most likely quite a bit more going on. As with the best books of this type, the matching of photos makes each one richer than it would be standing alone.

The book also seems broken into chapters, noted by an occasional blank page on the left. Chapters appear to have loose themes, but, again, none seem too obvious or programmatic or forced. They're simply there to help organize and make effective the huge abundance of shots. (Aspiring street photographers take note: Just because you've found a few matching circle or triangle shapes on the street, and put them next to each other, you're not really telling us anything at all.)

And there are many, many photographs of wonder and richness. I'd say every shot in the book is worthy of being there, but some, of course, are better than others.

The first spread that really hit me hard comes twenty or so pages in. On the left is one of the trademark extreme close-ups: this time part of a man's hand, lying flat on a pocked sidewalk, three unhealthy fingers with orange nails visible; and in the extreme foreground of the photo, two copper pennies ... just out of reach. Across from that unsettling shot is a city street in the Chelsea section of Manhattan, a photo that looks down through a car window on two people in the front seat of a black sedan (taken from the back of a bus?), the driver holding up his left hand in a Stop! gesture, the woman next to him hiding her eyes with her hand. A great photo, of surprise and manifold unknowns.

And both shots ones I wish I'd taken.

And the thing is, I might have. I, too, wander the streets of New York (or wherever I am), always with my beloved Fuji X100F. (I haven't yet figured out how to take a good photo with my iPhone; don't really want to.) I'm always looking for the photos I know I'm there to shoot. I take many photos that are far different from Mermelstein's, but I also have some similar shots. The odd thing is, I found photos in *Hardened* almost the same as ones I'd previously taken. Indeed, Mermelstein shoots a line of plastic grooms ascending a set of steps in a store window. In my book *Sorrow Street*, from 2019, I have an ascending ladder of plastic brides in green dresses also in a store window. (I recall a line of grooms in the window of the photo I took, so who knows, maybe the same one?) In another *Hardened* photo, a winter sidewalk is two thirds walking boots, one third shirts and pants reflected in a large puddle. In a couple of my books I have sidewalk-puddle reflection shots, including my *New York Street* (2017) and the cover of *Sorrow Street*. (Oh, and one more connection: There's a wild photo in *Sidewalk* of a monkey atop a dog all while sitting on a smoking dude's left shoulder. That shot was taken a block from my apartment, right by my subway stop. And, like, how come *I* wasn't there that day?)

But photos both Mermelstein and I have already taken isn't the full extent of photographic connection. A curious note: As I was walking down East 57th Street, on my way to Mermelstein's gallery to get a copy of his book, the last shot I took, after a day taking my own kinds of photos, was very much in Mermelstein's mode: a bright redhead looking back over her shoulder at me, and pointing to her right, eyes dancing with youth and color and fancy. Was I already falling under his spell, half a block from picking up his book?

Another curiosity: When I first got *Hardened* home, I thumbed through it, took it in, admired it, and let just a whiff of its power into my head. Then I went out with my own camera to do my own work, but for the first half hour all I saw were Mermelstein shots, oddly telling moments on the street, quirky juxtapositions, a layer of comedy, a strong note of its opposite. Like a fog, Mermelstein-vision, as I think of it, lifted after that half an hour, and I was able to see the street my own way.

But, again, that's what makes any street photographer great. We see *their* vision, over and over, in every shot. Of course there are quirks and tics. Daido Moriyama owns red lips (though to my delight, Mermelstein has included in *Hardened* two pages of lip shots that feel like his own, a comfort to me since I also like now and then to shoot a good pair of colorful lips). Mermelstein himself has great purchase on the intensely in-your-face street portrait, that close-up of mouth and eyes that is his alone (different, indeed, from other in-your-face masters such as William Klein and Bruce Gilden). In *Hardened* we get some memorable ones: an older woman, photographed only from mascared eyes to wrinkled chin, with a bulbous nose and red lips reminiscent of Joaquin Phoenix's Joker. A page later, a black man's right eye and a white woman's pursed lips, a pimple on her nose ... just that, in a close-up so tight it's hard to imagine how Mermelstein got it. (Not to mention a whole lot of shots of nothing but bristly leg hairs or eyebrows over skin.) Oh, wait, there's also a hint of the perils of in-your-face street photography: a dumpy woman with a takeout coffee cup in her right hand, and with her left a raised, jaundiced-looking middle finger flipping the photographer off.

Compared with *Sidewalk* (and the somewhat one note of Mermelstein's last book, *Arena*, photos all shot at the Barclays Center in Brooklyn), *Hardened* is less determinedly clever and witty, though the wit does shine. But in its essence *Hardened* is richer, wilder, more suggestive, more mysterious, and in these benighted times, far more cultural and political. Another striking shot: a wide-eyed dark-haired woman with her palms up before her, "HANDS OFF" written on her right one, "MY BODY" on her left. (This shot hopefully paired with a slab of writing over an ad shot of black-and-white hands: "LOVE STILL WINS.")

I always judge photobooks as if they're works of art and/or literature, and *Hardened* is a long, powerful novel of images, like an *Underworld* or an *Infinite Jest* in photos. As with any great book, it rewards rereading; you always see something new, get taken on a different journey each time through. Photos pop in new ways, pairings yield new meanings, new characters appear, the plot twists and turns.

And all the while Mermelstein, and his editor, Campany, are in control.

So there we have it, that simple truth, again: Most street photographers go out and take pictures of the world. The masters, the true artists—like Jeff Mermelstein—go out and use the street to make worlds of their own.

Far More Than "Pretty Vacant"
Joji Hashiguchi, *We Have No Place to Be*

April 2020

THERE ARE PLENTY OF photobooks of punk rock days, it being such a visually wild time that it's hard to not have them filled with vibrant photos, skinheads squeezed in at the front of a Ramones or Sex Pistols concert, tatted-up bodies leaping left and right, fists flying, teeth bared, blood erupting ... powerful shots, but most of the books made from them are essentially music and star shots from clubs. CBGBs from the stage, other louche downtown dives with ripped-stockinged women smoking and drinking (and for the fancier set, lines of powder on the table), guys with mohawks lurking nearby, all very early-'80s ... and, for better or worse, oh so long ago.

Give 'em props, though: That early-'80s generation was unique, a pinnacle blend of alienation and nihilism, not the long-haired, consciousness-expanding hippies of the late-'60s; not the back-to-the-land earth-shoe-wearing '70s kids; not their temporal cohorts, the bow-tied Gordon Gecko–wannabe yuppies; and certainly not today's youth, who seem to think dying their hair in a first-flash-of-color-in–*The Wizard of Oz* palette to help them get Instagram or TikTok hits is their highest calling. Nope, the young adults of the Thatcher-Reagan years were seriously disaffected. My guess is that with "Pretty Vacant," the Sex Pistols tune that gives this piece—and for some, the whole generation—its title, the band was being a little ironic with the word "pretty."

Kids back then were also part of a true subculture, a concept that seems to be either lost or breathtakingly co-opted. (We all know CBGBs is now a John Varvatos clothing store.) A true subculture means there's one normal, highly conventional world, and then there are smaller distinct cultures outside it. Subculture denizens usually lurk in their own hood, dress in their own coded ways, and are shunned if not feared by the predominant culture. (What passes for subcultures now don't go out every night, don't bang heads; they curl up on their couch and jack into the dark corners of the Web, Reddit, et al.) Back in the day, being part of a subculture meant you had to be all in, soul and body. (No skinheads working at J.P. Morgan.) All the way in. No place to call home. No place really to go. As the title of Joji Hashiguchi's new book, *We Have No Place to Be*, has it, under Thatcher's and Reagan's reign, there really was no place for these people, no jobs to be had, no world to accept them, only a blank nihilism to embrace for whatever consolation it could bring.

Which probably wasn't much. And in Hashiguchi's book we're there with them. The kids, that is, with no place to be, or as the first iteration of this book from 1982 is usually translated, *We Can't Be Anywhere—Teens in the Turbulent World*. Not the celebrities, not that bands, not the stars who would never admit to being stars. No, the young denizens of this gritty world, in all their confused and doomed and proud glory.

And for that, the book is all the richer.

And beautiful. It's a large book, 8.25 inches by 11.25, with all its heavily chiaroscuro'd photos printed full-bleed in deep black and white. (Session Press published it; that's all you need to know, to know you need the book.) Through 1980 to '82, Hashiguchi traveled the world, first to Liverpool (he was a stone Beatles fan) and London, on to Nuremberg and West Berlin, then to New York City, and finally home to Tokyo. A long *Wanderjahr*, an artist chasing disaffected youth, warmly exploring these subcultural haunts, always with sympathy and a passionate eye.

And one who's indubitably a powerful photographer in his own right. Hashiguchi is simply not the person with the camera in the right place to capture a time soon to be lost, he's a real photographer making some great pictures. That is, the book is far more interesting than just a document of its time. Indeed, moving through the book, as it goes from country to country, I got a distinctive Ed van der Elsken *Sweet Life* vibe. I'm tempted to crack wise and say that Hashiguchi's book could be called *Sour Life*, and for a lot of the photos in it, the title would fit, but hardly for all of them. Sure there are plenty of tough-looking skinheads, and in Berlin at least a few junkies with their

The Mysteries of Light

dope paraphernalia, but there are also a pair of cheerful young women in Liverpool in their Wimpies uniforms ... I know, how happy can you be working at a Wimpies?, but there they are.

Like van der Elsken, Hashiguchi's book covers the wide world, and the photos are in a similar highly-contrasted black and white. There's a lot of Daido Moriyama in the book, too, but there's also Hashiguchi's intention, which seems to be about 70% not to just take good pictures but to capture these youth worlds he's clearly so fascinated by.

By my calculation, Hashiguchi would have been in his early 30s when he had this *Wanderjahr*, which raises the question of how much he observed what he's shooting, and how much he participated in it. Probably a bit of both, and probably in similar proportions to the ways in which the book is a photobook of powerful shots as well as also a documentary.

Each chapter starts with a quote from a person in the different cities that tell us in a quick bite the essence of what Hashiguchi found with his groups of teenagers there. Liverpool: "I don't have any money. I don't have any work. It's like I don't even have a life." Nuremberg: "I didn't have anything to do, I was bored. Back then, the only thing around me was heroin." And from the far less desperate Tokyo: "I want to have fun, too. Normal people have it so easy." And just as each quote has a different tenor, so do the subjects and kinds of shots that follow. I find the New York City section particularly impressive. Hashiguchi looks to have hung out with young Latin toughs, and young African-American toughs, and the shots have a definite *Mean Streets* feel, just less Italian. More photos in this chapter are taken straight on, somebody clearly projecting their own force at the photographer. In other chapters Hashiguchi is taking a wider range of street shots, groups of kids hanging out, regular people walking along the street, and one beautiful shot of six boys gazing forth from a Liverpool roof. Still, I think he's best when he's focusing in. In the New York section the press of bodies fills the frame, giving it an added intensity. Which is interesting. I find the opening Liverpool section not quite edgy enough. London is tougher, Berlin perhaps toughest of all with its drug focus. And when he gets back to Tokyo, the shots, while all strong photographs, are mostly of kids being kids, getting together with friends, driving cute motorbikes, smiling a hell of a lot more than in England and Germany and the States.

Another photographer I see in *We Have No Place to Be* is Anders Petersen. Petersen, photo by photo, has taken more intense, telling, often downright upsetting shots, and in his more focused books such as *Café Lehmitz*, made works that deeply document a particular world in all its messy and tawdry vitality. Hashiguchi is more spread out, perhaps not quite the artist Petersen (or Daido) is, but then again, I can't think of any book quite like *We Have No Place to Be*.

Indeed, the deeper I look into it, I realize it's not really that much of a punk book at all, just a great collection black-and-white photos, not even all of them of disaffected youth. (I love two different kinds of shots in the Liverpool section, one of a bonfire, just a big splash of light in a wholly black background, and the other of the menu from the Golden Square restaurant. Ah, England, which I first went to as a poor twenty-four-year-old, eating, as I'm sure Hashiguchi did, at places like the Golden Square, such culinary delights as: Chop Suey Roll, Sausage Dinner, Curry and Chips, Chips and Peas, and that delightful British mashed pea goop just by itself for 14p!)

Which puts *We Have No Place to Be* firmly in the league of classic Japanese photobooks. The book bears long study, and great pictures keep turning up. There are intimations of Provoke, a couple energetic shots in the New York section almost as strong as two of my favorite photos from Shomei Tomatsu's masterpiece, *Oh Shinjuku* (the young man furiously pounding a punching bag, the other the student in white before a perfect blurred background). *We Have No Place to Be* isn't quite in the same poetic league as Tomatsu or Daido at their best (who is?), but Hashiguchi's book is a more stirring historical document, as well as the work of a photographer worth rediscovering in his own right.

Daido's Progeny: "Subway Diary" by Masakazu Murakami and "The Dreaming" by Yasuhiro Ogawa

July 2020

I WASN'T ANYWHERE CLOSE to Japan when Daido Moriyama's first book, *A Photo Theater*, dropped in 1968, but I like to think its effect on the Japanese photography world was like the Beatles' "I Want to Hold Your Hand" hitting America four years earlier. As in, "What was that? Wow, everything is different now—and always will be."

A few years later came the *Provoke* books, Daido participating from the second one on, and, yes, everything in Japanese photography was different. Soon the high-contrast, murkily focused photos would spread to the world and things would be different there, too, though hardly as much as one might have thought, that grainy, rough, blurry aesthetic never quite upsetting the use-the-right-focal-length, keep-it-sharp expectations of Western photography. I'm sure you can hear the words in your own ears now: "That photo's no good, it's not in focus." Oh, yeah. Sure.

But many photographers remain inspired by Daido, his past revolutionary work and his present day marvels, from a late classic like *Pretty Woman* (2017) to his endless parade of *Records*. Two photographers clearly under his sway, yet nonetheless finding their own powerful visions, are Masakazu Murakami in his recent *Subway Diary* and Yasuhiro Ogawa in *The Dreaming*. Both are works of black-and-white photography, and both are striking and important.

One intriguing thing about Daido: His photos move along a continuum from the descriptive to the poetic. I like to think almost every shot he's taken is redolent of that special Daido eye, even seemingly banal street scenes, clusters of pedestrians, concatenations of signs. It's the way that any true artist imbues their work with their own way of seeing things, no matter what they're actually pointing the camera at.

And so with his disciples here. Murakami's *Subway Diary* is ostensibly about the Tokyo subway. That's where most of the photos are taken, at least in the early part of the book. We open with a shot outside two coupled trains, a glimpse of a commuter on his phone through the train window. On the title page we get escalator steps plunging those unimaginable depths to the trains themselves. (With my first trip to Tokyo a year and a half ago, written up in my Tokyo photobook-buying diaries at the end of this book, I was amazed, as a New Yorker, by how boundlessly complex and expansive even a minor subway station in the city was.) The next shot's a nice Provoke-like blur of bodies, an elbow in close-up, ascending one of those escalators.

O.K., so far, so good … we're getting a series of decent, often strong photos of the subway … a reasonably poetic description of it. The silent, glum man, eyes closed on his seat. A near Roman ruin of subway pillars along the track. A Bruce Gilden–like zoom-in on a brow-furrowed man, followed by a flutter of pigeons over a sidewalk … oh, wait, pigeons … nope, we're not down there in the depths any longer.

We're also moving further and further from just a photographic examination of the Tokyo subway. In truth, in *Subway Diary* we're basically where the subway goes, which of course is all of that huge metropolis. The book's subjects have widened, and though some shots return underground, at this point anything and anywhere in Tokyo is fair game.

As is the history of modern Japanese photography. There's a shot near the book's end of a highly-pixilated nude woman curled up, a face-covering flock of black hair, two arcing knee caps, and shiny sculpted nails most visible. It's a photo that immediately calls up Daido's famous shot from the 1960s of a highly-pixilated nude woman smoking on a bare mattress in a hotel room. Murakami's photo is compelling in its own right, so it's not even close to a rip-off, just a winking allusion and a shot that works perfectly in his book. Likewise the occasional shots of pigeons, not Fukase's devilish ravens haunting his northern train journeys but the "rat birds" fluttering through Tokyo streets. There's also a cracked and dirtied clock face that immediately conjures up the famous Shomei Tomatsu shot of

The Mysteries of Light

the unearthed Hiroshima wristwatch. And then to make sure we know we're looking at a history of Murakami's celebrated forebears, his subway journeys take us to a meter-high stage upon which the actual Nobuyoshi Araki is holding forth.

So right here we've left any kind of "Here's what the Tokyo subway is like" book. But yet there's much further to go, and that's deep into Murakami's own mind and soul.

In a few paragraphs at the end of *Subway Diary* he tells us this about himself: "There was always a sense of unease with me. It wasn't a concrete anxiety, it wasn't about anything real. It was an illogical, vague unease; a deep, disturbing resentment directed at myself for living and for spending my days so carefree.

"At some point, I began taking photographs to deal with my anxiety and oscillating moods....

"Pushing my way past the crowds I ride a long escalator down into the depths of the city. As I walk along the station platform, a swift wind sweeps by as the subway arrives. Its dull, steely eyes tear my unease apart...."

That in a few phrases is what separates a recording photographer from a poetic one. It's the way the external world, that serpentine beast, doesn't lie supine for the photographer, but comes at him, striking. It's not about what's actually out there. It's one's own deep internal state that chooses when the shutter is clicked, and what and how that which lies before the lens reveals itself, then is snatched. It's the world itself complicit with the photographer. It's about those artists, like Daido, Araki, Fukase, who make each shot their own. With *Subway Diary*, Murakami approaches their esteem.

One of the strengths of *Subway Diary* is how its width, and most important its depths, surprise; how his photo poems flicker in unexpected places and ways. It's as if the book just happened, compelled by inner need and not fully understood impulse.

Ogawa's *The Dreaming* on the other hand feels much more conscious, more intended. We sense his intent to be dreamy, otherworldly. The book is more a series of painted scenes than anything like the expression of how the world's "dull, steely" eyes rip into an artist.

Yet *The Dreaming* is also more beautiful, and at least as powerful as its city-bound pairing here.

And not actually the city at all, but instead photos taken in small towns and lost alleys on sojourns through China, Myanmar, Guatemala, Japan, Cambodia, Mongolia, Tibet (and even one shot from Ethiopia) that Ogawa took over the past twenty-seven years. The shots he comes up with are anything but tourist shots; instead, they're vividly mysterious, evocative, and private. The more time you spend in "The Dreaming," the more the living dreams of Ogawa's explorations become our living dreams, too.

The misty cover picture is of two black-silhouetted umbrella-holding women walking down a Guatemala village road, dark buildings framing them from the sides. The photo wraps around the whole book, and gives it its essential tone: dark, muted, somber, all in thick blacks that would've printed beautifully in gravure in its heyday more than half a century back. That's another very intriguing thing about "The Dreaming." Though Ogawa also has allusions in his work, a few hat tips to Daido and Fukase, the greatest debt seems to be to earlier masters of Japanese photography, in particular Ken Domon and his street children, Yasuzo Nojima's stark yet painterly formalism, and Hamaya Hiroshi's *Snow Land* … as in, there are some soulful portraits of young kids and other foreign denizens, and an awful lot of very snowy shots, images almost erased by flutters of flakes or blankets of white; again, all more a dream than an actual landscape.

This reference to far earlier photographers is something striking in a contemporary photobook. Rarely do you find photos that could have been taken before the mid-twentieth century, but it makes sense. If Bob Dylan over the recent decades can be inspired by the music on the radio before rock and roll, why not be a photographer reaching back to the past of snow-blurred landscapes and almost anthropological portraits of moody urchins in India, Guatemalan musicians in native dress, a streetside food market in Myanmar. Still, it is striking, like opening up the hot new photobook only to find Edward Steichen all over it.

The great news: Ogawa pulls it off. There's nothing old-fashioned about *The Dreaming* because, well, it's more about dreaming than anything historical. As with Murakami, Ogawa has rendered a strong personal and poetic vision. The portraits are all rich and telling, especially a Tibetan woman on pilgrimage, a Japanese woman on a train seat, and most of all an old Tibetan man, head tilted back, eyes closed, well-lined face redolent of all of history ... indeed, this distant soul could easily be spinning the whole book through his dreams even as he's at its center.

Some amazing trips Ogawa took over his twenty-seven years of taking pictures around the world. *The Dreaming* is a bit like Ed van der Elsken's *Sweet Life*, with just as strong photos and yet an even more otherworldly vision underlying the book's flow. An instant classic.

※ ※ ※ ※ ※

A COUPLE MORE THINGS.
With Murakami's subtle invocation of his forebears in *Subway Diary*, I started thinking of Koji Onaka's recent *Memories of Younger Days in Shinjuku*. The black-and-white book is basically a lot of crowds, dilapidated buildings pre-modernization, and guys hanging out gabbing. The guys, though, are Daido and CAMP and those circles; and the book is an evocative historical portrait of a lost time. It might not carry quite the power of seeing the Beatles walking down the Pan Am stairs at JFK airport, or shots of them pillow fighting in their Plaza hotel room while "I Want to Hold Your Hand" rips up America, but the shots in "Memories" are close to that magic moment when Daido changed his small part of the world forever. A fine keepsake of a stirring time and place.

※ ※ ※ ※ ※

AND FINALLY A quick apology, sort of. In my last review, of *We Have No Place to Be*, by Joji Hashiguchi, set in punk rock days, I referred to "today's youth, who seem to think dyeing their hair in a first-flash-of-color-in–'The Wizard of Oz' palette to help them get Instagram or TikTok hits is their highest calling."

A lot has happened since then. The worldwide pandemic,

then the eruptions of demonstrations for George Floyd and racial change in the U.S. and all around the globe. They show little sign of dissipating. Soon I believe we'll see the current youth as potent a political force as the '60s generation, quite possibly more so.

May we all carry on the good work.

A Plenitude of Novels:
Stephen Shore's *Transparencies: Small Camera Works 1971–1979*, Part 1

September 2020

IN THE 2017 BOOK *Stephen Shore: Selected Works, 1973-1981*, put out right before Shore's last grand solo MoMA show, the photographer Paul Graham writes, "When writing about photography, a constant temptation is to weave a theme from the images, to hitch them together like clanking boxcars tethered to some conceit, to suit ourselves, to suit the mood of the times, to suit the author's whims. Yet, though there are a thousand novels [in Shore's images], let us not do that, for all narratives are vulgar falsehoods in the end…. The still photograph on its own allows none of that. It is mute. It is multitude. You or I may see completely different worlds contained within. Its strength is precisely this."

Yeah, well, maybe. But for "vulgar falsehoods," how about *Don Quixote* and every novel that came after it? And how about the inescapable imaginations we bring to all kinds of works of art?

Now I'm kind of for not reading too much into photographs, though I'm also all for writing about photobooks—looking at how they work, what makes certain books great and meaningful. And Graham's perhaps too hasty dismissal of meaning in photographs (this by a photographer best known for creating small, elliptical narratives in his own books) does lead to an intriguing thought: The best photobooks actually are comprised of shots that easily turn into a plethora of stories, little novels on every page.

And in the best of Stephen Shore's work, a group to which we can add his most recent book, Mack's *Transparencies: Small Camera Works 1971–1979*, little novels abound. Along with so much more

Still, let's not discount Graham too quickly. I'm actually

happy to not tell you the novel that springs to mind from, say, this Shore photograph in *Uncommon Places*, the classic of large-format photography of which *Transparencies* is the 35mm Leica shots from the same trips. It's a shot of a room in the Sun 'n Sand Motel in Holbrook, Arizona, in August 1973, the almost perfectly made bed, the moody yellow-green light, the empty midcentury modern headboard (oh, not wholly empty: there's a Gideon Bible on a wood slat, and two desk lamps craning down), and most telling of all, the crookedly-hung cheap painting of a river below mountains ... and I won't even begin to speculate upon the denizens of this room, what they ate, drank, thought, who they combined with and what joy or miserableness they brought into the room, and probably left with same ... no, I am happy, as I am with all of Shore's *Uncommon Places* shots, and now this wondrous addition of wider-aspect and lower-res photos in *Transparencies*, to not read too much into them.

As in, I'm happy to enjoy the magic, no, the miracle of how Shore created such perfect shots, with so much emotion and simple order, with seemingly so little effort ... how all that driving around America in gas guzzlers, taking photos of other gas guzzlers, back in the 1970s became manifest in such a strong series of photos ... a series that, as *Transparencies* now proves, appears nearly inexhaustible.

Yet my imagination keeps working. So here's the deal. You should get a copy of *Transparencies* and look deep into these casual photos yourself and see what happens, enjoying the aesthetic pleasure, that special tingle of a perfectly (yet unexpectedly) framed photograph. I admit, not every photo in the book gives rise to its own short story, though many are rich and ripe enough to spur one's imagination. Let me describe a few of the photos as clearly and unembellished as I can, then see if you might create a short story or little novel around them; or at least, pace Graham, have to actively resist the impulse.

Shore has always been a master of color composition, and that's the case throughout *Transparencies*. On page 29 we find a shot of a small outdoor house with a gray shingle roof, a fake red chimney, white clapboard, green trim, a flock of daisies taller than the house, and in the door and the window pale-faced blonde dolls. What? There's another building next to it, its gray roof and weather vane above a cupola positioned exactly right in relation to our doll house. And again, the doll house has to be four feet tall at least, and it's stocked with the two dolls. Just staring out there at us in full Gothic glory ... wait, is William Faulkner clacking away on his Remington typewriter to shape this shot?

Further along, page 111, the photo is almost fully filled with a red-burgundy car hood, and in its center is a foot-high plastic-model wedding canopy with a plastic bride and groom in it. Arrayed behind this is a row of carnations, and before it longer green carnation stalks with the flowers cropped from the photo. The wedding centerpiece is held down by Scotch tape, and reflected in the car's hood ... and that's it. Look at it a long while, then close your eyes. Can't you just see the bride's dress, her bouffant hairdo, the groom with slicked-back red hair and a sunburn, stuffed into a rented three-piece suit. They're both pretty nervous. Their relatives are whooping it up. And then they have to awkwardly drive off in a car with all this wedding regalia on their front hood.

I'm not going on about this because I believe Shore himself is after a novel in every photo. Far from it. I'm doing so because that's one way photographs can work. (Look at Graham's quote above, even he admits "there are a thousand novels in" Shore's photos.) But that's part of what makes them great. All photos by definition lock down one moment in time, but in the greatest photos it's the right moment, redolent with meaning, implying a whole series of moments; and if those moments hold together, you have ... a story. Likewise, if you get a tiny sliver of a picture, but it's the right shard, as with the cover photo of a tan and brown-filigreed cowboy boot in a shaft of light at a booth in a diner, the muted stainless steel stool and the gentleman's slit-back-pocket blue polyester pants vivid, a blur of the diner window and two other customers reflected in the next stool over ... well, just this little piece of the whole picture and you can easily see the daily specials on the wall; Flo, the waitress, pouring a cup of coffee; the local paper open on the counter; and the breakfast sitting before him. (I'm betting breakfast, just as in

Shore's timeless image of pancakes, cantaloupe, milk, and water glass that appears in *Uncommon Places*, as well as on a T-shirt I bought a few years back from Uniqlo.)

Just that one little flash of boot.

One aspect I find remarkable with *Transparencies* is that, as I said before, these are the 35mm shots taken when he was doing the large-format work for *Uncommon Places*. (More on this in Part Two of my piece on *Transparencies*.) I'm the first to admit I'm not a camera geek, but apart from some quick shots probably taken from a car window early on in the book, I don't see all that much difference in the quality of the shooting here in *Transparencies*. (Though on the printed page the greater detail of the original *Uncommon Places* is spectacular.) The deal is, a large-format camera is soooo deliberate, a handheld Leica something you can just fling around. But as always, it's the eye that counts, and Shore's eye in these photos is at the top of his game.

One of my favorite photos ever is Shore's *Uncommon Places* shot of the corner of Beverly and La Brea in L.A., the one with the looming Chevron/Standard sign. I once had the chance to ask Shore how he took that picture, meaning specifically what his day was like. He said he was up early and at the corner, and that he spent a long time—as long as needed—moving the camera an inch here, an inch there until everything was framed perfectly. He even had a checklist he ran through, to make sure he'd considered every aspect of the photo; that he was being that deliberate.

Then, finally ... snap.

And it is a perfect picture. The longer you look at it, the more perfect it becomes. Nothing falls out, nothing seems extraneous, every rectangular sign fits the others in just the right way, and yet ... it's just a street corner in Los Angeles in 1975.

Same with most of the shots in *Transparencies*. There's a street scene in San Francisco looking down Columbus Avenue, the recently erected Transamerica Pyramid to the left, a yellow sign jutting out from a building to the right that reads HOUSE OF ECSTASY. As with the Beverly–La Brea shot, every car, building, sign, even the orange Union 76 ball in the distance is just where it should be.

Which to me makes *Transparencies* as strong and important a photobook as *Uncommon Places*.

And it doesn't get better than that.

Getting Your Kicks on Route 66: Stephen Shore's *Transparencies: Small Camera Works 1971-1979*, Part 2

September 2020

As I was planning out this second piece on Stephen Shore's new Mack book, *Transparencies*, I started thinking about the road trips that created the book, and, hmmn, decided I could call my piece "Getting Your Kicks on Route 66," after the Bobby Troup song from 1946, first made a hit by Nat King Cole, before it jumped into various generations of rock and roll, from Chuck Berry to the Stones to Depeche Mode. I worried, though, that tying the song in with Shore might be a stretch since his first road run was from NYC down to Texas, didn't seem to run anywhere near that route ... until I found a piece on Shore's website called "The Road Trip," in which he exalts the song's "magical litany of place names: 'Now you go thru St. Looey; Joplin, Missouri and Oklahoma City is oh so pretty. You'll see Amarillo; Gallup, New Mexico; Flagstaff, Arizona; don't forget Winona, Kingman, Barstow, San Bernadino.' " (Turns out that Shore himself, after my piece ran, let me know that in 1972 he drove from Winslow, Arizona, to Chicago along the actual Route 66. My guess he had Robert Frank's roadside shrouded-body car accident photo in mind.)

I go on about the song, and Shore's inspiration from it, because as I'm writing about the books from his 1970s' road trips, *Uncommon Places*, *American Surfaces*, and now *Transparencies*, I'm newly fascinated by those years as, well, road trips. In *The Road Trip* Shore writes about other inspiring road trips, including Kerouac's *On the Road*, Frank's *The Americans*, even the great Preston Sturges film *Sullivan's Travels*. Clearly all these landmark cultural moments, and more, were in Shore's head as he took off across the nation with numerous camera arrangements in that decade of wide-flare striped jeans, skin-tight polyester shirts, and faux-leather everything. He wasn't just out to take pictures (and change photography forever), he was coursing a great American theme, the epic journey, going back at least to Huck Finn on his raft or Ahab after his white whale.

As a novelist, I'm always interested in the day-to-day, how things happen, the before and afters, the minute details, the commonplace touches, the little triumphs and indignities we all go through ... simply, the lives we actually live. Road trips aren't simply sailing down Route 66, a rockin' song on the radio, a comely blonde on the seat next to you, storm clouds brewing over Tyler, Texas, in the most dramatic way. Nope, it's also worrying about running out of gas, digging up a few bucks somewhere to get something into the tank, all the coffee stops, pee breaks, hunting for an affordable motel (or pulling off the side of the road to crash), endless miles behind an exhaust-bellowing semi, getting dumbfoundingly lost (then with luck, wondrously lost), puzzling out maps, feeling a fool, feeling on top of the world, feeling a chump, feeling exalted.

To Shore's enduring credit he took the minute-to-minute dailyness of his road trip life seriously, setting out to photograph, as he puts it, "every meal I ate, every person I met, every bed I slept in, every toilet I used, every town I drove through." Which he did. The book that resulted from his first road trip, in 1972, *American Surfaces*, I've always found a little too random, unkempt, scattered, with little of the magical symmetry and glow of photos from his later trips that decade.

Still, the 1972 photos Shore took changed photography forever, destroying any contemporary expectations of formalism and high seriousness (Irving Penn), glossy-magazine fashionistaness (Richard Avedon), Family of Man bombast, even that search for *le moment parfait* (Cartier-Bresson). *American Surfaces* was as demotic as Atget's Paris, William Klein's *New York* and Frank's *Americans* (not to mention Shore's teenage mentor, Andy Warhol), but without any visible nod to what at the time was considered serious art. Indeed, Shore really did shoot everything, and well enough, though for me that only goes so far. As an ax into the establishment, I love the gesture, but I find *American Surfaces* a little too lacking in thoughtful and considered, well ... art.

Turns out Shore felt that way, too. When he went back to the road, he took a 4 x 5 camera, then later in the decade an 8 x 10. The photos would build off the random corners and happenstances of the first road trip, but they'd be far more thoughtful and worked out. That's what the larger-film cameras forced him to do, take every shot with da Vinci–like seriousness, and boy did he do it well in *Uncommon Places*, where the attention to light and detail with the huge "pixel" range of the 8 x 10 view camera gives an artistic magnificence to the often banal scenes he chose to shoot. The new book, *Transparencies*, offers the 35mm Leica photos he took on those road trips when not wielding the 8 x 10.

In a postscript to *Transparencies*, by Britt Salveson, while discussing the differences between the smaller frame 35mm slides and the large format work, she drops in the casually perfect sentence: "[Shore] is recognizably the same person in both languages."

Indeed. He's also the same guy who worried about running out of gas on the road, and where to sleep, and whether to have pancakes—again?; well, why not—for breakfast. He's the guy who, as we find out in detail in a piece in the book *Stephen Shore* by Christy Lange, on July 7, 1973, checked into a Holiday Inn in Gaylord, Michigan, ate a plate of roast beef and smorgasbord at the Sugar Bowl restaurant, and "out of habit, he photographed his surroundings." The resulting picture, from *Uncommon Places*, is uncommonly lovely, an early-evening light spread over Formica tabletops and vinyl banquettes. Later that evening, we learn, he watched *The Mary Tyler Moore Show*. (Can you imagine ever knowing what Robert Frank watched on TV after shooting the New Orleans trolley car? Maybe if it was a Monday, *The George Burns and Gracie Allen Show*, or if Sunday, the appointment-TV lineup of *Ed Sullivan*, *GE Theater*, then at 10 *Alfred Hitchcock Presents*.)

What am I getting at here? That at the least Shore is a complex, innovative, and wide-ranging artist. He's as preoccupied by ways of seeing as he is by what he sees, and the life that leads up to all that seeing. On these later trips Shore evidently was particularly interested in the differences in the distinct ways of seeing between his various film formats. *Transparencies* reflects this, a wider 35mm frame than the large-format squarer frames, a lot quicker on the draw. Perhaps that's what he was thinking about during the commercials in-between the antics of Mary, Rhoda, Ted Baxter, et al.

Which means that for all of his common, everyday life Shore is willing (if not driven) to share with us, he's always Stephen Shore the artist, with one strong and unique artistic vision, "recognizably the same person in both languages." While he's the man tooling down the road shooting everything, he's also an artist of near Italian Renaissance purpose and design.

No matter what they're shooting—in Shore's case, bad paintings in a store window, a pile of broken bricks (two shots in *Transparencies*)—artists must always aim as high as possible; and yet also never forget, even the most "important" ones, that they're most of the time regular people ... or at least they should be. Especially photographers, who always have to make their art in the here and now, wherever they are. They can approach their work with ideas and concepts and even high-art theory rattling around in their heads, but when it comes time to snap the shot, they're in a moment, and they have to give the moment all they have. It would be interesting to ask Shore how many shots were ruined because he couldn't get last night's sitcom out of his head. Or maybe he couldn't quite decide which camera to use that day. Or the grill cook burned the pancakes.

The miracle, of course, is that in finding true art in the most common of photos, Shore made so much great work; and that *Transparencies*, for its differences of detail and color, is still a most valuable and essential addition to *Uncommon Places*, in all its iterations.

As much as the new book moves me, in a way I'm most touched by Shore's own short postscript, in which, before he thanks his publisher, Michael Mack, and others who brought *Transparencies* to fruition, he writes simply, "I met my wife, Ginger, in the middle of the years covered by this body of work. We've now been married for forty years. Our relationship has been the most significant one of my life."

That's why, as Rod Stewart put it, every picture tells a story, as does every photobook. It's the story of the photos, of course, but also implicit within the book is the story behind the making the book. Shore takes us far closer than almost anyone else to this hidden story, letting us know the meals eaten, the street corners he parked on, the weddings he stumbled upon, the cowboy sitting next to him at lunch … and so much more.

It's not really a wild ride for him, this kicks-getting on Route 66, but it's a complete one, of the low and the high, of endlessly interesting and inventive photographs, and, inarguably, of boundless significance to the world of photography; and now it turns out, even greater significance to Shore and his own life.

News That Stays News: Gordon Parks, *The Atmosphere of Crime*, 1957

November 2020

I'M ALWAYS INTRIGUED BY how a timeless photobook comes together. Most often it's the artist setting out to create a book following their personal vision, and after a lot of work—and perhaps many hours on press—accomplishing that. But sometimes great photobooks come from just a bunch of photos lying around, then edited down to the right shots and put in the right order by someone else, and it works. A prime example is William Eggleston's *Guide*, in effect created as a book by John Szarkowski. Not so successful is Garry Winogrand with his stand-alone photobooks such as *Animals* and *Women Are Beautiful*. His real strength as a photographer was not in somebody's discreet selection of some of his subjects into a book but the whole crazy spread of his genius across all manner of subjects and forms. It's a question of how advertent a photographer is, how much she or he intended their photos to become a book.

Then there are the very rare books that hold together perfectly with no input from the photographer at all because they have passed. A classic is of course *Diane Arbus: An Aperture Monograph*. Her vision was so vivid, personal, and definitive that that simple collection of her photos makes as strong a book statement as can be.

A photographer in many ways connected to Arbus (similar dates of working, connection to big-time national magazines, unique qualities of subject and vision) is Gordon Parks. There are approximately a dozen books of his photos (some with his poetry), but most are collections. In his own time he was too busy working to put out artistic books, which led the way for Steidl in 2012 to publish a five-volume set of his *Collected Works*.

Now Steidl has followed that up with a new book that holds together as tight as any classic photobook, with no input from Parks other than that he was on assignment for *Life* magazine six decades back and took lots of shots, some of which ran in the magazine.

The result is *The Atmosphere of Crime, 1957*, and it's spectacular. The photos themselves are not only unsung landmarks in color photography—we're two decades short of Eggleston's purported invention of serious color shooting—but they also tell a photographic story far richer than anyone would expect from a national magazine even at the top of its game, as Life was throughout the mid-century.

What do we see? The cover photo, a Black man's left hand extended wrist-length through gray jail bars, an ash-rich cigarette held loosely between his fingers, all before a depressing yellow and green jail wall, lightly crisscrossed by shadows of further bars ... the hand and its smoke that perfect detail that implies the whole, the harsh tedium and sadness of incarceration. On to the first of the book's plates, the dark silhouette of an on-duty cop shot from behind before a rich cobalt blue evening sky, all in the middle of Times Square. A quiet, majestic shot ... and no, that word didn't pop into my head because one of the theater marquees is for the Majestic theater.

Then we get really arty. Three photos of another silhouette of a man, in the left front seat of a car, probably a policeman, eating an apple, all before the colorful wash of streetlights through the windshield. It could be a Daido Moriyama photo in its angle of focus and general blur, yet these shots were in the national American magazine, with tens of millions of readers across the land.

It's to the *Life* editors' credit that, though they no doubt sent Parks out to do a documentary feature on crime, which he handles with masterful skill, they also ran photos of such strikingly virtuosic color use. (Though norms of the day made *Life* not run Parks's shots of dead men, nor three powerful sequenced photos of a man shooting up.)

Still, the crime photos are certainly there, and they're as dramatic as can be. The most intense is two suited detectives, one with his pistol pulled, kicking down a door off a narrow tenement hallway. The furious grimace on the closest detective's face speaks to the fury and heedlessness of police going about their business. Then comes more moody, half-blurred silhouetted shots, one with a man in a Panama hat with his hands held high in surrender, another holding a drooping gun before an orange glow. There have been countless reporter ride-alongs with police over the decades, and of course the flash-bright bloody sidewalks of Weegee, but I've never seen, nor could have imagined, a documentary series as hauntingly beautiful and striking as what Gordon Parks shot, and Steidl has put together for us here.

Indeed, *The Atmosphere of Crime* is a kind of textbook on how to shoot a documentary subject. There are basics such as fill the frame with a telling detail rather than show too much (that cover shot), and try to capture intense action, those cops kicking in the door, but also don't be afraid to be quiet and still (two cops on a cigarette break, talking to a handcuffed man). You gotta cover the waterfront, as they say, and Parks does it, with photos of arrests, bookings, prisoners leaving a paddy wagon, a body slid out of a drawer in a morgue, and then the book's final two photos, flocks of men lining the narrow catwalks outside their San Quentin prison cells, and a moody beautiful yet chilling shot of Alcatraz Island, when it held the notorious prison in the middle of the San Francisco Bay. Parks's book is not just the atmosphere of crime, it's as deep a dive as could be taken into that world.

Yet it's so much more. The key is to be an artist, always an artist, letting your own vision move the photos, rather than simply showing what's in front of you. So with most of the photos I've described above we get Parks's strengths with shadow and light, color and form, clarity and that always evocative Provoke-like blur, here a decade before anybody in Japan put it all together.

It's Parks's artistry in every shot, as well as his fearlessness and denial of any kind of conventional shooting, that makes *The Atmosphere of Crime* a towering example of Ezra Pound's definition of literature: "News that stays news."

That said, the book is unusually timely today, especially with the protests and debates in America over racial justice, and preponderance of people of color in our prisons; and now movements to let many of those souls, convicted of no more than selling cheap drugs, out. In more than one way, the atmosphere of crime, as Parks's book has it, is the atmosphere everyone in America, from the top down, breathes every day.

So props again for Steidl for bringing this important photobook out in 2020.

Interesting, too, is how they've done it. As someone who waits eagerly for, then snaps up the deluxe versions of classic rock LPs put out fifty years after the fact, such as what Giles Martin has done with the Beatles' *Sgt. Pepper*, *White Album*, and *Abbey Road*, I can appreciate the whole package here. Besides the grand extent of Parks's photos for this *Life* magazine assignment, this great photobook on its own, we get numerous useful essays, and—best of all—the actual pages from the September 9, 1957 issue of *Life* that ran the article, then titled "Crime in the U.S." There's the *West Side Story*–redolent illustrated cover (one gang member wearing a SHARKS jacket), and the full story as it appeared in the magazine, from pages 88 to 111. These pages include even the ads from the time, including ones for Gleem toothpaste, Fruit of the Loom socks, and (my favorite), a full page introducing the Edsel automobile from Ford Motor Company (wonder how that'll work out, eh?).

As a model of how to resurrect the past, yet be as current as this morning's Twitter storm … as history, as a primer on the documentary photo essay, and most of all simply as a photobook of exceptional beauty, drama, and power … Gordon Parks's *The Atmosphere of Crime* is essential.

Shelter from the Storm:
Jesse Lenz, *the locusts*

November 2020

IN A WAY I'm surprised there haven't been more recent photobooks about America falling apart. Sure, we skated the first three years of the Trump administration with little manifestly amiss but timeless national ills and (relatively entertaining) madness in the air, but since spring when the Corona virus hit, we've had one plague or disturbance after another, the pandemic, vivid police homicides and racial protests, the chaos of the presidential campaign, as well as all the daily national traumas of a president who, as he told journalist Bob Woodward, who used the phrase to title his most recent book, "I do bring rage out. I always have."

Of course things have to happen before they can turn up in photobooks. And also it's not the first job of serious photobook artists to tell us the news, though when they capture a historical moment or mood in an original way, that can be quite powerful, witness the late photographer Paul Fusco's *RFK Funeral Train*. Still, events as momentous as those we're all living through should no doubt inspire equally towering photobooks.

Which makes those books' alternatives, antidotes to the lunacy, disruption, and rage all the more important. To the ranks of books of quiet certitude and timeless succor add "the locusts" by Jesse Lenz, put out by his own Charcoal Press. This is a book of, as the promotional info puts it, a home in "rural Ohio where his children run wild in the fields, build forts in the attic, and fall asleep surrounded by lightsabers and superheroes."

Home, children, dreams of superheroes, all middle-America basics ... yes, the beautifully printed black-and-white photos in "the locusts" provide both an anchor in how things should be and an escape from how in the wider world they are.

"the locusts" is in a tradition following Lenz's mentor Emmet Gowin, who back in the 1970s pretty much invented the photobook capturing the rich, intimate world of one's home and family. "the locusts," with its many shots of Lenz's own children gamboling about the countryside, is also a direct descendant of Sally Mann's powerful family photos in books such as *Immediate Family* and *Still Time*, in which she conjures up the full, even more complex world of her family on their country land in Virginia. (Noteworthy: None of the children in *the locusts* are nude, as some were in Gowin's '70s photographs, and many more were in Mann's *Immediate Family*, which caused Mann no end of troubles, which she wrote about in her lovely 2015 memoir *Hold Still*.)

Lenz on his website describes his book well: "*The Locusts* is a project about the microcosmic worlds of plants, insects, animals, and children, searching for grace and healing within the brokenness and imperfection of life." The book is also a vision of home, and raising children on a farm, and the passing seasons, and life and death right out the front door. Indeed, there are a few shots redolent of birth, including the placenta from the home birth of Lenz's daughter and the first Morel mushroom of the spring sprouting, not to mention a strong shot of a bird's nest built atop an outdoor light, with three wide-open baby beaks poking out above the straw. (Note to Jesse Lenz: We had a bird's nest above an outdoor flood light at our country place that caught on fire and almost burned the whole house down.) Another shot with babies is more disturbing, a bristly furred possum dead on the side of a road, its tiny breathless fetuses strewn about. Life and death always present out there on the land, with this possum shot followed four later by the baby birds, and four after that by a skew of bones, the spine and limbs of a long-dead raccoon.

There are many shots of play, Lenz's children inventing games on the open fields, and in one case burrowing into a snow cave with a basketball hoop visible over the flood of white. Another has a cat focusing in on a tiny field mouse, ready to pounce. And in a notably strong shot, one of the boys holds a dead screech owl by its wide wings in front of his two plies of cotton shirt, apparently not quite sure what to do with it.

There are many other impressive photos in their own right, a sleeping dog on a bare field, a boy looking away; rows of corn husks on a snowy field, capturing a whiff of Van Gogh; two water-filled canning jars, one with a polliwog swimming in it, the other with a child's hand blurred fully behind the glass; a boy burrowed into that homemade fort beneath a wall of large boxes; that same boy looking startled amidst the branches of an apple tree. But for the most part *the locusts* is a photobook whose meaning and power come from the accumulation of photos in the book, of the daily lives lived, and our journey through them. (A journey that, each time I take it, I feel extends a little too long; the book's powerful hold on me wanes ten or so photos before the end.)

To the book's credit it's not sentimental in the least, about growing up, nature, or anything else. Neither is it harsh or troubled or overtly emotional much at all. Simply, here are some of the things that happened, a boy playing with chalk, a girl waiting bemusedly at a front door, a pumpkin in the foreground; here are some of the fauna around the land, a chicken, a dark flock of starlings in the sky, a small raccoon climbing a spindly tree. As far as drama goes, well, there's one of the boys, shirtless (which suggests he's at home), getting his mouth worked on by a set of dental picks.

Which makes *the locusts* the quiet book we need now. There's not too much fun, not much grief, a lot of normalness. And it all works because throughout our read of the book we always sense, in the faintest of ways, our troubled, chaotic, collapsing America just beyond its domestic boundaries.

I do have one question, though. The title, *the locusts*, confuses me. Locusts suggest many things, including Biblical plagues, as well as one of my favorite novels, Nathanael West's "The Day of the Locust," in which a Hollywood screenwriter goes mad amidst a mob of deranged people, and ends up howling along with the siren of the ambulance he's inside of as the book ends; and also a not that well-known Bob Dylan song called "Day of the Locusts," whose chorus line is: "The locusts sang, and they was singing for me." (I've picked this review's title, of course, from a far better known Dylan song.)

That's the thing, locusts really don't conjure up home, family, a safe place; more like madness, terror, and dark swarms (not of starlings) out there waiting to get you.

None of which I see in Lenz's book. Again, *the locusts* is in no way a sentimental vision of a home, but neither is it dark and disturbed, at least any more than any daily life has moments of uplift and moments of boredom and of course daily chores that have to be done.

Which leads to the question of whether there's an undertone to the book that I'm missing. I don't think so. There is a great beauty and simplicity in the accumulation of Lenz's photos—what you want from any important photobook—but not necessarily a larger vision other than the one that, as the book's epigraph on the final page, from the American poet and theologian Frederick Buechner, says: "Here is the world / Beautiful and terrible things will happen / Don't be afraid."

Maybe that's what Lenz at bottom is up to: Showing us the world. And telling us to be not too afraid.

In this time of fleeting beauty and looming terror, maybe that's enough.

So Long Photography, Hello East Orange: A Reissue of Daido Moriyama's *Bye Bye Photography*

February 2021

IN HIS NINTH DECADE, at age 82, Daido Moriyama keeps on trucking. If anything, he seems busier than ever. Working with his gallerist and publisher, Akio Nagasawa, in this last pandemic year he's put out *Record No. 45*; released the eighth of his series of older photos grouped by subject or theme and placed between luscious covers of silk-screened photos; and according to Simon Baker, curator of the Maison Européenne de la Photographie, Daido and Nagasawa designed every inch of an ongoing show, devoted to both Daido and his brilliant mentor Takuma Nakahira, at the celebrated photography center in Paris.

Oh, and as Baker recently said in a webinar about the show, when he last met Daido a couple years back, for all his illustrious reputation, all Daido really wants to do each day is go out and take photos. *Snap, snap, snap.*

Along with all the above busyness, this year Akio Nagasawa has published a new version of Daido's masterpiece, *Bye Bye Photography*, which for the first time has presented the extant photos from the original 1972 book not divided by the gutter mid-page but laterally so you can easily see the whole photo as it was shot.

Recently I bought copies of *Record No. 45*, one of the latest in the silk-screen books, *Kanban*, as well as this new *Bye Bye Photography*. With these three works sitting next to me, it's a good time to look again at Daido Moriyama.

For photographers who can't stay home, well, they take a lot of pictures, and it's always a question of how to get those shots out to the public. The best way, as Daido has found (and more recently the American photographer Matt Eich) is to surround your major book releases with an ongoing series of work put out as it gets finished. Daido's *Records* go back to the summer of 1972, the same year as *Bye Bye Photography*, and from the beginning have recorded his wanderings. The first edition is only 16 pages, including the covers, and is very much in the spirit of his most Provoke-like photos, rough, blurry, out of focus, as the refrain goes. Ditto the next four *Records*, released as a Reprint Edition in 2008, and well worth owning. They fulfilled Daido's idea of "a small, self-published personal photo journal." As he further explains, "Without any ties to work or any fixed topic, I just wanted to continue publishing a 16-page booklet with an arbitrary selection of favorite photos among the pictures I snapped from day to day. By nature, it was directed first and foremost to myself rather than other people. I wanted a simple, basic title, so I called it *Kiroku (Record)*."

The *Records* resumed in 2006 with No. 6, and the style of that and all the subsequent *Records* reflect what Daido was up to at the time. Those "favorite photos" from day to day. From No. 6 to the present the shots have been far less Provoke-like and much more representative of the world his eye sees. Some have been in color, though most are black and white in that high-contrast style he deploys so well.

The latest, *No. 45*, holds a special place in the whole series. As Daido explains, "Around the middle of the year [2020], I got slightly ill, and eventually spent some time in hospital, after which I got to stay at my home in Zushi. Except for some business and a rehabilitation program that I did in Tokyo, I spent most of the days that followed walking in the streets and taking the occasional snapshot in the Shonan area.

"But there's one particular thing about Zushi/Shonan. It is for me a location that necessarily reminds me of Takuma Nakahira. Now that I was staying in Zushi for the first time in years, quite naturally there were various opportunities for me to reminisce about my days with Nakahira, which is already more than 50 years ago."

At the same time Daido was reading a book of Nakahira's reviews, and so spent his evenings silently debating his departed dear friend, then heading out to the streets to take photos to continue that dialogue. *Record No. 45* is all-Daido, mannequins,

The Mysteries of Light 277

a strange clown face projected on a store window, the stark angles of a parking garage, and it's also very 2020 with people in masks and girls lost to their iPhones. There are also snaps with the spirit of Nakahira's masterpiece, *For a Language to Come*: a blur here, a patterned wall there. The volume is fully Daido's, but especially intriguing since it's also this communion with his self-stated mentor.

By my best calculation, the series of books issued with those great silk-screen covers began in 2013 with a two-version reprint of Daido's *Another Country in New York*, the work that he famously custom-made in a copy shop back in 1974. The series really took off with *Pantomime* in 2017, and is now up to number eight, *Tiles in Aizuwakamatsu*. I have a number of these themed works; indeed, during my trip to Tokyo in 2019 I went to the Akio Nagasawa gallery in the Ginza district, which was wall-papered with giant Daido lips photos, and so of course I bought *Lips*. There's also *Plastic Love*, devoted to his mannequin shots, *Tights in Shimotakaido*, full of photos of women's legs in tights. I haven't yet sprung for *Tiles in Aizuwakamatsu* because, well, it's nothing but shots of tiles, but I did get *Kanban*, filled with black-and-white and a few color photos of signage around the world.

Kanban is classic Daido, every poster-festooned wall or street-level assemblage of signage fascinating. The book itself is a joy to read, not only all the great photos but every few sheets in, the page folds back to uncover a double-sized spread. These are dense photos, collage-like with their abundance of street signs and photos on billboards, yet mysterious, too. (They remind me of Robert Rauschenberg at his strongest.) No photographer fills a frame with better signs than Daido, from giant heavily-lipped models glowing along the street, to a stern-looking Steve McQueen on a well-ripped poster amidst of timeless sea of other well-ripped posters, to a red silhouette of a hands-on-hips woman next to a sign that reads RED HOT MAMA above a red-chartreuse locked door. Daido even sneaks in a self-portrait of himself shooting into a mirror next to a huge poster of Johnny Depp as the Mad Hatter in Tim Burton's *Alice in Wonderland*.

I also simply love the feel of the silk-screened covers, on roughly pebbled cloth, photos printed in rich blacks and whites.

Among their own intrinsic joys, the covers take me back to the fun I had at Aperture's 2011 Printing Show—TKY, in which everyone there compiled their own Daido book, which was then hand-stapled in a silk-screen cover by a swarm of minions, then signed by the master himself.

Which brings me to this reissue of *Bye Bye Photography*. The original book is arguably one of the most important photobooks in history, right up there with such epochal works as Robert Frank's *The Americans*, William Klein's *New York*, and Diane Arbus's Aperture Monograph. It's no exaggeration to say that photography jumped forward upon the book's publication, and as it became better known around the world truly changed things. The book is all the more fascinating because it's driven by Daido's desire to exhaust photography, to push the medium as far it could go.

I'm fortunate enough to own a first printing of the 1972 book. One of the reasons we love photobooks is that the best can have powerful force simply as objects. They're not just a collection of photos, the books themselves radiate the singular magic of art. I first learned this when I bought my first expensive photobook, Brassai's *Paris de Nuit*. The one from 1933 with black gravure ink so thick it's like it was laid on with a trowel. With bursts of light so intense it's as if the whole book is plugged into an electric current. The blacks as stark as the nights they chronicle, the whites glowing as if filament bulbs ripple through the paper. The original book captures truly mystical incarnations of photographs; further printings are just inert pictures.

I have the same feeling with the original *Bye Bye Photography*. It's a totemic presence; I open it with a sense of mystery, care, respect, even caution. Simply, this book has the power to change lives—indeed, it's changed mine. I was ready to shoot in a way inspired by Daido even before I discovered him, but afterward … well, I knew then that anything I printed on a sheet of paper was fine and dandy.

I just pulled the original off my shelves. It's an inch-thick heavy block of a book. Open it, and there's photo after photo of indistinct blur, flurries of images, strange movie stills, shots of Tri X Pan Film (not prints from a roll of the film, the actual film

The Mysteries of Light

itself, sprocket holes and all). There are photos messed-up in the camera, and there are photos nearly destroyed in the development and/or printing. I'd say roughly sixty-five percent of the photos have something recognizable in them, the rest are that purest essence of photography: nothing but an ever intriguing mix of light and dark.

It's also a tough book to read, the photos laid out in no discernible order, and the content as rich and complex and personal (and nearly unreadable) as Joyce's *Finnegan's Wake* or Ezra Pound's *Cantos*. O.K., maybe that's unfair. Maybe Daido's book is more like *Ulysses*, groundbreaking in style but exhilarating to read. Or maybe *Bye Bye Photography* is really a work of Beat literature. It's known that Daido has read Kerouac's *On the Road* over and over, and *Bye Bye Photography* is certainly a road book, a number of shots taken from cars or trains; and even when the photo is a close-up of a person's face, it's usually so distorted as to be simply a vision of that soul hurtling past.

There are bottomless wonders in *Bye Bye Photography*, and every time I look at the original I find my sense of photographic possibility expanding. One reason: None of the photos are very clear; indeed, they're hardly photos at all. Some could be anything, which means I can photograph anything, too.

Now we have this new edition. As I noted above, the new version lays out each photo laterally and fully, with a small white border around it (as opposed to the original's full-bleed shots stretched across two pages). This makes the photos feel more as if they're hanging on a gallery wall. The new book is also printed on thin and slightly glossy paper; the paper in the original is much thicker with far less shine. The photos in the new book are much crisper, too, which is interesting because for me it goes against the spirit of the original work. Finally, we're confined to those photos from still extant original negatives, as well as some others Daido discovered from that time period that didn't make their way into the original book.

All this makes the new version feel like a redux version of a great movie, as Francis Ford Coppola's been doing with *Apocalypse Now* and *Godfather III*, cutting them differently, throwing in scenes that didn't make the first theatrical releases (and arguably slow the film down). Those are different movies from the classic version, and the new *Bye Bye Photography* is a different book, for better or worse.

Of course good luck finding an original, or affording it. There have been numerous reprints, and for budgetary purposes the 2009–10 pocket book–sized editions of Daido's classic books published by Kodansha can get you a few steps closer to the original book experience. One of the selling points of the new Akio Nagasawa version is that there is no gutter cutting the photo in half. Interestingly, in the original the binding is such that each page opens fully and lies flat, thereby letting you see the whole photo. That's not the case for the latter reprints.

So the new version does serve a purpose. It also has one of those luscious silk-screen covers as with the handmade book series that includes *Kanban*"; and while I adore the silk-screen covers (and wish I could drape all my own photobooks in them), here in the case of *Bye Bye Photography* it takes away from the force of the book as an actual book. In a sense it's just another addition to Daido's ongoing series.

Which is fine. *Bye Bye Photography* is one of those few books I want to own multiple editions of, like *The Americans* and *Ravens*. Books so rich and essential that even the slightest variations of ink flow or cropping, as in the various copies of Robert Frank's masterpiece, are worth looking at and enjoying.

Like collecting different pressings of great LPs, which I've also been known to do. Which lets me segue into my title for this piece: "So Long Photography, Hello East Orange." That's a play on Bob Dylan's second recorded original song, "Talkin' New York," on his debut album back in 1961. The idea being that back then Dylan might've given up on New York City, but he didn't stay away for long, keeping on coming back till he created some of the greatest songs in his oeuvre. And that even if Daido meant it in 1974 that he was giving up photography, he never even began to stop.

I've always thought there are a lot of similarities between the two artists, their brilliant, coruscating imagery; their roots in Beat culture; their quasi-outlaw poses, but a new reason to tie them together is their longevity. They're both still crankin' out the work, Dylan with one of his greatest albums ever at the age of 79, *Rough and Rowdy Ways*, and Daido with his endless parade of books, including the new *Record* and the new silk-screen books at the age of 82, not to mention the masterwork of all-new color photos, *Pretty Woman*, from only four years back.

Blessed us, that Daido just keeps on going. That all he wants to do each day is go out and take new snaps.

The Endless Afternoon:
Mimi Plumb, *The White Sky*

April 2021

It's been well over forty years since I lived in California, but when I hear about 117-degree days last summer in the suburb of Woodland Hills, only miles from where I grew up, I think back to my own 100-degree-plus summer days, the sun a big ball of white in the sky, the heat pounding down so hard it was like it was creating walls you'd bounce off of, those summers little but boundless dizzying waves of light and heat ... yeah, I know where the title of Mimi Plumb's new photobook, *The White Sky*, comes from.

Plumb's previous book, *Landfall*, was full of pictures from the 1980s. In *The White Sky*, from Stanley/Barker, she rolls back a decade, to give us shots from the '70s. Important to note that this is not the current California that, with climate change, simply exists, as authorities say, to burn up. It's more a world of the ostensible California Dream, not the 2020 nightmare; though that decades-ago California was at least for teenagers hardly a paradise. What Plumb's book captures so well is what we called "the endless afternoon," those boring suburban days with nothing to do, a world around you so blank and empty that even grand imaginations could hardly begin to fill it.

Plumb grew up in the Bay Area, not the L.A. suburbs, and a few years after me, but the world of *The White Sky*, the parched hills and endless days of aimless teens hanging out, is one I recall well. Indeed, there's a guy driving a car in front of a big Standard gas station who, with his beard and plaid shirt, looks a lot like I did back then (though I don't remember ever going out with a girl with quite the beehive hairdo as the one that blooms on the date sitting next to the dude in the photo).

That Standard gas station, of course, is an inescapable California motif, from Ed Ruscha's paintings to Stephen Shore's famous shot from West L.A., and Plumb captures other essences of the Golden State, such as the broken-down Pontiac in the middle of a parched field, its left front tire flat, the driver's side door and trunk flung open. That tribute to car culture gone bad is printed on the front cover and is a fine introduction to Plumb's California, not the Beach Boys' sun, surf, and hot rods but the endless parched expanses and things that don't quite work.

What else is in her California? Well, those imaginations trying to lift into the nothingness, such as that of the young boy lying flat on a stark rock outcropping, his most-likely Evel Kneivel motorcycle toy leaping in his hand off the rock's edge. Or the photo right before it, a torn-up newspaper feature between pieces of McDonald's detritus, especially a foam Big Mac container no doubt helping in its small way to bring on global warming and those 117-degree days.

There are numerous photos of kids hanging out, in large clusters on a hillside watching a Motocross rider, and in a smaller bunch gathered for some reason on a bark- and rock-filled island in a Safeway parking lot, many gazing upward into who knows what. Toward the end of the book there are a few photos of swarms of trick-or-treating tikes parading under the hard sun, followed a few photos later by a teenager in shorts lying prone on clay-y land so parched it's broken into vivid chunks. That parched land is another motif of Plumb's book; earlier, right after the somewhat melodramatic title pages ("The" alone on a black page; a few photos, then "White" alone of a black page; a few more photos, then "Sky" alone on a ... well, you get the idea), there's a shot of just this broken-up land. And to make sure we get it, the final shot in the book is a wide unpaved dirt road lined with white concrete sidewalks, probably that of a subdivision coming along, but perhaps just a road to nowhere.

O.K., it's not all manifest bleakness. There is some reasonable life in Plumb's array of photos. Fairly early on we get seven most-likely family members squeezed into a toy choo-choo train about to head along the rails, and just before it a shot of two men in suits, of which all we see are their hands and the open Bible clutched by one of them. Right after that we're at a celebration, looking at two photos of Miss Bicentennial 1976, one of her smiling grandly, the second of her looking pensively right at the camera. Right before these two shots is one of the few photos in the book strong enough that I'd consider hanging it on my wall: a small boy with a large cone-shaped something (horn? traffic marker?) looming in the foreground as a parade float of four women in a boat passes behind, pulled by another of those huge, wide, white-wall-tired '70s cars.

All of the shots are evocative of Plumb's California emptiness, and many supply apt metaphors, especially the trike and empty wood TV box behind a house, and most of all the set of concrete stairs of a no-doubt burned-out building that lead to nowhere, but there aren't that many that say great photo. A few others that do: four boys playing amidst a mountain of discarded tires; a teenage boy in a sleeveless T-shirt gazing toward the camera; another strong portrait, this one of two teenage girls, one smoking and smiling provocatively, the other rising blurrily out of the frame, one leg of her jeans stenciled with the Zig-Zag cigarette papers guy.

Back when I was that teenage California kid I used to use Zig-Zag papers to roll joints, and who knows how stoned everybody (except Miss Bicentennial) in the book is. My guess, pretty damn blown out. That was certainly one way to confront the Endless Afternoon. (For the record, I realized a few years after my teens that I never really liked smoking pot, and haven't touched it since.) But back then there was a whole lot of nothingness, all capped by the beating-down sun, to swim through every day; and it's that aimless, pretty pointless existence that *The White Sky* captures so well.

And that's my small issue with the book. Though as a whole it definitely connotes its specific aimless California-in-the-'70s world, there are a number of photos that are just kind of there. That picture mentioned above of the cracked, parched ground ... it makes the point, but it's hardly an interesting photo. Another has a smiling kid on his bike, his white dog running alongside him. A couple more long-snouted dogs behind a thin chain fence. A couple kids dashing across a suburban street. Not even much of a point to any of them. Would the book be stronger edited down? Probably. But that's the thing with a book of photos from forty-five years ago, you're kind of stuck with the shots you took back then.

Fortunately Plumb took a lot of other shots that are both strong photographs and fit her book's theme well. A boy in glasses lying on his back blowing smoke in the air. A clutch of long hairs sitting on a concrete slab getting high with their dogs—looks like everybody's got a dog in *The White Sky*—with a row of three wooden crosses in the picture's foreground. The flank of a new subdivision home that has the stark elegance of a Lewis Baltz shot. A coyote, teeth bared, atop a picnic table. The backside of an elevated sign for 101 MOVIES in a now vacant lot, signifying what looks like the death of a drive-in theater. Another huge '70s auto upside down, its roof crushed.

Roofs crushed, imaginations beat down, spirits washed out under unforgiving skies. That's what I remember from my California youth, and why on the exact day of the American Bicentennial I spent my first full day in New York city, where I've lived ever since.

I spent that first day watching Tall Ships float down the Hudson, then the evening in Central Park, where Leonard Bernstein conducted the New York Philharmonic for everybody for free. I knew right then I didn't want to be anywhere else, and could never go back to California except for short visits.

According to her website, Plumb now lives in Berkeley, Calif., the home of my alma mater and a far cry from the empty suburbs of *The White Sky*. We've had some parlous decades since the burst of light and freedom of the 1960s, including those punked-out '80s, which Plumb, in her previous book, *Landfall*, captured so well, with much stronger photos than in her new book. But when it comes to penetrating and capturing a certain kind of American ennui and blankness, Plumb is a master. *The White Sky* is a worthy addition to her canon, even if it's not her most important work.

Which leaves me wholly curious what she could do with the past four benighted years in the U.S.

Vermeer Around the Corner: *Forever Saul Leiter* and Dorothea Lange's *Day Sleeper*

June 2021

WHAT A SAD AND JUBILANT career Saul Leiter had! From some success shooting fashion (and fashioning his own groundbreaking color shots) back in the 1950s and '60s, he went quiet as a photographer until 2008, when Steidl put out *Early Color*, in which we got one lovely, delicate, mysterious color shot after another. Every photo in the book was strong, and Leiter's reputation was made. He was suddenly celebrated widely, and in effect he became an overnight Old Master of the photobook.

I use the phrase Old Master purposefully, because more and more we should consider greats such as Robert Frank, Berenice Abbott, William Klein, Walker Evans, Diane Arbus, William Eggleston, Nan Goldin, Daido Moriyama as just that, Old Masters. (Ready to fill up the forthcoming photobook wings of the Met and British museums, yes?) And Leiter of course fits right in.

I also use the phrase because for nearly ten years after 2008 pretty much the only Leiter photos we knew were the ones in *Early Color*. Which made him in ways the Johannes Vermeer of photography, not simply for the way they both focused on the quality of light, and had their own singular palettes and delicacy of vision and touch, but also because there were so few known works by both artists. Certainly the chance of a new Vermeer turning up after 350 years is near impossible. Saul Leiter? Well, read on.

First, though, a personal turn. For most of his adult life Leiter lived on East 10th Street between 2nd and 3rd Avenues. During my first ten years in New York, I had a $90-a-month (not a typo) apartment on East 11th Street between 1st and 2nd Avenues, which meant that anytime I was out walking the neighborhood there was a good chance I might pass

The Mysteries of Light

Leiter. I was living the literary life back then, working at *The New Yorker* magazine and going to parties with the likes of John Updike, Norman Mailer, and Kurt Vonnegut, so I wouldn't have noticed Leiter even if I had run across him. I also wouldn't have known him because he was so far out of any mainstream eye. Just another middle-aged guy in the hood. I have no doubt I did walk past him, maybe even sat next to him, when he was hanging on his favorite bench in front of St. Marks Church (where in 1977 I saw Allen Ginsberg and Robert Lowell give a reading together; fancy that!).

Ah, the East Village in the 1970s and early '80s. You were in the center of a still breathtaking artistic ferment even as you prayed never to get mugged or robbed. The Ramones, Blondie, Talking Heads at CBGBs. Jean-Michel Basquiat and Keith Haring at the FUN Gallery on East 11th, just west of me. And there right in the middle of it was old Saul Leiter working away painting and photographing in his apartment without any particular recognition.

Who knew? Well, fortunately we all do now, and thanks to the great work of Margit Erbe and the Saul Leiter Foundation new works appear all the time. There have been black-and-white nudes, gouache paintings, and more and more photographs. I can't say there have been huge surprises—Leiter is an artist with his own powerful, focused, essential vision—yet each release widens the scope of his work, and furthers our understanding of how rich and complex his achievement is.

Perhaps no book does this as much as the recently released *Forever Saul Leiter*, put out by the Japanese Manga publisher Shokakukan to accompany exhibitions at the Bunkamura Museum of Art in Tokyo and the Kyoto Museum.

In a way the book is a counterpart to 2017's *All About Saul Leiter*, from Seigensha. Both books are the same size, with similar paper stock and type on their obis. And both books purport to cover a wide breadth of Leiter's output. But while the earlier book, in a way one more introduction to Leiter, repeated a lot of the eminently well-known shots, *Forever Saul Leiter* adds photo after photo we have never seen before, always broadening our understanding of his work, his ambition, his accomplishment.

(It also has a whole essay by Otake Akiko about, yep, living around the corner from Saul Leiter in the East Village.)

Yet what we have most of all in *Forever Saul Leiter* is that most elusive of photographic qualities: shots from a clear, distinct, unique eye. There's not a photo in the book that doesn't feel as if Saul Leiter took it. (Even a couple self-portraits as shadows on the ground; Lee Friedlander trademarks, though Leiter's were evidently taken a decade earlier.) There are many more snowy and rainy scenes, often with boldly colored umbrellas, though none feel redundant from the well-known ones. There's a beautiful photo, as great any Leiter shot we have, of snow falling around a street corner, a woman and man crossing the street in front of a two-tone green-and-white '50s sedan, a large black pawn shop sign, and most of three quarters of the frame filled with the side of a building in that special red tone famous from Leiter's Rothko-like shot ("Through Boards, 1957") of layers of red, black, a thin slice of a car, then more black. (The building looks to me like the one on the northwest corner of Third Avenue and East 13th that I'd pass all the time on my way to the subway, famous for the doorway in the flick *Taxi Driver* in which teenage prostitute Jodie Foster plied her trade.)

What makes *Forever Saul Leiter* such a revelation is all the different sections. There are new-to-us fashion photos, and more of those beautiful smoky or weather-blurred street scenes, pedestrians floating through them, this time in black and white as often as color. I think I prefer the color ones, like the ones from *Early Color*, because Leiter's palette is so singular and expressive; but the black-and-white photos pack punches. One entitled "Freckles" from 1958, a girl in a cap and winter coat, with a pinched, furious glare, has the urgency and intensity of Robert Frank's black-and-white shots from London around the same time. This is followed by a wooden car before a brick wall with a simple Goyaesque magic.

We also get a whole flock of self-portraits, not just the two street-shadow photos mentioned above, but a lot of shots through store window glass, Leiter's reflection almost lost among mannequins and other forms. I did a photobook awhile back called *Eye and Eye*, which was all self-portraits shot into various surfaces that made me virtually unrecognizable. I count that off to my own way of shooting, as well as a bit of modesty, lack of interest in spreading my image about; and I believe Leiter, in all his quiet East Village perambulations and just-another-guy-on-the-bench life-style, shares those qualities. The self-portraits certainly do.

Then there are the women, particularly his partner for decades, Soames Bantry, a professional model. A whole swarm of new photos of Soames, photos always dramatic, original, with a lovely and well-loved woman at their center. As Leiter says, "I shared my life with Soames. We had moments where, in spite of all the problems, we had an inability to concentrate on misery properly, and a tendency to enjoy life. And I don't think that's such a bad thing."

I can't think of any photographer with such a complex, joyful, and lovely relationship with a model partner. Soames nude reaching for an ashtray out of bed. Soames laughing gleefully in a man's white shirt. Soames "listening to music," pensive through a diner window. Soames even more pensive, possibly troubled, with nose resting on knuckles in close-up. Soames back in model mode in a fur and velvet coat, mock-playing a violin, a wistful look on her turned-to-the-side face, two dogs at her side.

Yes, some shots in professional model mode, but most drawn from telling moments day-to-day. Photos that are simply ways for Saul to say, I love you.

There's a lot of love in Leiter's work; that might be its animating secret. And there's also a lot of deep understanding of photography. I used the word *master* before, and let me try to say this book is a master class without stirring the banality of the phrase. For it is. Wonder how to shoot a couple kissing in a hallway? There's a lovely chiaroscuro pair going at it on page 162 in a black-and-white shot redolent of Frank's use of illuminated bulbs, Leiter's photo taken a couple years before *The Americans* was published. Shoot a Lower East Side street? Pull the camera back, get two pigeons to perch on the asphalt, and flood the whole thing with bountiful falling light. Light? You students have heard that's the key to photography, control the light. Well, here's a, um, master class.

It's tempting to go on and on with all one can learn from *Forever Saul Leiter*, and they're a lot of the lessons we all took from what other of his work we've seen. The thing is, though, we're blessed now with *Forever Saul Leiter*, with all its new-to-us photos; its stretching of his subjects and styles; the contact sheets; the self-portraits from 1939; the introduction of Leiter's first personal subject, his sister Deborah; a range of lovely almost Japanese black-ink washes; a first glimpse of what are evidently legions of color slides (note to the Brooklyn Museum: after your hugely successful 2019 show of unseen Garry Winogrand slides, how about one with Leiter's?); and perhaps most important this wide range of heretofore unknown photos of lover and muse Soames Bantry ... yet in a way as you think you're discovering a new Leiter, really you're just in the presence of a vastly more complex and expansive soul.

That artist, who through his cache of beautiful photos published thirteen years ago in *Early Color* struck us as a Vermeer, turns out, by the end of *Forever Saul Leiter*, to be much more like a Picasso: ever creative, ever changing, ever venturesome, working in various media, and overall informed by original takes on love and new visions of beauty.

The respect and admiration for Leiter's life and work only keeps growing. *Forever*, indeed.

ANOTHER Old Master we've recently learned more about is Dorothea Lange, thanks to photographer Sam Contis in the powerful book of Lange's work, *Day Sleeper*.

Think Dorothea Lange and you immediately think of migrant workers, especially the 1936, Farm Security Administration–supported photo of the troubled woman, fingers to chin, two of her children's faces turned from the camera, another child swaddled in her arms. It's the picture of the Depression. (And like all iconic photos, it's fascinating to see the outtakes: photos of some strength and intensity, but nothing close to the one we know so well. That's what makes the masters: they can grab that one photo that transcends all the others shot that day ... or any day. And know it.)

The Mysteries of Light 291

In *Day Sleeper*, we see vast ranges of Lange's subject matter and moods. More Depression shots, many African-American portraits, personal photos (a body entangled in bed sheets), a guy on a cable car in a Navy uniform who looks a lot like my own father in his Navy uniform. There are a few nudes, and a shot of a woman testifying in a makeshift revival church, head back, palms up, the Holy Spirit almost palpable as it ripples around her.

There are also a lot of surprises. I love the wit of the sign that reads, SEE THE WORLD BEFORE YOU LEAVE IT! BUY YOUR TV SET TODAY," followed by two striking and intense Black professional women striding down a city street, stylish pencil skirts just covering their knees, pocket books waving. Lange also goes much farther outside. There's a photo of a wild white horse kicking up dust, followed by undulating hills outside San Luis Obispo, California. There's really every kind of photograph. For one, a posed shot of a young woman from Lange's portrait studio, the most successful one in San Francisco in the '20s and '30s. That photo is two shots after a disturbing photo of a blue eagle tied to a barbed wire fence, its wings spread; and between the two shots just mentioned is one of Japanese-American women making camouflage nets for the war effort even as they're being "impounded" (read: literally imprisoned) during WW II.

Yep, Lange got around. Every photo in *Day Sleeper* is powerful, many revealing, some as great as any photograph ever taken. Contis's intense and sympathetic edit and clever and helpful notes make the book far more than just more photos by a photographer we may have known more by name than the full bloom of her work.

May our culture's continuing fascination and study of the Grand Masters of the photobook keep bringing forth works as revealing and essential as these two here.

Night Prowl:
Joshua K. Jackson, *Sleepless in Soho*

August 2021

I LOVE COLOR PHOTOGRAPHY. That's all I shoot, and whenever I can get a rich explosion of color into a photo, I feel like I'm doing my job. I also love color shots at night. I often joke that I spend more time in Times Square (at least pre-pandemic) than any other New Yorker. The furious abundance of colors, the neon energy, the packed-in souls out for fun or at least diversion … pictures galore!

Which means that Joshua K. Jackson's *Sleepless in Soho*, from Setanta Books, is right up my alley (or at least my narrow twisting street). London's Soho of course is not exactly Times Square, but it is the night part of town, with its clubs, restaurants, sex shops, theaters, and flocks of people on the stroll, either tourists or natives. And in Jackson's eyes it's a place of lovely, mysterious, artful photographs.

One thing I like about the book is it's not any kind of guide or overview of Soho, the square-mile district in Westminster, as much it's the night area as backdrop for Jackson's singular photos. What's he after? First of all, those bursts of night color, the rich swells of neon reds, burgundies, greens, and turquoises (particularly vivid on a high-heeled woman's legs as she strides down a brick walkway). He's also masterly in the way he captures floods of interior yellows and oranges. One striking photo—actually the book's power is that every photo is striking!—has a hatted, phone-toting man in front of glowing restaurant window.

Which leads to a second subject matter, those night denizens of Soho. There's an intensely smooching couple in a doorway, passion in this dark photo as rich as the swaths of color in others. There's a man's head in silhouette before a slash of orange neon sign. Many of the people who do appear are not so much the subjects of the photos as much as, say, foredrops for them. In a sense, that is, there is no direct subject matter here, just arrangements of forms and color....

Which is only partly true. There is a vivid emotion underlying any number of photos. I'd call it loneliness, anomie, those night-haunt hopes that almost always crash by dawn. Here's a shot of a woman and a beglassed man through a café window, her hands grasping his lapels, going at him intensely. Here's a full-on shot of a cabbie waiting stubbornly for a fare. A close-up of a man, eyes alarmed yet empty, too, filling nearly half the frame beside a few smudges of color. A woman, arms folded over her breasts, a deep pensive look on her face. Perhaps she's ruminating deeply on the explicit message of a photo that appears near the front of the book: a beautiful near-empty room of rich cherry-red light, two dark chairs, and a glowing neon sign that reads, LOVE IS THE DRUG.

More on that in a minute, but first I want to talk about how *Sleepless in Soho* is made. The book is in Swiss binding, and is composed of four sewn signatures, with each signature's first and last pages full-bleed abstract shots on thinner paper, glued to the next signature or, at the end, bound tight to the back casing. This lets the whole book of photographs set comfortably into an open spine.

Swiss binding ... about as wild as the Swiss in general, I suppose; yet still there is something both clever and sweet about the way *Sleepless in Soho* is put together. Certainly the book's form makes it all about the photos. Can't ask for more than that.

Now back to those photos. The woman mentioned above is not the only pensive one. There's a personal favorite of a woman in the back of a cab, only her wide, alarmed eyes visible between layers of light on paint and metal.

This photo is on the cover of the book, inset in thick black board, so it's clearly a key shot. The layers of light and dark around her remind me of Saul Leiter, whom I've written about recently. Leiter, the master of photos of layered color, as with his famous shot "Through Boards, 1957" of stacked layers of red, black, a car on the street, and more black. Jackson looks to have learned much from Leiter, with his powerful silhouettes (smudges of people as means to define colors), his way with a blur (a woman and two metal-rimmed folding chairs in a very unfocused swarm of yellow and blue reminiscent of Leiter's shots of Parisian waiters), and the way Leiter could make a simple detail sing.

Throughout *Sleepless in Soho* Jackson makes his photos sing, too, and tunes that even if at times they recall Leiter's, also range far from his. A child in an open doorway with four pale blue balloons. A woman's red skirt and ghostly shoes ablur in a frame. A woman with a purse before a few thin neon bulbs in the lower left of a photo that is three-fourths a dark cloud.

Well, that last one is back in Leiter territory. Jackson's also learned a couple things from William Eggleston. There's a grill in the corner of a restaurant that's of a similar tenor as Eggleston's famous green oven; there's even an upward-peering shot of a bare light bulb among a swarm of wires before a red ceiling.

My guess is Jackson couldn't resist the homage. And why not? With *Sleepless in Soho* Jackson proves he's his own master, and shout-outs to those photographers who inspired and brought him here, well, that's simple courtesy.

And deep feeling. That neon sign might read LOVE IS THE DRUG, but Jackson knows love, and desire, and sadness, and loss are all so much more. Not drugs, no escape at all, just essential human emotions.

Which leads to the true point of strong, expressive color in photography. Used right, bold color leads to deep feeling. New realms of expression. Photos that move you like the best music.

As much as any photobook I can think of, "Sleepless in Soho" has soul.

The *Raised by Wolves* Bootleg Series No. 2: Jim Goldberg, *Fingerprint*

October 2021

WHEN IS A PHOTOBOOK not a photobook? Not a riddle, but instead a way into a discussion of all those works containing sequential photos that aren't actual books, with covers and pages and binding and such. Specifically this piece is a look at Jim Goldberg's recently released boo ... well, his not-a-book; instead a collection of forty-five 4-inch by 5-inch Polaroid or Polacolor prints on cards, comprising what we might call the *Jim Goldberg Bootleg Series Vol. 2*. I'm of course both making an allusion to Bob Dylan, whose authorized bootleg series is up to fifteen by my best count, and Goldberg's own official *Bootleg* version of his book *Raised by Wolves*, from 2019 (the only way he could get the book back into print; rights are held by the first publisher).

The original *Raised by Wolves*, from 2007, is arguably Goldberg's most essential book; and it's no surprise he's mined it for further work. *Fingerprint* is simply these forty-five cards in a lovely and disturbing aqua-and-black cardboard box, with a striking photo of a young man with an eye patch riding above his right eye as he uses three fingers to show Goldberg his face's damage. The cover photo isn't one of the cards in the book, but the boy, ZHodI, is, as he glares at Goldberg's lens, the inscription "My black eyes from fight" written along the lower white frame of the card, crude arrows swooping up from the text to the eyes in question.

ZHodl and the other subjects of *Raised by Wolves* are deep in their subcultural world, and Goldberg is, too. Indeed, he's a most original photo documentarian. To make his best books he immerses himself in a singular world—teenage street runaways in *Raised by Wolves*, the rich and the poor in, well, *Rich and Poor*—then stays longer and digs further than anybody else than, perhaps, Bruce Davidson in *East 100th Street* or Mary Ellen Mark. Unlike those two, Goldberg gets his subjects to write about themselves in their own handwriting, and works these sheets into the books. Hence we get this gutter-scrawl near-verse, "Born a wicked child / Raised by wolves / A screaming kamakazi / I never will crash," which gives his earlier book its name. We also get the perfect-penmanship of the Rich section of *Rich and Poor*, revelations such as "This is an elegant photograph / My life is luxurious and my taste is refined. / I don't worry about what people think of / me or my lifestyle. I am a nice person." Both word excerpts are revealing, though obviously (and not wholly unexpectedly) there's a lot more poetry in the writings in *Raised by Wolves*; that is, a lot more Verlaine and Rimbaud than smug country-club braggadocio.

That's certainly one of Goldberg's many gifts, the way he draws out his subjects and enlarges our understanding of them by their own words and snapshots of the objects they cherish, such as a favorite skateboard or a red-tape-wrapped broken-bat truncheon. (Yes, a truncheon; these kids don't mess around.) In *Raised by Wolves* he also works in a personal diary, in which he tells us where he's been, and recounts conversations there. *Wolves* especially is as multimedia as a photobook can be; and in truth, there's nobody out there doing anything quite like what Goldberg does, going so deep and so wide.

Which is why it makes perfect sense to get this *Bootleg Series* release of more *Wolves* photos in the form of the 4 x 5 cards. The new work definitely mines rich material, and gives us a new and in some ways more immediate take on his teen subjects. Also, many of the cards are in vivid color, whereas the vast majority of shots in *Wolves* are in black and white. Many cards are straight-on portraits, sometimes with a name scrawled on the front, others with words on the back. Some are just photos (there's one of a lonely guitar case by a civic pool), and yet every last one is fascinating. Like all of Goldberg's photos, each is deeply revealing, of character, situation, and simple or elaborate doom. Some shots are manifestly startling. I'm thinking of the hand reaching down to pull a shiv from its holster by a heavy black boot, and another card of a guy asleep on a mattress on the floor, his nickname Morbid inked below his written comment on his current state: "to [sic] drunk to fuck."

The Mysteries of Light

Any way you take *Fingerperint* as a photobook it's a powerful work. Yet of course it isn't a book but a collection of repro Polaroids.

Which is just the way it should be. On my own shelves I have a small white box by the powerful photobook maker Jason Jaworski called *Thinking of You* that's full of cards. Next to it sits a bright-red mock Chinese cigarette pack with what looks like actual cigarettes inside, covering an array of photos capturing the importance of smoking at Chinese weddings, the brilliant *Until Death Do Us Part*. And on another shelf is Antony Cairns *LDN EI*, which re-purposes an obsolete Kindle to show the full range of those ghostly LDN photos he's taken for years, simply by swiping away.

My feeling? The more ways artists find to make photobooks that aren't books, the better. The further we stretch the definition of the book, the better. And the more times any photographer can turn one artistic project into a wholly new and mindblowing one, the better.

So props to Jim Goldberg for *Fingerprint*. And a simple suggestion for what's next for his guttersnipe cast of characters.

How about a musical?

I'm serious. As Broadway opens up again, *Raised by Wolves* the musical would be the perfect next iteration of Goldberg's masterpiece, *Rent* meets *Three-Penny Opera*.

I'd sure go see it. At least if the tunes and score were as rich and complex and deep as the Polaroids in this very special bootleg box.

Pick a Card, Any Card:
Daido Moriyama, *Random Walk*

March 2022

I'VE WRITTEN BEFORE, IN "Daido Moriyama's Never-Ending Tour," about how much I learned—and how much fun I had—at the 2011 Printing Show–TKY at Aperture Gallery in New York. That was the Saturday a roomful of Japanese-photobook lovers strode back and forth all afternoon before four-sided sheets of Daido photos on a wall, picking the ones we liked best and writing their numbers on a card, so that student volunteers could put the sheets together in each singular order, bind them in a classic Moriyama silk-screened cover, and each person would have their own unique Daido book.

I don't know if Daido's photos more than any other photographer's lend themselves to this make-your-own book practice, but there's no question his photos do. Witness the new Moriyama release, *Random Walk*, from Ibasho/the(M) éditions. This is a 5½ by 10–inch white box; inside it is a gray-cloth-bound book, with blank black pages except for small silver dots in rectangles, and underneath the book lie two cellophane-wrapped packs containing 100 mock Polaroid cards, 62 in black and white, 38 in color.

It's time to make my own Daido book once again!

Now the Aperture event had a few uniquely cool things about it. For one, Daido was there, and as friendly as could be. (He even took my picture with my camera. An original Daido portrait ... of me!) And two, the books were 9¼ by 11¼ inches, the photos grand, and because each sheet was a folded-out four pages of photos, the ordering of the shots in the book was far more chess than checkers: You picked front, backs, insides ... and since each photo was full-bleed, they all whispered or shouted at every other photo in the book. Or at best simply cooed.

But the true fun was in the way you ordered the photos. I was just getting going with my own photobooks, and what

The Mysteries of Light

I learned that day about the process of finding the best way to work shots into a book was a fundamental lesson for my own work. (When I look back at my Printing Show–TKY book now, I'm baffled at why I put the photos in the order I did; another good lesson of bookmaking, each iteration is a, um, snapshot of how the book feels to you at that moment you're making it. At least to you. If you get it right, as, say, Robert Frank did with *The Americans*, the order becomes timeless and transcendent, at least to the world, no matter how the artist's own feelings might change.)

I've been assiduously making photobooks, and thus ordering and reordering my own photos, for over a decade now; and I teach a university course called Writing the Photobook, in which that's what each student does: Choose the best (or at least the right ones) of their photos, arrange them in a certain order, rearrange them, and rearrange them again—when I taught writing, I used to say that you have to rewrite everything you do at least three times; it's probably more like dozens of reorderings with photobooks—then lay them out on the page.

That is, they make a book.

And now with *Random Walk*, making your own unique Daido book is the book. An inspired idea.

Let's crack open the white box, gently pull the tape off one of the glassine envelopes ... what do we find? The cards inside are Polaroid-like; that is, they're more or less the size of an old-school Polaroid print (in two sizes here, $3^{3}/_{8}$ by $4^{1}/_{8}$ inches and 4 by 4 inches). All but a couple of the smaller prints are in black and white, the larger ones are the color photos. The photos take up most of the card; the white space below the photo sports a printed Daido signature. (The box itself carries an actual signature, along with which copy out of a thousand you possess.) The black-and-white prints are not the most dynamic. Indeed, the tones are various washes of pale grays, almost vague enough to make it not exactly clear what you're seeing.

Look closely, though, and what you get are shots of streets in Japan, buildings, alleyways, signs ... pretty much what you'd see on any given random walk. At first glance they don't look all that distinguishable as Daido photographs. They do have the unexpected angles, that sense of his camera just flicking itself around in any old direction, but they're a little too washed-out and aimless to be strong works.

Which is curious, since the magic of Daido's photographs is that virtually every one I can think of, no matter how banal, is unmistakably shot by Daido Moriyama. Indeed, this is the magic of any great photographer, especially those such as Frank or Garry Winogrand or Lee Friedlander known for their work on the street: Every photo we see is an expression of their eye, their sensibility, their art. For a great photographer the camera becomes simply the tool through which flows the way they, and they alone, see the world.

Which is not to say that the black-and-white Polaroids in *Random Walk* could be taken by anyone else. It's just that they're not Daido at his strongest.

The color cards are better. Even though the photos here are also a bit washed-out—in truth, more washed-out than actual Polaroids—they're also more striking, original, and demonstrably Daido photos. If I were doing *Random Walk*, I would have made it all of color shots. Why not? I have a copy of *Bye-Bye Polaroid*, the book from a show of Daido's actual Polaroids in 2008, and each photo is original, striking, indubitably one of the master's. And they're all in color.

The cards in *Random Walk* create another dilemma: the mix of black-and-white and color shots. In my photobook course the question always comes up: "Can I mix black-and-white and color photos?"

My answer: Well, you can, many photobooks have done it, but it adds another level of complication and can easily backfire. That is, you at the least have to find a rhythm in your blend of the two media so neither the color nor black-and-white jump out too much or feel misplaced; and you also have to have a pretty good reason to do it. At first blush, with *Random Walk*, I can't see the good reason, and also don't see why we need that added level of complexity. Ditto the two sizes of Polaroids. At least the publishers set out their silver dots on each page to give guidance to both sizes of cards, but even before I've started to make my own book, I'm a little anxious at knowing I have to

The Mysteries of Light

mix the black-and-white and the color shots, and also mix in the two different sizes.

Anxious because the whole point of any photobook is that it's not simply a random collection of photos but instead an ordering to the shots that makes sense, has its own logic, rhythm, and correspondences (real and metaphorical) between all the photos in the book. Indeed, that's one of the comforts of making a photobook: The resulting work of art does not rise and fall on the power of a bunch of distinct photos standing on their own, as they would in a classic monograph, but instead in the way all the photos flow together, talk to each other, gather their power from the accumulation and order of the shots, the complete whole. When I take a particularly strong photo out on the street, I don't only say, Oh, that could be a great shot; instead I tell myself, That will fit well into one of the books I'm working on.

That is, it's all about sum of the work, not the separate parts. The book, not the photo.

Back to the book in front of me, *Random Walk*. If the book you make is truly a random walk, then you could simply shuffle the cards and paste them higgledy-piggledy onto the black sheets. But anybody can do that, shuffle a deck of cards then lay them out on a table, but where's the magic? The magic comes from the card somebody's thinking about being in exactly the place it's supposed to be. Get it right ... and the audience gasps in wonder.

So the title in truth has to be a misnomer. It only seems like a random walk. If we're to truly make our own unique photobook, what we come up with must be anything but random....

Which means we have to deliberately take a first step, head off in one direction. That is, we 100 photos. Question 1: Which one do we start with?

I know I'm going on a bit here, but this is important. Because every book starts somewhere, and there is a first page to our blank book. Again: Which of Daido's shots goes first? And then, of course, which one goes next, and next, and next, and—

A woman in last semester's Writing the Photobook class, struggling to find a subject for her own book, finally came up with just that: a random walk. She started off one afternoon in lower

Manhattan, then walked home to Queens, taking a lot of photos along the way. Her book was pretty good, the photos interesting, angled well, not too common or blah. The shots had a definite energy: Here's my eye capturing what intrigues me on my walk. It was also easy to do. This is the first thing I saw, here's what came next, and finally, here's my neighborhood, I'm almost home.

But Daido's *Random Walk* isn't that. We have no idea what order the photos were taken in. We assume they were taken at different times and all over the place. And with the color shots, they're not all street photos; as we'll see, many simply show a woman's feet or her bum.

No way our own book can be random in any way. As I face getting started, I realize this. I need a plan.

A deep breath. Nope, can't imagine the whole book in my head now, or even much of it at all. I realize I will basically be making it up as I ramble along.

Still, we're not going anywhere without that first step, that first photo.

So, again, where to start?

Daido in *Random Walk*'s foreword gives us some help. "After all," he tells us, "it seems like when I walk the streets, I am looking for somewhere other than here, in other words, I probably release the shutter only when I feel I have found the entrance to that 'alien world.' "

Which makes sense. Any good or great photobook is about a journey into another world, the photographer's; even as, of course, the photos themselves reproduce some aspect of the common world that the lens sees. Daido also talks about his love of black-and-white photography, how those photos hit us "right from the start with their transferred 'extraordinariness,' instantly stimulate our imaginative understanding of the imagery purified into shades of black and white, and let us experience a different reality through the encounter with the 'alien world.' "

That is, photography for Daido is never at bottom about the actual world but instead a dream world, an unreal world … a world that only he sees.

So, again, which photo to start us off on our own "ran-

The Mysteries of Light

dom walk"? I'd say the one that most clearly ushers us into the "extraordinary" world of our own photobook. The one, to quote another visionary, William Blake, that will knock down the "doors of perception" and show everything "to man as it is, Infinite."

A lot to ask from just a few faux Polaroids in black and white and color we're to arrange in an order to our liking; and yet at bottom the exact job of any and all works of art: To ground us in the real, yet also show us extraordinary worlds … the way things are, and then the way they truly are, infinite.

But still … come on, really, where do we start?

Ah, that's where creative faith comes in. And confidence. And a sense that we're not alone in our endeavors; that, indeed, there are forces in the universe that want us to make art, and to see things as they really are. That is, we just have to take a leap and pick a card and….

I start flipping through the first stack. I don't even look at every card, a lot are pretty similar; and I don't believe you kick open the doors of heaven by overthinking things. Nope, you just lean back, feel the lifting, soaring force of eternal truth at your back, and … simply pick one of them.

I'm starting with black and white because the preponderance of cards are in black and white, and I want to set a tone. The card I choose depicts both sides of a narrow alleyway, a restaurant's globe lamps to the left, a row of bicycles to the right, and the backs of two men far down the alley, almost to the next street. Pretty much a nothing photo, like most of the black-and-white ones we're given in *Random Walk*, and yet, at a closer look, with that perfect Daido balance, lamps high to the right harmonizing with the globes, a rectangular-patterned wall giving the photo geometric structure, and those two men going somewhere, maybe randomly, maybe not.

They're on the move, and now so are we.

And yet I'm not about to paste this photo into the book. I actually haven't decided if I will ever paste photos into the book's black pages. More likely I'll affix them with a light tape or a removable glue or something, so I can make another version of my random walk if I feel like it. But that's a decision for later.

For now I have a start.

I've pulled the card out of the deck and set it aside, and I'm looking for photos that will follow it, though I'm doing that mostly in my head for now. I'm also not thinking or looking too hard. Most of the black-and-white shots are of undistinguished streets, and if I were walking in my home of Manhattan, say after having lunch in Chinatown up to the Strand bookstore a mile or so north at Broadway and 12th Street (a trip I make all the time), I'd have a number of different ways to go; and which specific route I took would be of no particular matter to me, I'd just start wandering, taking this left, this right, crossing if I have the light, and going down another block or so if I don't. That is, my exact route wouldn't matter, just my beginning and my end points, and, well, maybe spots along the way I might linger and try to grab a photo or two of my own.

As in, ah, I now have a strategy for my *Random Walk*. I flip through the Daido cards quickly and look for ones that stand out, that have special significance—that are worth a longer stop.

Ah, there's one of Daido photographing himself, that inimitable shadowy shape, dark torso, hand raised with camera, Beatle haircut swooping down to his ears … a special photo, and I put it aside. There's another self-portrait-in-window shot, and I put that aside, too. I look quickly for a third self-portrait, thinking those shots of Daido himself will be a good way to punctuate the flow of the book, but I only see the two. Still, I can drop them in at signal moments.

There are also a few other shots of open streets somewhat like the one I chose for the first, and I set them aside, too. I'm looking for beats here, photos that will help me pace my walk (and the book). The more I thumb through the cards, the more I notice that the vantage point changes, it opens up to the road or closes in on something alongside it. Look, there's a chain-link fence, a bicycle before a tall stack of wrapped bumbles, a store foyer and window. I group them, too. Yes, this idea for the pacing of the book could work. We walk down a common street, then we stop and linger for a moment, then we head down the street again. Those open street shots will imply movement, perhaps a new chapter.

The Mysteries of Light

So far, so good. I haven't put any of the cards in any order yet, just kind of sorted them next to my computer, but I'm getting a strategy. Oh, and look, here's a shot of three women waiting for an elevated train. That one will have to have a special place in the book, because to be there we'll have to have left the actual street.

The gray, faded, black-and-white street....

Which brings me to the stack of color photos. Each larger than the black and whites, and of wholly different subject matter ... and, yes, in color.

I glance at them, then quickly put the whole *Random Walk* package aside.

I'm not ready to deal with color. Let me sleep on it. I'll tackle those color photos tomorrow.

✵ ✵ ✵ ✵ ✵

ALL RIGHT, BACK at my computer to write, cup of morning tea by my side, and ... on to the color photos. Oddly, two of the black-and-white-sized shots are in color, two angles on a wide-eyed, ruby-cheeked plasticine doll with a 1930s Myrna Loy golden bob; but all of the other color shots are in the larger size. Intriguingly, fewer than half of them are street scenes—that is, views we might see on our random walk. A number of photos are of women, either nude or wrapped in bright red. There's a classic Daido lip shot, that is, a lot of red lips on the wall behind a hanging T-shirt sporting a Daido photo of another T-shirt with big lips on it. (Too many lips—and too meta—to even considering thinking more about.) There are also a couple toe shots, and more Daido lips. There's Daido shooting himself in a tiled mirror in a courtyard, and again in front of a billboard for restaurant menu dishes.

Ah, so some of the color shots follow the black-and-white ones. Good. And look here, there are long street scenes from pretty much the same vantage as many of those in the black-and-white pile. A river, a bridge. A two-story clothing store front. A tangle (and abstraction) of power lines.

Got it. Some of the color photos can play a harmony with the flow of black-and-white ones, others will be so different as to be a quick change into another key, a lift, say, from the day-to-day wanderings in Eb to the jolt of fleshy buttocks a bright, ringing E major will bring!

Further strategy is revealing itself. My personal random walk will, by necessity, be a run of the black-and-white Polaroids, mostly following instinct, but it will be all these other types of photos, too: Daido's self-portraits (O.K., it's not only my random walk, is it?), and then the range of color shots. The streetscape color photos will be subtle brightening, an enrichening, but still on the walk. The other ones, the toes, butts, and lips, will be as if Dorothy just clicked her heels and left Kansas behind.

Pacing. It's all going to be pacing, right? When to zig instead of zag, when to walk up to a window instead of just down a street, and then when to blow up the whole black-and-white "alien world" with an even more far-out color shot.

So I have a plan. Makes sense. Now it's time to hit my dining room table, start laying the photos out as they'll be in the book ... and see how well those plans hold up to the actual show.

✳ ✳ ✳ ✳ ✳

I'M AT THE long table, my laptop computer in front to me so I can keep writing, and I've placed my first black-and-white street scene on the table to my left. It's the one I chose the other day, and right underneath it in my stack is one of the Daido self-portraits, and—why not?—I set it to the first card's right ... and immediately say to myself, Hmnn, maybe the self-portrait should come first. Makes sense, right? It's Daido's walk, why not start out with his image?

Easy to do, I just slide the cards around, look at the new order, and immediately think, Nope, too strong. Too declarative. Too much of a statement. I quickly go back to my long-chosen first card, and move the self-portrait out of the way. I want to start walking, and I want to just keep walking, so I pull out cards that reasonably seem to fit that walk, don't worry too much about what's in them other than street scenes; and I set five of them down till I come across a shot of two young women on the

The Mysteries of Light 307

sidewalk, their backs to us. Great ... that'll be the sixth photo. Time to get some people in here.

And time now to talk about all the ways photographers physically work with their photos to get them into book order.

I'm kind of new-school. I do all my ordering on my computer, mostly in Lightroom, where it's easy to move photos about with the flick of the cursor, and where I have photos of cards that read tentative end, following photos still possible and following photos not in book, which I use to demark which photos are in, possibly in, or out. (And of course as I make a book, photos slip in and out of each category.)

Most of my friends are old-school. They work with actual photos on paper. Either they print them out, or if they're way old-school, make work prints of them in the darkroom. These cards are usually not that much larger than the faux Polaroids in *Random Walk*. Some sort their photos on a table (as I'm doing now), but the classic way is to pin them to a special wall (yet of course I don't want to put pin marks in my Daido cards).

The good thing about a wall is that you can walk back and forth and easily take in the book's order. A reordering is a simple unpinning and moving a photo. One friend "walks" his board first thing each day, fresh eyes trained on what he's come up with, and does this for years before putting a book out. Other friends have their own times of the day, their own mindsets, and their own lengths of time working their boards.

There are other ways. I'm working now with a designer who digitally lays out each spread, prints them out, then folds the spreads into lose pages, which she manipulates around to make the book. This spread not feel quite right next to that spread? Flick, and it's moved, or even removed.

The key, always, is instinct. There are no rules to a photobook. Truly, not even a basic strategy one can learn. Like the idea of separating your photobook into implied chapters, and thinking of using pictures of flags to do it? Good luck. Robert Frank's covered that move for all eternity. You might as well think of cutting off your ear.

Think of starting with small photos and building to large? Makes sense, but why is that any better than starting large and moving small? Start with people then go to places? Or the opposite? Or blend them all in together in a way that … makes sense?

That's the idea: to have your photobook make sense in its own unique way. Each new photobook starts wholly from scratch, and the way it develops can only be by that rarest of qualities: artistic instinct. As in, I'm trying to do something that's never been done before. So I simply go ahead and … do something that has been done before?

No way. Once you have the general idea of your photobook, and, of course, the photos themselves, how can you make that book except by feeling how each photo sets next to the one next to it, and how that photo links to the one after that and that and….

It's true you can learn a lot; that is, that the more you work on photobooks, the better you get at it. It's like cooking; moving from literal measuring to knowing how much a pinch of saffron should be. It's basically feel. You learn that each photo has numerous qualities. Weight. Gravitational pull. A set of expectations of what should surround it. A fierce demand about just where it belongs.

That Daido self-portrait leading off my version of *Random Walk*? It was simply too heavy, carried too much with it. I felt the shot tug the book down right off the bat. Again, this was just a whisper of instinct, the way seeing the photo placed there felt as palpable as a finger pressing my skin, no, a nail digging into my skin. It just was not right.

So how do people begin to set out their photos to arrange them into books? I assume the way that each photo or spread speaks most clearly to them, allows their instincts to immediately sense what's going on, and address it.

For myself, I move from Lightroom to InDesign, put the pictures on a two-page spread, and look at it as a spread. It always amazes me how vivid and palpable two pictures sitting next to each other can be. Or not. And then the ultimate question: Do we want each spread to be vivid and palpable, or do we want some that quiet things down, skip along, lead to another crescendo?

Yes, it's all pacing, as in a concerto or symphony. Which is basically whether the photos, like musical notes, are in the right

The Mysteries of Light

order, or the wrong one. Whether they harmonize or clash, and if they do clash, is it interesting enough to keep.

And always, how to make the book better.

In my photobook class we spend a lot of time helping students move photos around. One of our basic questions is: "Do you see a good first photo?" We don't always get the whole class to agree on just one, but we do get a lot more consensus than you might think. And we're also constantly revising. Somebody has a better idea, and we try it. Then we try something else. That's how a good photobook is made.

And what I'm back to now with the Daido shots. The six black-and-white ones in a row, culminating in the two women's backs.

All of a sudden I know we need a color shot. A quick shuffle of that deck, and the next photo in our book can only be one of the two shots of that woman's nude buttocks. One photo is of both cheeks, a colorfully manicured and ringed hand on each of them. The second photo is of the same ringed hand on just the right cheek, shot from the side. The first photo, with both cheeks, is more stark, more jarring, and that's exactly what my book needs now. Swing that baton, hit those cymbals. Boom, it's there, next to the two black-and-white women on the sidewalk, this splash not only of color but of nudity.

I look, I look ... and it holds up. Six black-and-white shots and a color butt.

Not bad, a good morning's work, and yet just as I had a rule when I was writing novels never to get up from my desk before I knew what the first sentence of the next day's work would be, I need to know now which photo will follow the nude buttocks. Back to black and white? Another color one? Wait, that card is perfect. It's a color Polaroid, but it's of a roadway, two men at the far end (just as with my first photo). Literally, this photo coming next puts us back on the road and also lets us know that color shots will loom large in the book. Maestro, take your bow.

※ ※ ※ ※ ※

THE NEXT DAY. All set to head back to the table and lay out more *Random Walk* cards, but all the work on Daido's photos has gotten me pumped to work on my own, so I go to Lightroom and start editing and moving around photos for a new project.

A few weeks before Christmas 2021 I came up with a new way to get shots from buses, a manipulation of focus and lens coverings, and psyched with how the photos were coming out—nothing as normal as people standing on street corners, but instead a phantasmagoria of blurred and mysterious street life—I started taking buses every chance I had. Normally, I'm a subway-er, at least north and south in Manhattan, but now I took long bus trips from down in Soho up to where I live on the Upper West Side. I'd aim for the back row of the bus, the seat on the right facing forward. If that was taken, I might take one a few farther to the front, or maybe the first seat on the right as you walk into the bus. Then I'd point my camera through the window and just blast away.

I did this for the few weeks around the holidays, and came up with hundreds and hundreds of shots. As usual I pushed the shutter when it felt right, trusting my instincts and the camera to do me right. Now as I sort the photos in Lightroom, I find a number of them are really good, a lot pretty interesting, and of course an awful lot of duds, too.

I'm moving all the at least O.K. ones into a Lightroom folder named "From the Bus," which for now will also be the name of the book I'm planning. Interestingly, just as there was something liberating with working with somebody's photos other than my own (Daido's), now I'm excited to be back at my own screen.

Also, I'm doing a whole different kind of photo work: taking each photo I shot, and if it seems worthy, working in Lightroom to make it the best it can be.

That is, with the Daido book I was simply sorting already finished photos into the shape of a book. Here I'm going back to an earlier step, and a more singularly focused and basic one: editing one photo at a time.

Am I thinking of the whole book? Some, not that much. That's a different muscle, the one I was using for days with Daido's book: the big picture. Now I'm enjoying just worrying about this one photo in front of me, then the one next to it.

Which is one of the fun things about photobook making: how there are so many aspects to it. You have to take the pictures. You have to initially sort out the worthy from the less so. Then you work with a whole other skill set to make each photo look as true as it can. And then, and only then, you begin to shape them into a book.

That was the initial joy, and ease, of moving Daido's photos around: It was only the final part of the process. (Well, the final part of one part of the process. When I make a book, I then have to get it published, distributed to stores, and sold … whole other cans of stinky worms.)

But now I need to do my own work.

So for now, Daido's *Random Walk* is stopping for a tea break along the way; that is, it's back on my desk in its white box.

And my own Random Bus Trip is rolling along.

✳ ✳ ✳ ✳ ✳

By now it should be clear that this long kind-of review is actually far more of a piece on how photobooks are put together, all the ways artists can think about doing it, the ways I think about doing it: the sorting, the pacing, the laying the book out … and the mysterious winds of inspiration that swirl around the process. For me part of the joy of working with *Random Walk* was that it was not my own book. Low ego, low stakes. And since I'm not under a too-compelling deadline, I've been waiting to get tired or burned-out on my own photo work before getting back to Daido's.

And how's this for further incentive: The package of Scotch Restickable Glue Stick I ordered showed up. This is, purportedly, the same kind of nonstick glue on the back of Post-it notes. Should be perfect for formally attaching the Daido cards to the book. If the glue sticks just enough, but not too much, then I can go through and redo every year. Hah. Enough to get through it once.

✳ ✳ ✳ ✳ ✳

It's actually been a couple weeks now since I was last on the Daido walk, weeks I spent on a handful of my own books. I tabled my bus photos and went back to a couple books comprised of shots from 2021 that I plan to put out in a trilogy called *NYC 2021*, following last year's pandemic trilogy, *Woodstock 2020*. The new books are *Naked* and *Cool Struttin'!*, following one already printed called *Shuttertown*. That'll be the set. I've also been working on a book called *Red Balloon*, title from an old Tim Hardin song. It's a kind of phantasmagoria of shots of balloon-looped streets in Lower Manhattan. Oh, and another book called Masks, photos taken on Fifth Avenue of people with, yes, masks. And even one more: Swing Street, a special selection of shots from my bus trips, all photos from December 2021, and dedicated to the memories of Bill Evans and Dexter Gordon, and Eugene Atget. (The bus trips continue into the new year.)

Busy busy. I've been picking photos in Lightroom, ordering them, exporting them into Photoshop, tweaking them, then bringing them into InDesign to lay out the books. Same muscles as with *Random Walk*, same skills, just more exciting because they're my own photos, my own books.

And yet that Restickable Glue Stick keeps sitting there next to the white box, waiting for an impulse to get back to Daido and finish it up.

I lace up my figurative walking shoes and hit the living room.

My last move was introducing the first two color shots into *Random Walk*, then stopping. I set the photos I've already chosen on the table, look them over, recall my plan: mostly be on the city walk, but shake up the step-after-step with new angles and color shots.

I decide right away to drop in a Daido self-portrait. It's my walk, but it's also his … or really his, or maybe really mine? Well, they're his photos, and if somebody were shaping one of my books, I'd hope they'd work in a self-portrait shot of mine pretty soon to establish proprietary rights. (I did toss a photo with a looming shadow of my head into *Cool Struttin'!*) So there Daido in his window is. It's also very Daido-y to have a self-portrait. That fine book of his *Novembre* has one as its cover,

The Mysteries of Light

and his *One Picture Book* is all photos of him in mime makeup.

Now where? This is a significant moment. I've established a sense of order and rhythm to the photos, and yet I've only laid out nine of them. That leaves 91 to go. As I know from work on my own books, there has to come a time when you figuratively just close your eyes and jump; that is, you turn the ordering over to impulse and intuition, even fate. Indeed, I just did that: The Daido self-portrait shot I put ninth was simply the one on the top of the pile when I looked below the book in its box.

Yet it felt right. And made sense.

So now that's the plan going forward. Just pull out photos and put them in an order, quickly, feeling locked in to the book every moment, of course, but in no way overthinking it.

Boom! Off I go. I move fast, the whole maneuver takes maybe ten minutes, maybe less. I'm mostly just throwing photos out there. I have a few new ideas along the way. One, I'll end with a self-portrait; let Daido own the book. Two, I'll lead up to that final photo with a flurry of Daido-y color shots, lips and things. Three, the book is titled *Random Walk*, and most of the black-and-white shots are just that: shots from a random walk. So I'll mimic that in my ordering, just putting whatever photo comes up next down on the table adjacent to the one before it. Then break it up now and then with color shots. But keep on moving. Don't think, just pick up on whispers of instinct. Trust the ordering of the cards as they fall from my fingers. Get them all out there!

And I do. They're all sitting on the dining room table, in a definite order, just as when I'm working on one of my books all the photos I'm planning to use get lined up in Lightroom in their own definite order. An order just waiting to be changed.

Which I plan to do. Probably later today. Let them sit awhile, that is, then go look at them fresh. I hope I won't have too many changes, but I hope just as hard that I'll have some. I'll bring fresh instincts, and maybe another new idea or two, to my own version of *Random Walk*.

※ ※ ※ ※ ※

Well, here's the honest truth, as they say. I put all the photos into two stacks, put them back into the cardboard box with the empty book, and let it all sit unattended on my desk for the last few weeks. I'm still busy with my own books, not only laying them out, but sprucing up the photos in Photoshop, getting them into InDesign, ready for the printer. I just didn't have any calling to go back to Daido's walk, all those little cards, and worry about them again.

Indeed I kind of feel I'm beyond it. That's how I am with all of my own books, they get my full attention, then a break, then more full attention, and more … but then they're done, printed, and that's it. I'm out taking new pictures, and off to new books.

But something's nagging me. Before I glue the photos into the *Random Walk* book, I really should go through them at least one more time, check my hurried ordering the last time.

Which I do. I move through the cards swiftly again, taking them in as I would scenes on a brisk walk. They're of course mostly the smaller black-and-white street-ramble shots, and I simply check that the journey through the cards feels as if I'm out on an actual walk, and one that's holding my interest. Then I come to one of the larger color shots, this one the first of two photos of actual dolls, and I'm stopped. Nope, that doll photo is too jarring where it is. I move it back a few photos, till it's behind a color Daido self-portrait, then think it's even a bit of a jolt there, and move it farther in my deck amidst a flurry of color shots, putting it in-between a photo of a statue of two golden beasts, a smaller gold dog riding the back of a golden steer, and a show-lamp-lit shot of a woman in a red dress standing on a small platform. Less jarring, more of a blend. Sweet.

The other shot of the yellow-capped mannequin throws me, too, and for a second I don't think it's going to fit in anywhere. I kind of wish it weren't in the box.

But it is. For now I move it farther back in the second stack, and then … oh, wait, this is an interesting idea. Tomorrow my studio manager, Bruno Jansen, is coming by. He has great judgment, and he's always tossing a good idea or two my way for my own books.

So we can go over *Random Walk* together. Maybe he'll have a better place for those creepy sleek-skinned golden-yellow dolls. Maybe he'll have a whole other notion.

But for now I'm pretty satisfied. As I went through the cards, I found the plot was gripping me. For real … I was totally waiting to see how the book would end. I couldn't recall which cards I put last those weeks earlier, and I found I was hoping for a self-portrait—a color self-portrait—as the final photo.

There it is. Daido in an outdoor courtyard, shooting into a wall made up of diamond-squared mirrors. He's holding a genuine Polaroid camera right under his chin, looking forward, a large roll of white paper under his other arm. Casual, a black jacket over a T-shirt, his mop-top haircut in full Beatlesque bloom.

It's like Hitchcock popping up not as a cameo in one of his movies but in the final scene, as if he's the guy hanging off the edge of Mt. Rushmore.

The perfect ending. Nope, that won't change. But we'll see tomorrow what Bruno has to say, and then I can start gluing the Polaroids into the book.

✳ ✳ ✳ ✳ ✳

ACTUALLY, NOTHING WILL change. My studio manager, Bruno, went through the cards and thought the order was fine as I had it, which was good to hear. He did have one thought that hadn't dawned on me: All these Daido mock Polaroids are going into a book. Of course, you say. But what he meant was that all the shots are going to sit on pages, facing each other, each with their own dynamics. For instance, I saw I had a run of five of the larger color shots in a row. Each page has room for four photos, eight per spread. So should I keep four of the color shots on one page, not have one spill over to the next? Will my current order even place those five color shots on one spread? Will I want it to?

Good questions, and ones that will only be answered when I pull out my Scotch Restickable Glue Stick and start placing the photos into the book.

Oh, and one more thought from Bruno: Do I want to use every photo in the package? That is, what if I just put one or two photos on a page for pacing?

Hmnnn. A good point. I think about it for a moment, then shake my head. Doing that, not using every photo we're given, feels out of the spirit of the book. Indeed, I like the integrity of the full *Random Walk* package, and also that I'm making my own Daido book using exactly what he gave to me. Also the challenge of using all the photos. And above all the sense that this is a random walk, yes, but also one that even as the specific path can be anything I make of it, still needs to touch every stop out there. I will absolutely use every last Polaroid.

So on to the book itself.

The glue stick has a not unexpected smell, a faintly chemical acridity with a touch of cheap mouthwash. I'm debating whether to spread it first on the back of the Polaroids or on the black paper itself. I guess it doesn't much matter, so I give it a try with a dab on the paper. Then I put down my first photo.

It feels kind of momentous. That's the thing with making a photobook, you can pick photos, sort them, begin to lay them out in your head, but when it's time to make the actual book, the whole thing rises up in the air and floats untethered. When it's time to make the book real, photos will fall where they will.

That is, the book itself exerts its own desires, its own expectations, its own will. I've found with books I've made that the finished product isn't vastly different from what I laid out ahead of time, it's just that two photos that seemed to sit well next to each other in Lightroom don't have that same energy in book form. Often the one I thought would be on the left needs to flip with its counterpart on the right. A fix as simple as that. Other photos just won't fit at all, and an earlier discard will insist on being worked into the actual book.

In other words, as I begin to paste the Daido photos into *Random Walk*, my labors are far from over.

Still, I decide I'll make the actual book as I did the later orderings of the photos outside the book: that is, rapidly, with full intuition flaring, not stopping to second-guess myself unless something simply feels wrong on the page itself.

The first photo, of the backs of two men walking down that narrow alley, goes in well. It sticks nicely to the glue, yet can also easily be moved. And it looks good in the book.

I did put the glue for the first photo pretty much in the middle of the Polaroid, and the edges are floating up from the paper. Hmnn. Let's try putting the glue on the corners of the actual photos. O.K., that works better. The second photo sits more rightly on the page. I lift off the first one, dab the glue stick on its corners, and position it again. And now the second photo seems a little loose. Well, livin' and learnin'. I lift that up—the Post-It Note–style glue works perfectly—apply more glue, and press it down again. Ah, a good, tight fit. Excellent.

The small silver dots on the black paper help immensely in squaring up the photos. And now the work is a lot like scrapbooking, an activity I can't remember previously participating in. Well, maybe in elementary school or summer camp.

But there it is. I'm busy pasting pieces of paper into a book.

Or procrastinating about doing it. It's been over a week since I glued in that first photo, just couldn't bring myself to get going again, simply sitting there gluing and placing, but yesterday provided a good opportunity. Two photographer pals, Jeff Rothstein and Harvey Stein, came over to use the same dining room table on which I laid out the Daido Polaroids, to together sort out 5 x 7 prints for a new book of Jeff's. O.K., two fine photographers in the room working on a book. That gives me just enough incentive to pull out *Random Walk* and start in on the final lap.

Yep, it's as boring as I expected. Swab some glue stick on the back, line up the faux Polaroid with the little silver dots, and press it down. Plenty of glue and the cards still keep lifting off the black paper. I figure they'll stick when I get them all in and close the book on them, and that turns out to be the case. So I sit there, listening to Harvey and Jeff say things like, "That goes together nicely, doesn't it?" and "I don't know, maybe that other photo will fit better here," and even with all my own handicaps as a crafter, I'm able to finish the job.

I do make a few changes from my order of photos going in, but very few. On one spread I make the mistake of pasting in the photos first on the righthand side, then realize that that kind of works, so I glue in the next two on the left. On one spread I put two color shots that were supposed to follow each other on the upper left and the lower right parts of the two pages—a better balance.

The next day I check the book. As a novice scrapbooker, I did pretty well. Some of the photos are a bit crooked, but that magic Restickable Glue Stick means I can easily peel up a Polaroid and set it down correctly. I also see that I missed a couple pages, though I used every photo; weird, since I thought the book would simply hold every card, and that'd be that. I guess the designers factored in the thought that, um, novice scrapbookers like me would go too fast and miss a page or two.

But that's about it. I like the book, the run of washed-out black-and-white street shots, the bursts of color and weirdness. Happy also that my general idea played out well: a simple walk, a random walk, but my random walk, interrupted only by those flashes of Daido Moriyama color and obsession. Not a bad walk indeed. I'd say even better than the vaunted High Line here in Manhattan.

I hold the book proudly, then come up with one final thought. I worked hard on *Random Walk*, so it's not simply a Daido Moriyama book any longer, it's partly mine.

For my final act I sign it, in black ink right under Daido's own signature on the white box.

That's the deal, right? It's now a photobook created by the two of us together.

Out on the Street: Rules of Street Photography

BACK IN JANUARY 2020 I wrote about Jeff Mermelstein's *Hardened*, his grand exploration of all things shot out on the street. I mentioned some coincidences between Mermelstein's street work and my own, and also wrote about what separates photographers simply snapping pictures on the street from those who create masterful books of street photography. After spending so much time with Mermelstein's book, I want to set down some of the rules of street photography I've gleaned from his work, as well as from others. I'll start with a general rule, then talk about what we can learn from Mermelstein, and finally add a number of ideas of my own.

1) The first rule, indeed, commandment of taking shots on the street is to ignore any of the dumb rules you've read about what you should do on the street. Here are a few: Only shoot with film, never digital. Don't crop. Don't shoot into the light. Don't shoot color, it's not serious. Always shoot people, and always their faces. You've probably heard more. Twaddle. There really are no rules for street photography, there are only interesting photographs and boring photographs. Indeed, it's always a good idea to not photograph what everybody else seems to be shooting, and it's also probably reasonable to ignore everything I'm saying here, too. That is, as Bruce Springsteen puts in the song that gives this piece it's title, *When you're out on the street, you gotta walk the way you wanna walk.* Go out with confidence, purpose, swagger. And always shoot what *you're* interested in, not what somebody else says is interesting; do your best to make it truly compelling; and don't have too much in your head while you do it. Instinct is all!

On to what I picked up from Mermelstein's *Hardened*, leavened by some thoughts of my own.

1) Details! Study and learn how just a whiff of the right detail can most intriguingly evoke the whole shot. I just now opened *Hardened* to a picture of a hand holding both a white-filtered cigarette and a long cucumber, with a women's shoe in the bottom left corner. There's oddness, tension, and not a waste of a millimeter of space in this photo. Here's a spread a few photos on: a woman's hand with a diamond ring and green nail polish holding some bright orange feathery thing. That's the whole photo, except for the perfectly color-harmonized pale-blue sky. And next to it? Another of Mermelstein's close-ups of near-phantasms, this time a black-and-white chancred foot, with gross nails and a blistery red sore. Yuck! But also far more effective as a photograph than a full shot of a small-in-the-frame destitute man.

2) And next ... more details. I titled the Mermelstein piece "In Your Face," because that's often what he shows us. Not a bunch of people full-length with a lot of negative space around then, but souls in orifice-popping detail, hands, feet, pore-cavernous skin, even just hairs on a scalp. And not just people. Here's a shot of a skin-puckered red bell pepper lying by a curb in a Little Italy street, the pepper taking up almost half of the page (with a smoked-down cigarette butt next to it). Why a red pepper in a gutter? Because it's a striking image, an intriguing play of color and shape, and as is usual with Mermelstein, evocative of its origin story, as in, What's that damn pepper doing in the gutter, how'd it get there? Details like this both command our attention and invoke little mysteries.

3) And one more time, Get up-close ... even right in people's faces. There's a video out there of Mermelstein shooting on the street where he does just that, time after time, just walks up to somebody and throws his camera

in their faces. Sometimes he gets yelled at. Sometimes flipped off. But that's how he gets those vivid, personal, revealing shots.

4) Be fast. Strong street photos might only make themselves manifest for seconds, even milliseconds. You have to see the shot, then manipulate your camera/phone to capture it. (And you're of course picking up on all the hunting words associated with street photography; obviously no coincidence.) Some of the photos in *Hardened*, like the title shot, are of actual signs ... ah, signs on the street. They don't go anywhere, don't move, you can focus and simply take the photo. People doing interesting or exceptional things? Not so simple, not so slow. That red-headed girl, eyes squinched, mouth howling, as she gets her hair grabbed just right? Flash, you got it; blink, it's gone. That great third-eye shot a few pages later, two men talking, the left eye of the man facing us captured in the eyeglasses of the man facing him ... that eye floating there, yes, a third eye ... I've gone for shots like that myself. A whisper of a breath later and the floating eye is bisected by the rim of the glasses, or simply not there. Fast ... yep, up-close and fast, and—

5) Then know when to pull back. Mermelstein is out there shooting without any agenda other than to take pictures, so when he sees something compelling, he goes for it. Most often they're the close-ups of people or vegetables or even cutlery and broken glass (as in one shot), and the closeness helps make them interesting. But in other photos it's simply what's going on that makes it worth our attention. A woman in a wide bell-shaped hat before a Chinatown nut and candy store, a bright yellow happy-face balloon in a corner. A woebegone girl between two puffy-sleeved arms. Another girl almost flying out of a taxi window, held back by her mother. Mermelstein knows also how to layer photos. Another striking one has a plastic cup and arm sleeve on the right, and behind it in full view a black man lying back while talking on a phone, what looks like a prone scooter between his legs.

These are all shots in the moment, photos grabbed on the street, something strange or interesting catching his eye and ... he goes for it.

6) Which leads to another important rule, you don't need (or even want) people to pose for you, or really even know you're taking their picture. You want to capture a consciousness that is about *their* business, not yours. I've rarely seen a posed picture that tells me more than, Here I am, posing for a picture. Or, Here I am, showing the world what I want to show them. Sure, we love posed pictures of beautiful celebrities (with their penumbra of presumed intimacy by dint of their fame), but the souls shot on the street are mostly just whoever's walking by, as interesting as Aunt Sue's shopping mall pal or an office worker scampering to lunch.

7) Though to be fair there are a few photographers who shoot set-up street portraits and are able to make each photo their own, to pull out of the characters they photograph something deeper and truer than what their poses want us to know. I'm thinking of Diane Arbus, of course, but also Jamal Shabazz, with his proud street shots, and Hiroh Kikai, in *Asakusa Portraits*, gentle and profound photos of the quirky souls who populate the Asakusa district of Tokyo. But powerfully revealing portraits as those from these masters come from a full-time pursuit by dedicated artists, not from just asking somebody on the street if they'd like their photo taken, then focusing carefully and snapping it.

8) Which means you don't actually have to look through your camera's viewfinder, or what passes for it on an iPhone. Just snap away with your camera or phone from any position. See what happens. Surprise yourself.

9) Which is to say, Why not shoot digitally? It doesn't cost anything, you can experiment, make terrible shot after terrible shot and delete them, and also get all kinds of effects less easy to come by than if you're beholden to actual film. (Just for the record, you can always use a digital camera as if, mentally, it's an old-school camera,

as in pretending that you're shooting expensive film, and upon each shot your dinner and rent depend.) Mermelstein went from a Leica to an iPhone. These days, Daido Moriyama shoots with a small digital camera. I only use my Fuji X100F, and with more pride than not, I know very little about how it works, just that I can wrench or conjure from it the photos I want.

10) What I do know, though, is that when I'm out with my camera, I'm always looking for pictures. Mermelstein has to be the same. It's a kind of vision thing, where you do your best to take in everything around you, always gazing about for what will make a good shot. Seeing the whole street is essential, and speed is all important, too. At bottom, I find it a joy to enter into a sort of Zen-like street-photography mindset, where I'm floating along the streets at heightened awareness, always looking, always ready to react with a snap of my shutter, both fully in the moment and yet artistically just a bit removed from it, too. All this is also good for you. Being fully involved in a scene or situation is a goal of all kinds of religious and New Age disciplines. Don't go away to a How to Embrace the World in All Its Wholeness retreat, instead put your money into a camera and go out and grab every smidgen of detail and motion and character of the world before you. Here's Mermelstein on the rewards of street photography: "In my opinion what is most important is to stay true to your personal vision and create a body of work that expresses that. I never believed in making pictures with the goal of showing those to obtain commercial work. Do what you do best and love the most and you will be doing all that you can to be happy."

11) And don't simply enjoy taking the photos, embrace the editing down, choosing, ordering of your street shots. Mermelstein also says, "Of course going out and making the pictures is exciting. But what is even more exciting is the feeling that I get in viewing pictures I made for the first time. Sometimes it is more than a month or two

before I first view pictures I have taken. There is a perpetual thrill of catching up."
12) All of which adds up to: love taking pictures; anticipate and delight in seeing what you come up with; and also love editing them into books. A complete life. What's not to like?

And all good lessons for street photographers. Now I'll add additional rules/thoughts wholly my own.

1) Move to New York City. O.K., that might be asking a lot, but there are reasons so many great street photographers live here, the always-ness of life on the streets, the endless parade of characters, the complex press of bodies moving in interesting ways, the abundance of different windows and materials to shoot through for different effects, the different ethnic neighborhoods (lots of quick trips around the world) ... I can go on and on. But of course one can find good photographs everywhere. I've done books set in Japan, Bangkok, Tuscany—pretty much wherever I go. So I shouldn't be so New York–centric. The basic rule is, Just get out there and shoot, and always—

2) Be hungry for photographs. I take my camera with me everywhere, and if I haven't been out seriously shooting for a couple days, I'm champing at the proverbial bit to start getting new shots. I also walk a lot, an added benefit; 10K- to 12K-step days is a norm when I'm out working. (Step count ... *that* I use my iPhone for.) I will also often tie in a lunch or dinner at a favorite restaurant, and a stop into a bookstore or two. At bottom, this rule is: Go out and take a long walk ... and bring along your camera, and your photo-head (see No. 7 below).

3) Here's another thought: expand the scope of photography you know. If you don't know Japanese Provoke-era-inspired masters such as Daido Moriyama and Takuma Nakahira, check them out immediately. Ideally, get the current reprint edition of Provoke magazine, as it was published 50 years ago. Then check out Moriyama's and Nakahira's and Shomei Tomatsu's books. The essential

The Mysteries of Light

lessons from these masters: focus is often irrelevant (it might even get in the way of mystery and magic); your own vision is key; and that you can do *anything* in a photobook ... even, as with Daido's *Bye-Bye Photography*, renounce photography altogether.

4) But don't stop there. Look at everything. Collect photobooks, and study them, the ones you like right off and others that you might not immediately get. Also dive into art as deeply as possible. Spend time in museums. And always ask yourself what you're responding to, or not, in a celebrated painting or photo. The ultimate idea is to find how to see arrangements of actual reality in the street that have the force of art. In the *Hardened* review I mentioned flippantly Winogrand's famous park bench photo; in truth, I've spent a lot of time gazing at it. Everyone in the photo is in the perfect position relative to the others, and making the perfect expression. Look at it hard. Take out one person and watch the shot fall apart. Imagine the girl with her hand on the back of her hair and the one next to her lowering her eyeglasses a moment later, no motion, glasses back where they belong—less interesting, yes? The deal is, to know photos when they present themselves you have to have looked at a vast amount of photos to get a feel for what works; then, of course, move fast to snap them. Just the other day I was walking through the East Village past a loading dock and from the corner of my eye saw seven or eight men there arrayed in a way that intuitively grabbed me. Before I gave my impulse a thought, I quickly spun and took two shots of them. The photos are still in my camera, and might not work out, but what if they do? (By the way, I'm hardly the only one fascinated by Winogrand's photo. Check out *The New Yorker* magazine article about "The Girls on the Bench"; in it, the author tracks down two of the then-young women in the photo.)

5) As I mentioned in Mermelstein Rule No. 8 above, go digital and shoot fast and intuitively. Film? I know, it looks great ... but these days it seems an unnecessary

hassle, or worse. Fast? Would I have shot the guys on the loading dock if I had to worry the cost and trouble of film? Probably not. But with digital, if it comes to nothing, so what. And then there's this: In the photobook course I teach, one of the students brought in her photos from a roll of film that was ruined by the place she had the film developed; something about processing the color film as black and white, or vice versa. Why worry about that? See what you did right away if you wish to. I delete photos as I go, enjoying making the decision as to whether the shot is hopelessly terrible or maybe, just maybe within tolerance of worth keeping and looking at more closely later when I dump everything into Lightroom.

6) And ... embrace mistakes! The woman in my class bemoaning her ruined film, well, the student next to her took a look at what she had and said, "This will make a great book, these messed-up photos." She was right. The student turned in two photobooks: a conventional one with nice photos capturing "solitude in the busy city," and the wholly unexpected one of blurs and seeping color and an intriguing abstraction ... which was far more moving. (Again, check out Daido's *Bye-Bye Photography* to see what I'm getting at.)

7) As I wrote above, broaden your horizons with Japanese photographers, but still study all the masters, Winogrand, Frank, Mermelstein, Levitt, et al. When I was first getting going with my shots on the street, I used a book I have of Walker Evans and Henri Cartier-Bresson photos called *Photographing America* as a talisman. I would pick the book up every day on my way out the door with my camera, both to look at great enduring photos and to jog my own mind into street-photography-think, that Zen-like floating state of seeing photos in the world instead of just seeing (or not seeing, you folk all the time buried in your phones as you walk along) the world itself.

8) And study the history of street photography. There are lots of good books out there on the subject, but I learned

the most from *Bystander* by Colin Westerbeck and Joel Meyerowitz. Pick it up.

9) Don't stop with just great photographers or their photobooks. I find I've learned as much, and fed my photographic ideas as richly, with great literature and even music. Read poetry, highly imagistic or metaphoric poetry (Keats, Shelley, Blake, Dickinson, Eliot, Plath for instance.) Listen to all kinds of music, but especially classical and jazz, the first for the sweep of musical tensions, the long emotional ride; the second for the rich complexities of harmonies and rhythms ... I mean, just try to fill up a photograph the way John Coltrane fills up (and batters and splatters) bars of music. Then there's Bob Dylan, who has written whole songs that can be read as photobooks—see, for instance, "Visions of Johanna," with its ladies playing blind man's bluff with key chains, night watchmen clicking flashlights, ghosts of 'lectricity howling in face bones ... three vivid, strange images, and that's only the second verse.

10) Back to Cartier-Bresson, you know, the Decisive Moment guy. Personally, I long ago stopped worrying much about decisive moments. Sure, if you can capture a once-in-a-lifetime image (that French guy leaping off a floating ladder, his foot floating inches above the puddle), go for it. But one of the beauties of photobooks is that they don't depend on one photo, but a string of them, the right ones in the right order. So shoot everything, and after the fact decide which ones belong in which book. And if your photo is of a decisive moment, great; but also keep in mind that Cartier-Bresson never liked that title, which Simon & Schuster slapped on the first American publication. Cartier-Bresson's title for the book? *Images à la Sauvette*, which roughly translates as images made hurriedly or furtively, a perfect instruction for the budding street photographer, as in: Get out there on the street, and grab photos as you walk/run about. Photograph them in the spirit of, There are targets out there, and you're shooting at them as they

flit past. Then back home you can hope that they're "decisive."

11) Which leads again to Mermelstein's point above in Rule No. 10. A lot of the fun of street photography is finding out later what you've actually gotten. As Mermelstein says, he gets as much or more thrill out of seeing his photos as taking them. It's the excitement of discovering you've actually taken some strong, good photos, and starting to think of what you can do with them. As I said, I use a digital Fuji, and I will glance at shots right after I snap them, and delete manifest duds, but mostly I wait till I accumulate enough new shots—usually hundreds and hundreds—then pour them all into Lightroom, where I can slowly start getting to know them, work to make them look a little better. It's always a delightful surprise to find a good photo amongst the ones I've overlooked the first few times through a new batch. Be quick on the street, but don't be hasty when editing your work. Take your time, then—

12) Make a book. The way I most often do it is, I get an idea, a title or theme, and I go looking through my Lightroom files to see which of my photos will fit it, in which order, etc. This editing is as much or more fun than taking the shots. Of course, I'm by background a novelist, used to spending all my working hours staring at an empty Word page and trying to fill it up from my imagination. Editing actual photos is blithe fun after that. Still, it is real work, making books, and the perfect culmination to all the wandering, snapping, and hoping that street photography demands.

13) Which leads to a final point: Have fun taking street photos. I mean, what's not to like, you're out on a nice day (or an intriguingly Saul Leiter–ish snowy one), sun's shining (that October light! That May, June, July, August, September light!...) or not, and you're filling yourself up with everything your eyes can take in and trying to do literal magic by stopping time. Think about it, you're out there actually stopping time.

The Mysteries of Light

14) O.K., one more thought. Like any good magician, don't think about your magic too much. Have I said this already? Bears repeating. The hardest work isn't taking the photos (or worrying about processing them), it's working to get your head into the place where you take in as much of the world around you as you can, then see photos within it. Fun, yes, but, again, work. This kind of full, abundant, ever-focused vision isn't our natural state. It isn't there on our phones. It's in learning ways of seeing. Study up, look at all the photobooks you can, dig into how masterful photographers see, decide what works for you, fool around, experiment, see where your own lens takes you ... and overall, remember: You do not want to take photos already taken. You do not want to take the photos everyone else will be taking. At bottom, you simply want to take the shots only you can.

That is, practice Mermelstein-vision, as I put it in my last piece. He has his way of seeing the world, Cartier-Bresson does, Robert Frank does, Helen Levitt does, Daido Moriyama does. That's any street photographer's ultimate task: to find *their* way of seeing the world, and then use some form of camera to capture that.

Easy? Nope. Simple? Certainly not at first.

But the more pictures you take, the more photobooks you own and read, and, well, again, the more photos you take, the easier and simpler the process becomes. You get into a flow. You stop obsessing about the photos you take, only the ones you miss. Yet with all of that, the joy increases, too. There's nothing like getting closer to what really matters, your own vision, your own singular body of work.

My Tokyo Photobook Trip

The following is my *Japan Journal* from my trip to that country in October and November 2018, when I took the pictures for my books *Shibuya Time* and *Lost in Tokyo*. The three-part *Journal* was first published in *Photobookstore Magazine*.

I'M TAKING A SHORT break from reviewing photobooks, off to Japan, traveling with my wife, with three main purposes: to look for classic Japanese photobooks to bring home; to take enough pictures to make a book of my own; and to write about it all here. The following is Part 1 of my Tokyo Journal.

So we're in Tokyo, staying at wonderful hotel a friend, Russet Lederman, recommended. Russet's the founder of 10 by 10, a photobook salon and book publisher in New York City, and an expert on Japanese photobooks. She's put us in the Hotel Niwa because it's a great place, and an easy walk to Jimbocho, the main used-bookstore district. Checked in, not too jet-lagged, and off I go.

My first book-hunting stop is a couple dusty shops on Sakura street, the block behind the major used bookshop street, Kudanshita. I go to those first because, after touring the Chiyoda gardens with my wife, and eating a mountain of not-bad sushi at a joint in Shibuya (where you order the fish from a touch screen and it shuttles its way to you on three tiers of conveyor belts—no humans evidently involved, and thus the whole filling meal came to about six bucks, maybe the only bargain I'll find in Tokyo), I'm primed to go hunt for those great old books.

Who knows what I'll find. This is only my first full day, and I'm thrilled that we've already figured out the subways (sort of) and found we can get our bellies full even if every menu item is indecipherable.

On Sakura, the first book I stumble on is Araki's classic *Oh Nippon*, a book that while beautiful (the naked women, the wild

The Mysteries of Light

layout, the, in 1971, perfection of an erotic style to be played out endlessly by him afterward) still seems to be just too many naked women. The price is decent, though the spine is torn, and I make a note of it. (There will be many notes on books and prices to come.)

At that first store seeing a classic photobook is a fluke. Next it's around the corner to the well-known mecca for photobooks, Komiyama. Those magical Japanese sliding doors pop open, and here I am poking around on the first floor, already a vast number of interesting books, though nothing yet I really want. Actually, the one book I'm determined to purchase here in Japan is Daido Moriyama's first book, *Japan: A Photo Theater*. I ask at the downstairs desk; a quick call, and I'm taken up to the fourth floor, where I find Keita Komiyama, the owner, whom I've met (and bought books from) during his sojourns to AIPAD and the New York Art Book Fair.

Keita greets me cheerfully, though the last time I saw him, a month or so back in Queens, he wouldn't meet the price I offered for a copy of Shomei Tomatsu's *Okinawa*, a book I'd like to own one day, though one I'm not as excited by as Tomatsu's other book from 1969, *Oh, Shinjuku*, which I do have a cherished copy of.

Keita has not one but two copies of *Japan: A Photo Theater*, one mint and another, well, less mint but fine—and signed by Daido. The price is not cheap, but I'm here to get a copy of this book, so I commit to it. I need my passport for tax purposes, and tell him I'll return the next day to buy the book.

Now *this* is the kind of place Komiyama is. I bring up *Okinawa* again. Keita brings out three copies, his assistant rushes up with another one, and there, under glass, is a fifth, which looks to be the copy I almost bought in NYC. (*Okinawa* is a flimsy paperback, almost 50 years old, and how many copies were printed? A thousand? Komiyama has *five* of them for sale.) Somehow the price has increased from what it would have been back home, so I pass again. I'm sure someday I can get it more reasonably. But ... five copies? Crazy.

The next day, after a wild, fruitless search for a monthly antique flea market that Google Maps puts in three or four different locations, including one purportedly in Yoyogi Park, which instead of antiques for sale takes us to the real deal, ancient scrolls and temples abloom with celebrants; and then an equally wild jaunt through neighboring Shibuya looking for the same conveyor sushi joint we ate in yesterday, and not turning it up, each street a jumble of indecipherable kanji, blaring signs for food, small storms of cute kids strolling about taking in the sunshine, then finally finding a restaurant that looks very similar inside but feels totally different, as if we've taken a quick turn into the Twilight Zone ... anyway, full of sushi and burnt out on Shibuya, I subway back to Jimbocho, my oasis in this wild town. There I head right back to Komiyama and purchase the copy of *Japan: A Photo Theater*.

Back in our lovely hotel, going through the book's heavy wheat-colored paper, thick slabs of gravure ink, each page an amazing photo (ones we all know well, since they're now Daido classics), the striking layout I've not before seen ... I'm reminded of why at bottom I love a great photobook: As with *Japan: A Photo Theater*, they're works of art in their own right, and to hold one in my hands, it's as if I'm not only going to an exceptional gallery or museum show, I actually *own* everything in it. All the prints in my hands! Indeed, I'd put the printing in Daido's first book up against any darkroom prints hanging on a wall. The ink is thick, palpable, the images richer, more vivid, more alive....

Ah, the magic of a classic photobook, and also of shopping at Komiyama for books I've only read about in the Parr-Badger series, or in Ivan Vartanian and Ryuichi Kaneko's *Japanese Photobooks of the 1960s and 70s*. I mean, you go up to the fourth-floor office, conjure up a book's name, and the store owner pulls it out. I mentioned the Tomatsu *Okinawa* book from yesterday, those five copies. Well, before I buy the Daido book I find a mint copy of Miyako Ishiuchi's *Apartment*, with obi, signed, just sitting on the fourth-floor counter, a book I certainly wouldn't mind owning, even if I don't pant for it. I handle it carefully. A bit more than I can even entertain a notion of paying for, yes? No problem. Here's another copy, sans obi, sans signature, in pretty darn good shape though, for about half the price. These are also books with print runs of, what, at most a thousand? And here are two of them for purchase just sitting there. Yes, Komiyana is that kind of store.

The owner and half the staff are getting ready to go to Paris Photo. I'm getting ready to head off to Kyoto in a few days, but I'll be back in Tokyo on my own for a week and a half (my wife heading to the mountains with a pal) starting on Halloween, to take photos and look for more photobooks. The Komiyama staff won't be leaving till November 5th, so I'll have more opportunities to weigh the value of buying books here and now in Japan that I might not ever see again even in New York City.

For that, stay tuned.

But on this second full day I'm not yet done. I head around the corner to Bohemian Guild, a slender used bookstore with an admirable (if not magical) assortment of photobooks. A little tired, I still pick up an original copy of Takuma Nakahira's *Adieu A X*, a fine work in the Provoke tradition, with obi, for a very decent price.

So far Tokyo, especially Jimbocho, is truly a photobook hunter's paradise.

And as I find out on our third day, I don't understand the half of it.

It's Monday, and my wife wants to go to a venerable paintbrush store in the Ginza (horsehair brushes! boar bristle brushes!), and I tag along to see the shopping street, and take my own photos. The picture taking goes well enough, especially as I've discovered one rule (of hundreds, thousands?) of getting around Tokyo: don't take the subway if you're only going one stop to make a transfer, as in, you'll be up and down five flights of stairs and probably walk halfway underground to the station you want. Better to stay aboveground and take it all in.

So I head over to a station that gives me a one-line shot back to Jimbocho. When I get off, I'm trying to find a store I heard about, discoverable, as the online article has it, "If you emerge from the subway at exit A4, you'll find Gyozando Antique Books just around the corner. The staircase that leads to this tiny bookstore (2nd floor) is between a massage centre and an adult magazine store." Well, I find the stairway, climb to the second floor; it's a dentist's office. I ask other booksellers where Gyozando is, and get pointed this way and that ... and still can't find it. (Another lesson of Tokyo: know when you're licked trying to turn up an actual location even when you have the address.)

O.K., I'll just head back to the center of Jimbocho, see what else I can find, when I make the discovery of the trip (at least so far). I see a sign that says something about art books but nothing about photobooks, decide what the hey and go into the shop, only to discover books as amazing as at Komiyama (and, as it turns out, a lot more affordable).

The store's a bit of a jumble, some classic photos on the wall, a bunch of rock and roll paraphernalia, but then rows and rows of photobooks. I'm nosing around when an old cardboard case catches my eye. Could this be Takuma Nakahira's *For a Language to Come*? I own a nice repro from the Steidl Japanese Box; could this be the original?

It is. I carefully slide out the book, it's pristine. Ask the friendly young woman behind the counter, um, how much it is. She looks at the label, then quotes me a price in millions of yen. "Got it," I say, "really expensive." She looks again. "Oh, I don't mean millions, I mean thousands."

I gulp. It's affordable, far less than half what copies online go for.

I keep looking. I remember my interest in Tomatsu's *Okinawa*, any chance she has a copy of ... oh, they did, but it's been sold. Sorry. Well, how about his *Nippon*, another book I'm looking—

And there it is, original mylar from 1967. Also pristine. Also less than half what an online copy goes for. I swallow hard.

I tell her I'm interested in both books, and she says I should talk to the shop's owner, who will be back soon. Fine. Meanwhile, I keep looking around. Almost hidden is a copy of Daido's *Light and Shadow*, another book I've always wanted.

Long story short, the owner turns up, and after saying, "I have cheapest prices," proceeds to give me an even better deal on all three books. A deep breath, and I go for it. This is why I'm here in Tokyo, right? To find books I might never even see in New York, well, maybe at a Swann Gallery auction, but probably never be able to afford.

Bookwise, the trip is already a success, but I have another

purpose: to make my own photobook. As I do at home in New York, I take my camera everywhere, and I've been snapping away. I've been taking pictures that feel like the kind of pictures I take, which is both reassuring and a little disconcerting; I think I was hoping for something wholly unexpected and new. Well, I've only been in Tokyo a few days, so we shall see.

(Actually, I've been in Japan over a week now, posting this from Kyoto, where we've been for three days so far. All photos accompanying this piece were taken by me over this first week in-country. In a few more days I'll be back in Tokyo for nine days, so Part Two will take in my photobook adventures and photos over that stretch.)

Part 2

WHEN I TRAVEL, I like to hit extremes, so here I am going from Kinosaki Onsen, a sedate town near the western coast in which the whole point is to wander from one hot-springs spa to the next (the only question being: how many baths does one person need, or can bear, a day? In my case, three) back to Tokyo for Halloween night. Shibuya, I'm told, is the place to be, and it's far wilder than anything I've seen in New York City, tens and tens of thousands of kids in costume, cutting up, drinking, being to my perhaps naive eyes for one night not all that Japanese. I have a fine (if at times anxious) time being crushed by bodies, swept along by crowd eddies as if in meeting streams, all the while trying to grab the best shots I can.

I meet by chance a British photographer who flies here for the holiday every year. He tells me the really good shots are only had after two a.m. No doubt, but I'm not his age and head back to my hotel a few hours earlier. I have to get up, get out and get to know Tokyo better ... and go look for more photobooks.

After a morning spent washing my clothes, I only make it as far as Jimbocho today. My main mission is to head back to Genkido books. On the first go-round before we headed to Kyoto, I had a great talk with Shinichiro Kawamura, the owner of the shop and a true photobook lover. I've long wanted a copy of Ed van der Elsken's *Sweet Life*, and of course in true Tokyo photobook store–style, Genkido has two, a U.S. version and the Japanese edition, which comes in a cardboard case. So this has become my idea of a good time: Shinichiro and I flip from page to page in the two editions trying to decide which gravure printing is the best. Hmnn, we go ... seems like more detail in the Japanese edition. Okay, I tell him, I think I'll buy it when I return to Tokyo. I also tell him I'm interested in the copy of Daido's *Hysteric #4*, the numbered limited-edition *Hysteric* (this copy number 69 of 300), and Shinichiro thinks that's a wise move.

But I don't actually get the books, so in a moment of worry in Kyoto I email Shinichiro and tell him I'll purchase both books when I return. He tells me he'll hold them for me, and now that I'm back in his shop, he has. Out they come. Genkido also has copies of the two other Daido *Hysterics* (one signed), and I don't, so now that I'm here I decide I'd better get those also. I also get a copy of Hosoe's *Man and Woman* the reprint of which I have, but here's an original for not much more than I paid for the new edition. (Insert head-whirling emoji here.)

I'm starting to fret about how I'll get these new books, plus the others I'm buying, back to New York City, so I ask Shinichiro if right before I leave Tokyo I can bring all my books to him and he can pack them and ship them. "Yes," he says, "no problem." He'll do it just for the postage. A big relief. I'm going to Bangkok after Japan and don't want to be schlepping valuable books along.

So I leave my new purchases with Shinichiro, with plans to turn up next week all books in hand, then head back to my hotel to rest. I was planning to go to Shinjuku this night but after my Halloween adventures I decide just to eat dinner and hang around my hotel room.

Which I do. But this next night I'm definitely planning to head off to Shinjuku for the first time. I'm sure climbers come to Japan to tackle Mount Fuji, which from our train to Kyoto was spectacular, the Mount Fuji of Mount Fujis. As a photographer, I think of Shinjuku as the Mount Fuji of Japanese photo sites.

The Mysteries of Light 337

Books by Daido, books by Araki, books by both of them combined ... all set in and called *Shinjuku*. What's to be intimidated about?

But first it's off to TOP, the Tokyo Photographic Art Museum, which as usual is a trauma of subway connections, which I'm always amazed I pull off, then the usual misdirection by Google Maps on my phone ... but finally I find it, and it's worth the trip. A couple good exhibits, a strong bookstore—I get the latest Daido *Record*, number 39, smoking off the press—and a nice library. I donate to them a copy of my book *New York Street*, and they seem happy to get it. That's followed by the only terrible meal I've had in Japan, beef fat and gristle (at a place called Kicks, what was I thinking?), then a quick touchdown at the hotel before I head off on that first trip to Shinjuku.

Evidently every day in Tokyo is lit by creamy, color-bursting fall light, and today's no exception. I get a lot of strong street portraits heading back to the hotel, but the light's gone gray as I head to Shinjuku. My target there is Photographers' Gallery, a co-op of Tokyo photographers. Shinjuku is more like Greenwich Village or London's Soho than other parts of Tokyo I've been to, though I don't really expect the district of Shomei Tomatsu's 1969 *Oh, Shinjuku*, when it was evidently mostly squalid student quarters. Now, of course, the first thing that hits me leaving Shinjuku Station is, *Boom*, the endless flood of shopping malls and departments stores and bright lights.

The good news: I soon hit actual streets, trusting Google maps to get me to Photographers' Gallery (a somewhat fluxible faith, but one that usually comes through), and I'm immediately in narrow, arcing ways lined with restaurants, Pachinko parlors, adult bookstores, what looks like sex bars. I finally find my destination, after overshooting it a few times, climb four flights of stairs, and there I am, a couple small galleries filled with strong winter landscape photos, and a small bookstore devoted to the gallery members' books.

Now I have had a tip-off. A New York City friend, Michel Delsol, told me last time he was in Tokyo he'd found the photographer Keizo Kitajima sitting right there in the space. There *is* a man in the office adjacent to the bookstore, and I start talking to him, telling him I like the series of Kitajima's *Untitled Records* sitting there, when I ask his name and learn that he is Keizo Kitajima.

Bingo!

I own his famous *New York* book with Mick Jagger on the cover, and in the course of our chat I tell him that I was living in the East Village during that period. Turns out I was on East 11th, he was on East 6th. We share some memories, mostly of how dangerous it was. I tell him how much I like his *Camp* book, reprinted by Super Labo, and look at a copy at the store. This is the record of the famous CAMP gallery founded in the late '90s by Kitajima, Seiji Kurata, and Daido Moriyama—one of those places, like the Marquee Club in the early '60s with the Brian Jones–led Stones, you just wish you'd been part of. I ask Kitajima who the four people are in the grainy, high-contrast shot midway through the book.

"Is this you?" I ask, about the man on the left who bears a resemblance to Kitajima.

"No, he was an important publisher. He's dead now."

"But that's surely Daido."

"Yes, and next to him is Araki, and on the other side is Tomatsu."

"So that means you took the picture."

Kitajima nods.

Ohh-kay. I might not have been there in 1979, but this ... this is a whiff of an electric moment in Japanese photography.

I talk about my own work, writing for *Photobookstore Magazine* and my photography. I show him a copy of my *Electrick Spirits* photobook, and he likes it.

Then I do something a little crazy. Years ago at a TKY event at Aperture I met Daido for the first time, and asked him if he minded taking my picture, and he said, "Sure I will." I explain this to Kitajima, and he graciously takes my Fuji and snaps three shots of me. So there it is: I have now been photographed by two of the greatest living Japanese photographers.

I don't want to wear out my welcome, and who knows how many bedazzled photographers turn up at Photographers' Gallery and bug him; so again I shake Kitajima's hand and head down the stairs into wild and twisty Shinjuku, where I

The Mysteries of Light 339

wander and snap and snap and wander for the next four hours.

Next day. Not sure what I'm going to do today, did a lot yesterday—over 20K steps recorded on my iPhone—and I'm slightly tuckered, though that won't keep me from wandering far and wide. Just went out for a couple rice balls (my glorious $2.25 Tokyo breakfast) so I can keep writing, and, yep, it's still creamy, color-bursting fall light, so I'm sure I'll be snapping away. I'm also looking for original Japanese Odeon Beatles LPs, so I think I'll go out hoping to find those, though in the way of things the used-record stores I've been to so far are way more interested in U.S. and British pressings than their homegrown ones. I found a store yesterday with six *Yesterday and Today* Beatles butcher album covers on the wall. Yep, Tokyo's that kind of place.

Okay, next day, and those record stores from yesterday were Disk Unions, a big chain around town, and after a few more stops at various outposts, I think my hope of getting original Odeons will be fruitless ... until I see a big black disc in a second-story window on my way back to my hotel after my long day wandering. I figure what the hey, has to be a record store ... and up the stairs, boom, I'm quickly pointed to a whole shelf of original Beatles lps. Long listening and debating finer points of vinyl pressings with the sweet store manager story short, I end up getting M or VG+ copies of the first eight Japanese Beatles albums, up through *Revolver*—at about what one or two might cost me if I ever saw them back home. (I stop back into the store a week later and find out it's been around for eighty-eight years, this info from three Aussies who fly to Tokyo twice a year expressly to go to this one store.)

But getting the Beatles LPs is enough for today, though I stop in for some very good Thai food, warm-up for my heading to Bangkok in five days, then back to the hotel. Oh, I've almost forgotten, I did pick up a few more photobooks. Stopped in first thing at Genkido again, was warmly greeted by Shinichiro, casually asked him if he had anything else I should look into, and walked out with three books, including Yutaka Takanashi's wonderful and mysteriously packaged *Tokyoites*, where pages of fine photos fold and unfold upon each other. A book I never knew existed. And in truth I didn't actually walk out with it; Shinichiro and I spent more time going over the big shipping day, when I take him all the books (and records), and he somehow gets them from Tokyo to NYC.

This Sunday morning I feel the book searching slowing down, though there are places I still want to get to in my five full days left. Instead I dig back into my own work.

In Part 1 of this Journal, I worried briefly that I didn't immediately have great new ideas of how to take shots in Tokyo. Well, now I simply don't worry, don't even think about it. Halloween night was a big moment. I went into it thinking I'd shoot it as I have Halloweens in New York (with their Miltonic overtones), but pretty quickly realized it was a whole different beast: brighter, shinier, cheerier, for Tokyo a holiday recently adopted for the dressing up and play-acting (and drinking). So I quickly started going at it that way. I'm planning to do a book of that night, think I have enough strong shots, and calling it *Happy Halloween: Shibuya Time*. Or maybe just *Shibuya Time*. We shall see. But the lesson is, don't have *any* ideas, or at least any conscious ones; instead just walk around and get fired up in and by the moment.

So I've been shooting like crazy, everywhere I go, and intuitively feeling that the best shots will hold together and make up another book on my Japan visit. Again, we shall see. But as with my work back home, I find that it's best not to have preconceived notions but to be as alive and responsive and quick as possible every moment you're out. Strong photos are everywhere, and I have powerful faith they'll come to me. As the owner of Genkido said when I showed him my *Electrick Spirits* book yesterday, "This is very good. Lots of colors, energy. I like it a lot. You have your own style."

My own style. I guess that's all as a photographer I can hope for. And that has always come from being as aware and focused and intuitive as possible in any given second.

The above written, and photos moved from my camera into my computer and Lightroom this morning, it's still Sunday, another whole day in front of me ... better figure out something to do. Part Three of my Japan Journal will let you know what (if anything) I come up with, as well as finish my trip ... and include talking about my photos from days other than Halloween.

Part 3

So in Part Two of my Japan Journal we left off with it being Sunday and my not knowing what to do. Well, I really didn't do much. Sunday, you know. Walked around some, snagged a couple strong photos, bought a couple more Beatles LPs, then went back to the hotel early to rest up for my final week in Tokyo.

Turns out Monday's not much better in terms of places being open. I'm sitting in my hotel room not at all sure what to do when an email pops up from Sayaka Takahashi, the director of PGI gallery and publishing house. We've met before at AIPAD in New York, and at her invitation I head out to her gallery. We have a fine time catching up. I show her copies of some of my books, and leave with her a copy of the one she likes best, *New York Street*. She gives me her latest publications, including a moody, highly textured book by Yuji Hamada called *Broken Chord*, which I'm happy to have. We also talk about how great it would be if Tokyo had a world-class photobook festival like Paris Photo or the New York Art Book Fair. I'm all for it: a good reason to come back.

I also want to check out Megutama, the fabled café with thousands of photobooks to peruse. Off I go, walking a long way from the Ebisu subway stop, only to discover the curse of Monday applies to them: the café is closed. I think. Either that or I can't find it. Or I might be standing in front of it and not realizing I'm there. Either way, I'll try to give it another shot but don't know if I'll have enough time.

It's Tuesday now, and my fantasy of endless creamy fall days and light is dashed. It's raining, and hard. I spend most of the morning in the hotel room, but soon I'm eager to venture out, even though it's still pouring. I have a destination, So Books, a highly curated photobook store near the Yoyogi-Koen subway stop. I find the shop easily enough and introduce myself to the proprietor, Ikuo Ogasawara. He knows about *Photobookstore Magazine*, but doesn't seem to know me or my reviews. He's also deep into inventory work. I poke about. A wide range of books, the preponderance from America and Europe. Everything very neat and tidy. The store reminds me of Dashwood Books in NY's Noho, where I spend a lot of time. I look around, don't see anything I'm searching for, then ask if he has a couple rare Japanese books I'm interested in. Turns out he does, and the prices are not unreasonable, but I suddenly feel spent out. This has been a looooong trip. So I take a card, can imagine myself back home, next month's rent paid, deciding I'm interested and reaching out to Ogasawara. But today ... nope, just can't buy anything more.

Which turns out to be not quite true. On my way to the hotel I go back to the first shop I stopped into, that first full day in Tokyo, and look again at Araki's first book, *Oh, Nippon*. I've been thinking about it, and since the store is less a bookstore and more a shop full of old and collectible skin mags (Araki right at home there, of course), I make the owner an offer twenty percent less than his asking price. "Cash?" he says. I tell him a credit card would be easier—cash machines? Haven't gotten that far yet in Japan—but he says he doesn't take credit. Why would he for old magazines the equivalent of *Hustler* and *Escort*? So I tell him I'll find a way to get the money (the book is priced at about a third of the best online price) and be back tomorrow. He takes my name, "Bob san!," and we shake on it

And feature this: the convenience store next door to the hotel simply pours out yen notes after I put in my bank card and pin number. And then it's a simple exchange the next day with the owner of the skin mag shop, and Araki's *Oh, Nippon* is mine. A clean copy. That wonderful gravure printing I'm such a sucker for. And on Araki's part a lot of wit, more so than with his endless bondage shots over the ensuing 45 years. Not to mention the old-school cut-and-paste work with the two naked (not nude, *naked*) models disporting away. Yes, another book from this trip I'll treasure always.

Big sigh. Okay, that's it, I swear, *no more books*. And right after I buy *Oh, Nippon*, I head to Genkido Books again to work out the plan for them to ship all the books I've bought home. My new good friend Shinichiro is a prince, and the whole deal couldn't be easier. A ten-minute walk to my Hotel Niwa, quick taxi with my books back to the store, weighing them, filling out the EAS form, paying the shipping cost, and that's it ... I'm bookless.

And later this day, it turns out, on my way back to Megutama, with the best possible guide meeting me at the subway: Yoko Sawada, the publisher of Osiris Books and all-around scholar of, and participant in, the Japanese photobook scene. While waiting for her in front of the station I snap what becomes the cover of my (alas, very appropriately titled) photobook *Lost in Tokyo*. We find each other easily, then we're off.

So here we are at the café, surrounded by the best photobooks in the world, all for tableside perusal. Yoko starts telling me about being the publisher of *déjà-vu*, the profound Japanese photo magazine of the '90s, and especially the issue they put out on the Provoke movement in 1993, thereby spreading the word universally of what happened in Japan twenty-five years earlier.

She pulls the Provoke *déjà-vu* from the shelves. It's lush, beautiful, dark and powerful. Yoko tells me it pretty much introduced the Provoke artists to the rest of the world, with results we all know. Daido Moriyama, Takuma Nakahira ... two of my favorite (and most personally inspiring) photographers ... I might not have known about them but for the work of the woman before me. *Oooh*, a slight, delightful tingle.

Yoko goes on to tell me that Provoke was not only a visual movement but a literary one, with great poets involved who haven't yet gained the recognition of the photographers. As a former poet myself (my first published work was a poem in *The New Yorker* magazine), I take note and plan to dig deeper into the words that bloomed along with all the *are-bure-boke* photos.

Yoko is now administrator of the estates of a number of photographers, including Nakahira, for whom she's just been in Hong Kong at a festival. We talk more about all the actual Provoke people, then we get onto Araki. She tells me Araki wanted to be part of Provoke but was working in advertising at the time and didn't feel quite worthy. Also, he was a few years younger. So he missed being an actual Provoke artist and instead went his own way, inventing his "I Novel," a fictive self he's lived to the hilt ever since. I ask Yoko if Araki was as wild as one always imagines, and she very diplomatically says, "I don't know if you and I have the same definition of *wild*."

Fair enough. I'd rather hold my own notions of the photographer, good or bad. We talk more about *déjà-vu*, and she shows me further issues from its prime. All the copies are stunning. What a coup to have created and produced a great artistic magazine with such high production values. Which leads to a story Yoko tells me on the walk to the Osiris office. Back in the day the beautifully printed glossy magazine was supported in part by a paper manufacturer who wanted to show off their paper stock. Then *déjà-vu* published a lot of Araki at his most Araki-est, and, well, the company pulled their support. Then the Japan economic bubble popped. And the magazine went the way of so many print magazines these days: *phffft*.

The visit with Yoko is great, and I only wished I'd found Megutama on my own two days ago, so I could have spent half the day there digging deep into all the books. Oh, well, next trip.

Which leaves me with one full day left. My wife has returned from her small-town mountain adventures, carrying tales of amazing stone gardens and a restaurant where the chef laughs hysterically as he ritualistically dissects crabs and passes them among riotous patrons, the whole meal capped by drinking sake from the crab's shell. I listen patiently. I'm allergic to crabs, they almost knocked me off once after my first trip to Baltimore. Oh, well, better off a hundred miles away.

I've sworn, *no more books*, but I can still take pictures, so at my wife's bidding we're off to Ginza so she can go to a venerable art supply store; it's been there hundreds of years. Pat's deep into brushes and rice papers when I remember that the Akio Nagasawa gallery is only a few blocks away. Daido's gallery. A place I definitely want to take a look at.

Off I go. I find it easily, take the elevator up to the gallery floor, the door opening on a whole wall of Daido lips. That's what's going on: Daido has a show there called Lips. Of course. And the wall of them looks a lot like the famous wall of Andy Warhol pink-on-yellow cows, which opens the question of whether Daido's somehow creating the very air that Warhol was.

The photos are colorful, crazy, vital, but I'm here mostly for books. I already own a lot of the recent Akio Nagasawa–published Daido works, but here's one so new I've never seen it: *Lips*, of course, one of his books of intensely contrasted photos with a textured silk-screen cover ... O.K., this really is it, *the last book*, and light and thin enough I can simply toss it in my suitcase. I buy it quickly and head out.

But not before chatting a little with the gallery attendant, who says that Daido celebrated his eightieth birthday last month, and now he's off in Paris. I take that in. I've come a little late in my life to my own photography, and Yoko Sawada paid me a fine compliment when she said that from my writing and my photographs she thought I was much younger than I am—"younger in spirit and energy."

Well, damnit, Daido is hugely younger in spirit and energy and brilliance than eighty. In my recent review in the magazine here of his book *Pretty Woman* I wrote about how lately he's been doing some of his best work ever. I also mentioned that the two times I've met him I told him I think of him as the Bob Dylan of photography, on his own Never-Ending Tour.

Well, maybe Daido's also like the 76-year-old Paul McCartney, who on Oct. 31 and Nov. 1 played three-hour-plus shows at the Tokyo Dome, only a hop from my hotel. Alas, I didn't know about the show in time to try to get tickets (I do manage always to see Macca when he comes to NYC), but how inspiring these artists are, charging ahead into the future no matter how many years they rack up.

It's a question of intense personal vision, undying commitment to one's art, enough success to keep going in the real world, and the drive always to take on new challenges. To that point I didn't just come to Tokyo to look for photobooks but to throw myself into a whole new world of (at least at first) boundless challenges, from puzzling out a language I couldn't begin to grasp to streets that curl and turn with no apparent sense, to an energy on the street that insisted on my finding new ways to photograph it.

I had endless fun digging up old and inspiring books, but mostly I took pictures. As I said above, my photobook of Japan did end up called *Lost in Tokyo*, but right then I'm not so sure of the title. By the end of my three weeks, I definitely feel far less lost than at the beginning, though I know I barely touched the enormous metropolis.

No, right then, in my final days (on this trip) in Tokyo, I'm not sure what I'll call my finished book. I trust clarity and inspiration will strike. But I know that even if I was dazed and head-spun by the city at first, I quickly found out how I wanted to photograph it. Perhaps from all those years studying the masters I've written about in these three pieces, perhaps because I'm used to city shooting in New York, or perhaps because in the same way I love these Japanese photobooks so much, from my first glimpse of a Daido book, in a way Tokyo has always been deep in my soul.

www.ingramcontent.com/pod-product-compliance
Lightning Source LLC
Chambersburg PA
CBHW020627220526
45464CB00001B/46